Fighting the Good Fight

Fighting the Good Fight
Two Accounts of Chaplains During the First World War

The Church in the Fighting Line

Douglas P. Winnifrith

In the Northern Mists

Montague Thomas Hainsselin

Fighting the Good Fight
Two Accounts of Chaplains During the First World War
The Church in the Fighting Line
by Douglas P. Winnifrith
In the Northern Mists
by Montague Thomas Hainsselin

FIRST EDITION

First published under the titles
The Church in the Fighting Line
and
In the Northern Mists

Leonaur is an imprint
of Oakpast Ltd

Copyright in this form © 2014 Oakpast Ltd

ISBN: 978-1-78282-317-9 (hardcover)
ISBN: 978-1-78282-318-6 (softcover)

http://www.leonaur.com

Publisher's Notes
The views expressed in this book are not necessarily those of the publisher.

Contents

The Church in the Fighting Line   7
In the Northern Mists   107

The Church in the Fighting Line

Douglas P. Winnifrith.

Contents

Foreword	13
Preface	15
Marching Orders	17
We Sail for an Unknown Port	21
A Field Ambulance	24
The Battle of Mons	28
Smith-Dorrien's Great Stand at Le Cateau	36
End of the Retirement on Paris	43
The Battle of the Marne	49
The Battle of the Aisne	58
The Race for the Sea	69
The Second Corps Bars the Way to Calais at La Bassée	77
The Winter Campaign 1914—1915	88
Appendix	102

To the Memory of the Officers, Non-commissioned Officers and Men of the 14th Infantry Brigade and attached units, who in the Great War have laid down their lives for their neighbours, the Belgians and the French, as well as for King and Empire, I dedicate this book
August 4th, 1915.

Foreword

This is a most interesting book. It ought not to need even a foreword, with such a preface to it as has been written by one of our greatest soldiers—Sir Horace Smith-Dorrien; but, as the author is anxious that I too should write a word, I add this foreword to say that readers will find here a plain, unvarnished account of a chaplain's experiences during the early part of the war.

Those who think that a chaplain's work is "an easy job" will find their mistake, but, on the other hand, they will find that it is a glorious bit of work to be called upon to do. Even as I write this, I see in the evening paper this sentence from a corporal's account of the recent battle:

> The bravest were the chaplains, who were with the boys all the time.

But what the chaplains feel is what the writer of this book feels, that nothing too much can be done, and no sacrifice too great can be offered, to stand by the glorious men who are fighting the greatest war in the world's history in the spirit described in this book.

The writer brings out vividly also the courage and the devotion of the whole surgical and medical staff, and not the least of the stretcher-bearers, who never flinch from their dangerous work under the worst fire.

I look upon it as an honour to have my name associated, in introducing this book to the public, with Sir Horace Smith-Dorrien's. The last time I saw him was sitting on Easter Sunday at the head of the army he commanded, surrounded by generals and officers at the largest Church Parade of all those which I addressed at the Front, not many miles from the German lines; and I shall not soon forget his encouraging words to me both before and after the service.

I know that he will be glad if our joint appeal should make many read a book which is a tale of simple heroism not often surpassed in history.

A. F. London.

Fulham Palace, S.W.
October 1st, 1915.

Preface

A short time ago I received a letter from the Rev. D. P. Winnifrith, asking me to write a preface to a brief account he was compiling of his experiences in France, in which he particularly hoped to describe incidents which would give some small idea of the arduous and fearless work performed by the Medical Services in this War.

I would gladly do anything which would help to bring before the public the gloriously heroic work performed by all ranks of the Medical Services, and as Mr. Winnifrith was with the 14th Infantry Brigade Field Ambulance from the commencement of the War, and was present with it at the Battles of Mons, Le Cateau, the Marne, the Aisne, La Bassée, Ypres, and Armentières—covering a period of eight months' continuous fighting—and was mentioned by Sir John French in his *Despatches*, I feel sure that there is no one better placed than he is to convey to their fellow countrymen some idea of the sort of stuff of which the Medical Officers and all ranks of the Army Medical Corps are made, and I therefore strongly recommend the public to read this book when it appears. It is probable that, from a sense of modesty, the account will not dilate to any great extent on the work of the Army Chaplains, and so I will myself testify to their splendid services.

It is true that they were not tested so highly as the skilled surgeons, who, day after day, under a deadly fire in close proximity to the enemy, with unshaken nerve tended the wounded and performed delicate operations; but they were always near at hand, and showed such devoted indifference to danger and hardship in their ministrations to the sick and wounded as to place them on the highest level of those heroes who are fighting that our Empire may prevent all that counts for Truth, Righteousness, and Honour from being ground in the dust.

H. L. Smith-Dorrien,
General.

July 31st, 1915

Chapter 1

Marching Orders

In August 1914, when Great Britain declared war upon Germany, I was stationed in Dublin, where I had charge of the 1st East Surrey Regiment, the 2nd Duke of Wellington's (West Riding) Regiment, and the 2nd King's Own Yorkshire Light Infantry. All formed part of the 5th Division, commanded by Sir Charles Fergusson, K.C.B., M.V.O., D.S.O., the last two being included in the 13th Brigade (Brigadier-General G. J. Cuthbert, C.B.) and the first in the 14th Brigade (Brigadier-General S. P. Rolt, C.B.).

I shall never forget the last, Sunday, August 9th, these regiments spent in Dublin. At the special celebrations of the Holy Communion large numbers of the officers and men attended. Though we knew it not at the time, many of those then present were, within a few days, to be summoned before Him Whom they were for the last time worshipping sacramentally. The morning being beautifully fine, a combined open-air parade service was held; there was a full muster of the regiments, and a large concourse of relatives and friends. I gave a brief address on the words, "*The Lord thy God is with thee whithersoever thou goest*" (Joshua i. 9). The reminder of the promise of Divine presence with them was, I was afterwards told by many, a great inspiration and comfort in the days of stress and trial that followed.

During the early days of mobilisation I was constantly being asked by my men, "Well, sir, are you coming out with us?"

I could, at first, only reply "I hope so." On August 7th, however, I learned with great pleasure from the War Office that I was to accompany the British Expeditionary Force, and to be attached to the 14th Field Ambulance, which was then mobilizing in Phoenix Park. Though I had no definite knowledge, I suspected, as afterwards proved to be the case, that I should have charge of the 14th Infantry Brigade. I

LIEUTENANT-COLONEL G. S. CRAWFORD, C.M.G.,
OFFICER COMMANDING 14TH FIELD AMBULANCE.

was very glad, therefore, not to have to bid goodbye to my regiments, but to be able to tell them, at their last parade service in Dublin, that on active service I was to have charge of one of them and should generally be very near the other two.

During the week August 9th to 15th I saw my regiments march away amid scenes of great enthusiasm, and embark on the transports. On Sunday, the 16th, I reported myself, in obedience to orders from the War Office, to the officer commanding the 14th Field Ambulance. It was a great pleasure to find he was an old friend of mine with whom I had served in Aldershot, Malta, and Dublin, Lieutenant-Colonel (then Major) G. S. Crawford, R.A.M.C. He had seen war service in India and South Africa, and, while I was in Malta, had been selected for the command of the British Field Hospital which was hastily despatched from that station to Messina for the relief of the sufferers from the earthquake. For his splendid work on that occasion he wears decorations bestowed upon him by the King of Italy, and the Order of St. John of Jerusalem.

His services in this campaign have been recognised by the award of the C.M.G. The other medical officers of the Ambulance, I found, were Majors G. M. Goldsmith, F. G. Richards and R. F. M. Fawcett, Captains Kelly and Crymble, Lieutenants J. H. Bell, Banks, and T. W. Clarke. Major F. G. Richards was another friend with whom I had served at Aldershot ten years ago. Lieutenant and Quartermaster T. Grenfell completed the establishment of officers. Attached to the unit, like myself, I was glad to find the Rev. O. S. Watkins, Wesleyan Chaplain, for, while I had not had the pleasure of meeting him before, I knew him well by name and had read of his good work in the Egyptian and South African campaigns.

I held a parade service for the Field Ambulance, and then, no definite orders as to the time of our embarkation having been received, I was allowed to return to my barracks in Dublin. I found them already filling with new troops, some of whom were billeted in the nave of the church. Pontoon sections of the Royal Engineers were busily engaged in completing their preparations for departure on the morrow. The old faces were sadly missed, and upon those of the wives and children who remained anxiety and grief were unmistakably written. But all were wonderfully brave. "I'm so glad you are going with the regiment, sir," and "Look after my husband," were typical remarks made to me after the evening service that day by the brave women, who had assembled to pray for their loved ones who had marched away and who were now they knew not where. Monday, August 17th, my birthday, I was able to spend quietly with my wife and friends, and then on Tuesday, the 18th, my own turn came to march away.

Chapter 2

We Sail for an Unknown Port

The work of embarkation was so expeditiously performed that by 6.30 p.m. on August 18th the equipment of a General Hospital and two Field Ambulances (the 14th and 15th), as well as part of a Bridging Train of Royal Engineers and an Ammunition Column of Royal Artillery, had been put aboard the S.S. *Benares*. At 7 p.m. we weighed anchor, waved our last adieus to relatives and friends on shore, and slowly made our way down the Liffey amid the cheers of the crowds assembled on the quays and every point of vantage. Even the lighthouse-keeper at the end of the long mole, where the river joins the open sea, clanged his bell as a farewell greeting. So far none of us knew for what port we were bound; but, when we were well out into the bay, the sealed orders were opened and we learned that Havre was our destination. Soon afterwards all the officers on board were ordered to assemble on the upper deck, where the senior officer read to us the following greeting from our King-Emperor:

Buckingham Palace.
You are leaving home to fight for the safety and honour of my Empire. Belgium, whose country we are pledged to defend, has been attacked and France is about to be invaded by the same powerful foe. I have implicit confidence in you, my soldiers. Duty is your watchword, and I know your duty will be nobly done. I shall follow your every movement with deepest interest and mark with eager satisfaction your daily progress; indeed, your welfare will never be absent from my thoughts. I pray God to bless you and guard you and bring you back victorious.

George R. I.

August 9th, 1914.

This was afterwards read to the non-commissioned officers and men, and the hearty cheers with which, on each occasion, it was received must have been heard in "dear dirty Dublin," and were an earnest of our determination to do, and die if necessary, for the cause espoused by our Empire.

We steamed quietly down the Irish Channel, and, as a precautionary measure, all lights were extinguished or shaded, but we slept well and soundly, feeling confident that the eyes of the navy, as well as He Who never slumbers nor sleeps, would watch over us.

Wednesday morning, August 19th, found us off the Cornish coast, and we sighted a small British cruiser which had been acting as our escort. She presently hove to, and, as we passed her, the members of the sister services greeted one another with hearty cheers. Henceforward we came under the protecting care of the French Navy, and steamed up the English Channel within sight of the Devon coast. The weather was glorious and the sea as calm as a duck-pond. At 5.15 p.m. the three Church of England Chaplains on board, F. A. Hill, J. Burrough, and myself, together with O. S. Watkins (Wesleyan) conducted a united service on the lower deck. Though we knew it not then, we were not to have another opportunity of corporate worship for many days to come. Later in the evening a most enjoyable "Sing-song" was arranged by Sergeant Plume, R.A.M.C., of the 14th Field Ambulance, I had known him in Malta and Dublin as a good member of the C.E.M.S. and of our Garrison Church choir in both these stations; I was glad, therefore, to find he was to be our Orderly Room Sergeant.

His assistant clerk was to be Corporal Burdett, another member of the C.E.M.S., the son of a Church of England clergyman. Both these have done excellent work in the clerical branch of the Field Ambulance, among other things keeping a very accurate record of the regimental number, rank, name, and regiment of all the sick and wounded cared for by the Ambulance. This alone has involved most strenuous work, but both made time to perform many acts of kindness, *e.g.* the distribution of parcels of clothing, tobacco, cigarettes, soap, notepaper, etc., among the personnel of the Ambulance and the patients, as well as to organise concerts and dramatic performances for their benefit. To both I am most grateful for the help which, as members of the C.E.M.S., they gave me in my work.

Early on Thursday, August 20th, we sighted Havre and soon after the breakfast-hour came alongside the quays and the work of disembarkation commenced. The horses, of which there were about 200 on board, seemed very relieved to be on *terra firma* again; the majority of them had suffered badly from *mal de mer*. The disembarkation completed, the two Field Ambulances marched to a rest-camp on the high ground behind the town.

It was just over a hundred years since a British Army had landed in France; then the British had come as foes, now as friends. Their landing in Havre and other ports awakened wild enthusiasm and joy, and though the people of Havre must, by August 20th, have grown quite accustomed to the sight of the khaki-clad men who had come to fight by the side of their countrymen, they gave us a splendid welcome, and greeted us with the cry "*Vive l'Angleterre!*" to which our men replied as heartily "*Vive la France!*"

Chapter 3

A Field Ambulance

A digression from the narrative may well be made here to give a definition of a Field Ambulance, of which frequent mention will be made in this book. It is really a mobile hospital which accompanies the fighting troops. Its personnel consists of nine medical officers, a quartermaster, and 242 non-commissioned officers and men. These last include men of the Army Service Corps, who act as drivers of the ambulance waggons, etc., and men of the Royal Army Medical Corps, who perform the duties of stretcher-bearers, nursing-orderlies, and specially trained theatre attendants. Its equipment, so complete that its work could be efficiently performed in a country, or locality, where it was impossible to utilise houses, includes the following: 10 ambulance waggons, 3 water carts, 6 waggons and 2 carts for stores and baggage, 14 riding and 68 draught-horses. A proportion of motor ambulances now replaces some of the horse-drawn vehicles. Both are equally necessary; the horse-drawn ambulance is best for work near the trenches, while the motor ambulance is best for conveying the sick and wounded from the dressing-station to the clearing hospital, or "rail-head."

Its organisation is so perfect that, on the occasions when the troops are followed into action, in a few minutes, either in one of the special tents carried for the purpose, or in some suitable building, an operating theatre can be set up with all essential equipment. Then, either in bell-tents, or in rooms or sheds upon the floors of which straw, when procurable, is laid, the sick and wounded are cared for by the doctors and orderlies, who do their utmost for their patients till they can be removed to a clearing or general hospital. By day the Field Ambulance, or "the hospital" as the soldier generally calls it, is distinguished by two flags, the Union Jack and the Geneva Red Cross on a white

In some suitable building, an operating theatre can be set up in a few minutes.

ground, which are hung side by side on a horizontal pole; at night, by two lamps giving a white light.

The Field Ambulance maintains constant communication with the regimental aid-post in front and the clearing hospital in rear. When a man is wounded in the firing-line he is carried by his regimental stretcher-bearers (the majority of whom are bandsmen in peace time) to the regimental aid-post, which may be a "dugout," or a house, or merely a place of natural and comparative shelter. Here he receives first aid from his regimental doctor. As soon as possible an ambulance waggon, accompanied by a medical officer and a squad of four or six bearers, comes out from the dressing-station, to which it conveys the wounded man. Here any operation, which the urgency of the case may demand, is performed, and wounds are re-dressed. Twice a day at least motor ambulances come up to the dressing-station and convey the sick and wounded to some clearing hospital.

Every morning batches of sick, who have generally first been seen by their regimental doctor, report themselves to the Field Ambulance. Some are detained for treatment, the remainder are sent down to the clearing hospital. Another very important work done in the Field Ambulance is the inoculation of the troops against enteric. Some four or five thousand men were thus treated by my Field Ambulance in a few weeks. The following table shows the numbers treated by the 14th Field Ambulance during the first three months of this campaign:—

	Sick.	Wounded.
Officers .	48	68
N.C.O.'s and Men	1,773	1,572
	1,821	1,640

These numbers were, of course, very considerably surpassed later on during the severe wintry weather and the heavier fighting in Flanders. Of the work done by the officers and men of the 14th Field Ambulance it is impossible to speak in too high terms of appreciation. They are heroes every one, and I count it a privilege to have been associated with them.

In this campaign, with its artillery duels between long-range guns, the Field Ambulance has been constantly under shell-fire, and the journeys between the dressing-station and the regimental aid-posts have always been perilous. But, whether it was across the open plain on the north side of the Aisne, upon which the shrapnel was constantly bursting, or along the cobbled roads of Belgium studded with "Jack Johnson" holes, they were always performed readily and cheerfully. Frequently in our mess at night when, in answer to the announcement "The waggons and squads are ready, sir," the colonel would ask, "Whose turn is it to go out tonight?" have I heard several officers answer together, "I should like to go out tonight, sir." I often accompanied these expeditions, and have, therefore, first-hand knowledge of the difficulties and dangers they involved.

My admiration for our fighting men, than whom there are no finer in the world, is equalled only by that which I have for these men of peace who so well deserve the motto of their corps, "*In arduis fidelis.*"

Chapter 4

The Battle of Mons

At midday on Saturday, August 22nd, we entrained at Havre. The men of the R.A.M.C. worked with a will and soon had horses and waggons on board our special train, for we were all eager to leave for "the front" as early as possible. Of what was happening there we knew little or nothing beyond the bare fact that somewhere in Belgium the allied British and French armies were coming to grips with our common enemy. We now know that on this day "French's contemptible little army"[1] was entrenching itself along a front of some twenty-five miles extending from Binche on the right to Condé on the left, with the historic town of Mons in the centre, to await with confidence "Old One O'clock's" attempt to "walk over" it with a force four times as numerous.

We knew that our Field Ambulance would be needed, and were all anxious to do our bit, hence we chafed at the tediously slow railway journey which had to be accomplished ere we could take our place on the field. By 11 p.m. Rouen was reached, and here hot coffee was served to us by the French. How glad of it we were! Breakfast, consisting of "bully" beef and biscuits, on Sunday, August 23rd, was partaken of in the train. The Rev. O. S. Watkins, an old campaigner, made us an excellent brew of tea. At noon we reached "rail head," Valenciennes, and immediately commenced to detrain. We all lent a hand, and by working hard in the heat and dust the task was accomplished in about two hours. Horses and men were fed, and we then anxiously awaited marching orders.

Some of us, in the interval, went into the town and sought refresh-

---

1. *Contemptible* by Casualty, an 'Old Contemptible' recounts the campaign of 1914 and *Doing Our 'Bit'* by Ian Hay are also published by Leonaur.

ment at the Hôtel du Commerce; the delicious omelet and coffee provided are things to be remembered. Here in a backyard closely-watched by the civil guard we saw our first German prisoners, an officer and five men of the *Uhlans*. The poor beggars looked very dirty, and were all sleeping heavily.

Simultaneously with our rejoining the Ambulance orders arrived, and at 6 p.m. we marched off in an easterly direction towards Bavai, which was reached about midnight. A distance of eighteen miles had been accomplished, a good performance for men the majority of whom were unaccustomed to marching. I shall never forget my introduction to the roughly paved roads, which my horse evidently disliked as much as the men, nor the hearty reception accorded us in the villages through which we passed. The children pressed upon us bunches of flowers, fruit, and picture postcards. The women would run into the road with fresh bread, and drinks of water for horse and man. The old men, for all of a fighting age had gone, would hand us gifts of their home-grown tobacco. The peasants usually hailed the Field Ambulance as "*La Croix Rouge,*" and the *padres* seemed always to occasion them wonderment. They would look at our clerical collars, at the red cross upon our left arm, and then address us as "*docteur*" or "*pasteur*" according to the decision at which they had arrived.

While we had marched on this memorable Sunday our comrades in front had been heavily engaged with the enemy. The first shots of the Battle of Mons were fired at forty minutes after noon. Our men soon settled down to their work, and wrought terrible havoc among the dense masses of German infantry which were flung again and again, but always in vain, against our position. Not infrequently, too, the Germans were given a taste of the bayonet and made to run like rabbits. The Second Corps, commanded by General Sir Horace Smith-Dorrien,[2] with our own division, the 5th, on its extreme left, more than held its own, successfully defeating every attempt of the enemy to cross the canal. One of my Dublin Regiments, the 2nd Battalion the Duke of Wellington's (West Riding) Regiment, suffered heavily; the commanding officer, Lieut.-Col. J. A. C. Gibbs, was severely wounded and taken prisoner, Major Strafford and Captain Denman-Jubb were killed. The tidings of the death of these two good friends of mine almost staggered me; it was difficult to realise we were not to meet again, and I wished so much I could have been with them at the end.

---

2. *Smith-Dorrien* by Horace Smith-Dorrien is also published by Leonaur.

'When darkness fell most of our line stood on the ground held at dawn. We had not suffered any great losses, numerically, while we had inflicted very severe ones on the Germans. The men had acquired confidence and eagerly looked forward to the renewal of the battle on the morrow. But the retirement of the French on our right, and the overwhelming numbers of the enemy which threatened our left flank, made the British retirement inevitable.

Before leaving Bavai, on Monday, August 24th, I was called to the civil hospital to minister to a man of the Dorsets who was seriously ill with pneumonia. The nuns who were acting as nurses ushered me into a room where there lay a man of the Royal Engineers who had been killed accidentally the previous day. By their request I said prayers by the side of the body, for the man was to be buried that day and I could not remain to conduct the funeral service. Even now, at 5.30 a.m., the Field Ambulance, having bivouacked but a few hours in the public square, was moving off. Not having had any breakfast, I remember how much I appreciated the coffee which the nuns made for me. Without a halt we pushed on, for tidings had reached us of yesterday's big fight and already we could hear the distant rumble of our guns. By 9 a.m. we reached a small hamlet named La Rosine near Dour, and could go no farther, because we were now in close proximity to our batteries which were in action.

The British had taken up a new line at dawn some five miles south of the Mons canal. General Smith-Dorrien had received a useful reinforcement to his command in the 19th Brigade, which had detrained at Valenciennes the previous day, and his task on this Monday morning, August 24th, was to hold the enemy while the First Corps retired to the Maubeuge position, and then to break off the fight and fall back to the new position, showing a bold front the whole time and striking back at every attempt of the enemy to interrupt it. This, the most difficult of movements an army can be called upon to execute, was most successfully carried out, thanks to the skill of Sir Horace Smith-Dorrien and the dauntless spirit of the troops under his command.

This was the general situation when at 9 a.m. we parked the Field Ambulance in a field and prepared parts of a large sugar refinery close by for the reception of the wounded. The first to come under our care was Captain Buchanan-Dunlop, of the Royal West Kent Regiment. He had been struck by a bullet which had entered his cap in front and come out at the back, making a nasty wound across the scalp, but, providentially, not deep enough to prove fatal. His wound having been dressed, he was intensely anxious to return to the fight; but this the doctors decided he was not fit to do. I then helped to make him a comfortable resting-place on some straw in the building above named. Many other wounded were brought in during the morning.

Here I first saw shrapnel bursting, and we received our baptism of fire. What were my feelings on this occasion? The novelty of the experience, thoughts of our brave lads meeting the onslaught of the foe, the desire to do what one could to help the wounded, entirely possessed me. Here, too, one first saw the pitiable sight of Belgian villagers hurriedly leaving their homes with a few treasured possessions, varying in their nature and number, and carried either on their backs, in wheelbarrows or waggons, according to their status. Their dogs were invariably included in the party, and how I blessed them for this! Many of the refugees would appeal to us to direct them as to the best route by which to escape: poor souls, how our hearts bled for them! They had trusted the British would secure the safety of their homes, and now we seemed to have failed them. But we had done our best, and an astonishingly good best too, with the small force then at our disposal. What a different tale there would have been to tell if, at this stage, we could have opposed the invader with not merely seventy but seven hundred thousand men! Brave and honourable little Belgium might have been saved incalculable misery and spoliation.

As it was, about noon on this day, we received orders to take our part in that great retirement which was to last, though we didn't know it at the time, for twelve days. The wounded were placed in the ambulance waggons, all equipment was hastily packed, and we moved back through some of the villages in which but a few hours earlier we had been welcomed by a grateful and confident people. Now one could see upon their countenances anxiety and fear clearly written. Oppressed though they were by a dread of the oncoming foe they would, however, momentarily forget their troubles and leave their preparations for departure to do everything possible for the troops marching by. Many a prayer did we put up that these generous, thoughtful, and unselfish souls might reach a place of safety.

The heat on this afternoon was intense, but on and on we marched with never a halt till dusk, when the Field Ambulance was turned into a field that horse and man might be given food and rest. We had partaken of the former, and were about to lie down among the shocks of corn to enjoy the latter, when we were warned that the Germans were close upon us. I need hardly say that it didn't take us long to pack

THE 11TH FIELD AMBULANCE MARCHING THROUGH A FRENCH VILLAGE.

BELGIAN VILLAGERS HURRIEDLY LEAVING THEIR HOMES.

up on this occasion! We owed our escape to one of the motor-bicycle despatch-carriers, a corps, consisting very largely of university men, which has done such valuable service in this campaign. A few weeks later we again met our cyclist friend, and it was a joyous surprise to him to find our Field Ambulance had eluded capture. It transpired that he had been instrumental in saving on this occasion not only ourselves, but an ammunition column and a squadron of cavalry.

We pushed on again, weary though horse and man were, till near the village of Villereau, just after midnight, it was deemed safe to call a halt. The waggons were drawn up by the roadside, the horses fed and rested with harness on, and we lay down fully clad so that, in the event of an alarm, no time might be lost in continuing our retreat. I, and a few of the officers, had just found a comfortable bed among some sheaves of corn in a field close by, and were falling asleep, when I was conscious of many dusky figures moving about the field. It was reassuring to hear them speaking in the French tongue and to discover they were troops of our Ally, and not of Von Kluck.

At dawn on August 25th we were roused and, without waiting for breakfast, trekked away again. How precarious was the position of the British at this time we now know. The enemy had been making very determined attempts to get around our left flank and surround us. Our commander-in-chief saw that no time must be lost in retiring to another position, an operation which he describes as "full of danger and difficulty" not only owing to the very superior force on our front, but also to the exhaustion of the troops. From 4 a.m. till 1 p.m. we marched, with only very brief halts, under an almost tropical sun, on the western outskirts of the big forest of Mormal, passing through pretty villages nestling among orchards, and scenes of pastoral beauty and smiling prosperity—so soon, alas! to be despoiled by the enemy.

During the morning I saw for the first time on this campaign our corps commander, General Sir Horace Smith-Dorrien. Always courteous and smiling, on this occasion he alighted from his motor-car, held up for the moment by a congestion of traffic, and chatted with us. We saw him frequently after this, and his face always bore the same confident smile. "Things can't be too bad, sir, for the general is smiling," the men would remark to me; and we all felt the same. Sir John French[3] speaks of the "rare and unusual coolness, intrepidity, and determination" of Sir Horace, but it was his evident cheerfulness on these dark days which helped to inspire those under his command, as

---

3. *1914* by Sir John French is also published by Leonaur.

GENERAL SIR H. L. SMITH-DORRIEN, G.C.B.,
C.C.M.G., D.S.O.

well as the mutual confidence existing between leader and led.

"You know, sir, it was Smith-Doreen who trusted the soldier at Aldershot; we didn't disappoint him then, and we don't mean to now," was a remark made to me, and one which I believe to summarise the attitude of the troops generally towards the commander of the Second Corps.

By noon we passed through Le Cateau, famous as the meeting-place of Henry VIII and Francis I of France, and halted in a cornfield about two miles west of it. A march of considerably over twenty miles had been accomplished; a splendid performance for "exhausted" troops. I rode into the nearest village, Troisvilles, and begged fresh bread, milk, and eggs for the wounded. Several of the villagers willingly assisted me to carry these commodities to the Field Ambulance. Upon my return I found the doctors busy dressing wounds and performing minor operations. This duty having been accomplished we sat down to the first good meal we had had since Sunday. We had never gone short of food—the splendid work of the Army Service Corps had ensured that—but we had been obliged to content ourselves with biscuits and cheese, which we ate as we rode or marched along.

Frequently, during the brief halts, we had lit fires by the roadside and set about making a "billy" of tea, and then, before the water had boiled, would come the peremptory order to march. How much, therefore, we appreciated the fresh bread, fried bacon, jam, and steaming hot tea of which our meal consisted that evening! We were warned that we should have to be astir at dawn, so we lost no time in seeking sleep. By the invitation of two wounded officers, for whom a bell-tent had been erected, I shared their shelter; and very glad I was of it, for the drizzling rain, which had commenced to fall while we were having supper, soon changed to a downpour.

CHAPTER 5

Smith-Dorrien's Great Stand at Le Cateau

The morning of August 26th broke fine and bright, a pale blue sky and thin mists rising from the wet ground giving promise of a hot day.

About midnight on the 25th the enemy had heavily attacked the exhausted troops of the First Corps at Landrecies, and the commander-in-chief arranged that during the 26th this corps should continue the movement to the southward, while the Second Corps, with the Fourth Division of the Third Corps (which had detrained three days ago at Le Cateau), and cavalry should follow the retirement and hold back the enemy. The second part of this plan proved impossible, for at daybreak it had become apparent that the enemy was throwing the bulk of his strength against the left of the position occupied by the Second Corps and the 4th Division. In face of such an attack General Smith-Dorrien saw that it was not possible to continue his retirement at daybreak, and he decided, therefore, to stand and face the enemy.[1]

The odds against him were overwhelming; the Germans must have had 250,000 men, while the British, making deductions for the First Corps, which took no part in the fight, and for the losses sustained at Mons, could not have numbered much more than 50,000. In the opinion of the German Generals the British had come to their hour of doom. They held on, however, for eight hours, and every attempt to break them failed. As an epic of resistance it was a feat of arms inferior to nothing in British military history. Our losses were necessarily heavy, but General Smith-Dorrien attained his object, and, as General

---

1. *Guns at Le Cateau* by A. F. Becke & C. de Sausmarez, the stand of the Field Artillery, 1914, is also published by Leonaur.

Joffre gratefully recognised, skilfully saved the whole Allied left.

Soon after dawn the 14th Field Ambulance moved from the scene of last night's bivouac and marched two or three miles in the direction of Honnechy. My horse had gone sick, so this morning I marched on foot. I mention this fact because, later in the day, the loss of my horse nearly proved my undoing. As I trudged along I passed the 108th Battery Royal Garrison Artillery, with its long 4.7 guns cleverly concealed by sheaves of corn, which soon commenced to work awful havoc among the enemy. I greeted two of my old Dublin Regiments, the Duke of Wellington's and the Yorkshire Light Infantry, as they were taking up their positions in the hastily dug shelter trenches. From the cheerfulness of the troops one might have thought they were entering upon a sham fight on Salisbury Plain. An officer friend shouted to me, "Good morning, *padre*; this is no place for you and the hospital. It will be a warm spot soon."

I assured him that the *padre* and doctors were not going to desert them and would be close at hand when needed. I watched, too, with admiration my own Brigade (Suffolks, Surreys, Cornwalls, and Manchesters) led by General S. P. Rolt, C.B., going into action, and often, as the brave lads passed by, did I re-echo the psalmist's words, *"We wish you good luck in the name of the Lord."*

Behind a hillock, on the crest of which we flew the Red Cross flag, our Field Ambulance took up its position in close proximity to the 14th Brigade. An operating tent was at once pitched and every preparation made for the reception of the wounded. About 7 a.m. the roar of the guns and the rattle of rifle-fire told us the fight had begun, so, from the ambulance, the bearer divisions of all three sections were despatched in charge of Major Fawcett, Captain Kelly, and Captain Crymble to bring in the wounded. In response to their urgent request, which soon arrived, several ambulance waggons went out to them, and it was not long ere they returned laden with wounded. Having deposited their burdens with us, they returned again and again to the field, where the above-named officers and stretcher-bearers pursued their work of picking up those whose injuries required their removal from the firing line. I went to the nearest farmhouse and assisted to convert several rooms and barns into temporary wards; straw was laid upon the floors, and hither the wounded warriors were borne as soon as they had been attended to by the doctors. A word of prayer here and there, the heating of water, making of beef-tea, and holding of a limb while a doctor bandaged, kept me fully occupied.

Soon after midday all accommodation for the wounded was overtaxed, and precautions had to be taken lest, a sudden retirement becoming necessary, we might have more patients on our hands than the waggons would carry. Colonel Crawford decided, therefore, to despatch such as could walk to Busigny railway-station, from which, we were told, a train would take them to a base hospital. The Rev. O. S. Watkins volunteered to take charge of them. We heard afterwards that he safely accomplished his task, but, before he could rejoin us, we had moved off and saw him no more till next morning in St. Quentin.

About 3.30 p.m. there came the order to retire, for overwhelming numbers of the enemy were working around on our left flank and threatening the three British divisions with annihilation. The wounded were placed in the ambulance waggons, all equipment was hastily packed, and, last of all, our hospital flag was struck and we left the field. And not a moment too soon, for shrapnel, intended for one of our batteries, was bursting in close proximity to us.

We had not gone more than half a mile when shrapnel began to fall upon the road by which we were retiring. The Field Ambulance, that the wounded might be got out of danger as quickly as possible, galloped off, and, being on foot and at the rear of the column, I was left behind! I had sheltered for a few minutes only behind a railway embankment when, luckily for me, a mounted man leading a spare horse came along, and I availed myself of this means of escape. I galloped between our artillery, which was in action, and the cavalry, waiting to cover the retirement of the former, and soon overtook the Field Ambulance near the village of Busigny.

Here we halted for orders which did not arrive,[2] and should probably have been captured had not some of our cavalry passed that way. The officer in command informed us that our infantry and artillery had all left the field, that the cavalry were being withdrawn, and he suggested we should follow him as quickly as possible. I need hardly state the suggestion was promptly acted upon! As it was, two of our medical officers, Captains Kelly and Crymble, were taken prisoners while they were caring for our wounded in the church of a neighbouring village.

About 6 p.m. we hastened away, determined that our waggons laden with wounded should not fall into the enemy's hands if we could help it. The farther we went the denser did the stream of traffic grow

---

2. Major Brunskill, R.A.M.C., the D.D.M.S. of the 5th Division, who would have given us orders, we now know, had been taken prisoner.

and the slower did our progress become. To add to the unpleasantness of the situation a drizzling rain commenced to fall at dusk, and later, in the inky darkness, we found ourselves in a confused tangle of guns, ammunition waggons, motor-lorries, cavalry and infantry. Progress was painfully slow; often we were compelled to halt for twenty, thirty, or forty minutes, and then could advance only a few yards. Fortunately, the enemy had himself suffered too heavily to engage in an energetic pursuit. The exhausted infantry lay by the roadside, and often on the road itself, and had to be roused before we could get through. The whole of the night I sat on the box seat of our foremost waggon and held in my hands the only lamp which would burn.

In the awful darkness it was impossible for the other ambulance waggons to keep in touch with us. To have dismounted would have been to court certain disaster from wheels or horses; I could, therefore, only stick to my seat, prod the driver, who invariably slumbered during the long halts, in the ribs, and, by dint of shouting "Please make way for the wounded," get my waggon on a few yards at a time. Many times during the night I pulled aside the curtain at the front of the waggon, from the interior of which the sound of intermingled snores and groans constantly issued, to inquire how the wounded were getting on. The wakeful invariably answered, "All right, thank you, sir." One man, doubtless thinking of his less fortunate comrades, replied, "I reckon we're in clover, sir." What wonderful patience and contentment were theirs! Packed like herrings in a barrel, covered with ugly wounds, hungry, dirty, weary, they sat in that waggon for sixteen hours without a murmur or complaint. And ever as I looked in upon them I saw the faithful waggon-orderly keeping watch over his charges.

About 1 a.m. we saw ahead lights moving in the fields, and fondly hoped we should soon be able to rest. But it proved to be a bivouac for the Infantry, and at the entrance, lantern in hand, stood General Sir Charles Fergusson, busily engaged in sorting the men out by regiments and directing them to their respective resting-places. He bade us, and all the wheeled traffic, push on as quickly as possible.

When dawn broke on August 27th the 14th Field Ambulance, as far as I saw, consisted of Colonel Crawford, myself, and one ambulance waggon! Our anxiety as to the fate of our comrades was not to be removed till some hours later when, in St. Quentin, there was a great reunion, stragglers coming in from all directions, each with a tale to tell of thrilling experiences on that never-to-be-forgotten night.

By the time we reached St. Quentin we had covered considerably over twenty miles, and on the way I had often feared the horses might not last out. They were overloaded and badly needed food and water, especially the latter. As soon as it was light, seeing clover growing in a field by the roadside, I dismounted, plucked an arm-full, and ran after the horses and fed them with it as they trudged along. Being wet with the rain, it was for them both food and drink, and if ever animals looked their gratitude those horses did that morning. Dear, faithful beasts, they, and others of their kind, had done good work in saving men's lives.

I had been too occupied to feel hunger or thirst; my water-bottle, therefore, contained a goodly store, and from it I was able to give a welcome and refreshing draught to a great friend of mine, a young staff officer whom I came across. But how terribly he had changed in a few days! I scarcely recognised him in the hollow-eyed, unshaven individual who rode along slumbering fitfully as he rode. He greeted me with "My dear *padre*, I am glad to see you, for I heard you had been taken." From him I heard some details of the fight, and, in answer to my anxious inquiries, learned the loss of many a friend.

I deeply regretted that permission could not be given me to remain behind to bury our comrades who had fallen at Le Cateau, and I know all chaplains felt the same. Had we remained to perform this duty we should have been taken prisoners and for many days to come, in consequence, the hale and hearty, as well as the sick and wounded, would have been deprived of a chaplain's ministrations. As a matter of fact, the Reverends J. T. Hales and B. G. O'Rorke, C.F.'s, were taken prisoners on this day and were not released from captivity till ten months later. However, we consoled ourselves with the knowledge that our dead lay in a friendly country, and we felt confident that the French priests and villagers would reverently bury them. We know that this was invariably done.

I myself on many occasions have witnessed the genuine grief and loving sympathy displayed by the peasants when they stood with me beside the graves of our comrades. They would cast flowers into the grave, plant others upon the mound, and promise to faithfully tend it, as, with eyes dimmed by tears, they expressed their thanks to those who had crossed the sea to fight and die for *La belle France*. The following tribute by a French priest, and one probably typical of many others, was paid while he buried some British soldiers, and reported by one who heard it. It proves that our confidence was not misplaced, and should comfort those who, like ourselves, regret that the British soldiers could not, in every case, be buried by their own chaplains. He said:—

> We are defending our soil, our homes, our wives, our churches, our children, all we hold dear and sacred to us. But with the English it is not the same. For them, they have no need to leave their sweet home, their green Ireland, their glorious Scotland, their grand and ancient England. Why have they left everything, sacrificed everything? Why do they descend upon our shores every day like a wave which nothing can stop? Why are they now at our side, armed, calm, intrepid, happy, and singing? Because they are men of honour. Honour was violated, the liberty of the people of the Continent was in danger. May the God of Honour and Right watch over their bodies. May He take care of their souls. May He give them what they deserve, having done their duty—eternal rest; because you, like us, believe in the immortality of the soul. Blessing upon them. Their memory will live among us. We will take care of their graves.

The whole of the 14th Field Ambulance had reached St. Quentin by 8 a.m. on August 27th, and no time was lost in moving the wounded from the waggons into one of the large public buildings, where they received much-needed attention at the hands of the doctors. I went around and said a word to each, distributed among them the last of my cigarettes (which were now almost as precious as gold!) and then assisted in taking them to the railway-station, from which they were despatched in a special train to a Base hospital. This done, we had some breakfast in a cafe, and soon afterwards continued our march, for the town had to be evacuated by noon, beyond which General Smith-Dorrien could not guarantee its safety.

Once more we were an ordered force, and, while we had lost at Le Cateau 10,000 of our best in killed and wounded, we talked with pardonable pride of the splendid achievement of the Second Corps assisted by the 4th Division of the Third. Were we "downhearted"? I say emphatically, No. The troops were footsore, weary, dirty, and war-worn, but absolutely undaunted. "Tommy" may be a "grouser" at home, but he is cheerfulness and contentment personified on active service. If he had any complaint to make now it was that he was not allowed to face the Germans again at once, to get, as he expressed it, a little of his own back. The fights at Mons and Le Cateau had increased his confidence; the small British Force had held the huge German army, inflicted upon it enormous losses, successfully extricated itself, and pulled itself together. All ranks now confidently felt that, though they might continue the retirement, the day would come when they would turn and rend the Germans again. Subsequent events justified this confidence.

Chapter 6

End of the Retirement on Paris

On Thursday, August 27th, we left St. Quentin at 11 a.m. and marched for eleven miles in a south-westerly direction as far as the village of Cugny, where we halted, about tea-time, all very tired, hungry, and dirty. I remember having a most refreshing wash in a bucket of water under a hedge, and my first shave since Sunday. As I looked into the small hand-mirror I could scarcely believe that the reflection was that of myself. Several of us were hospitably entertained at a farm; the fresh bread and delicious coffee they gave us were a most welcome change from the hard biscuits and water on which we had existed almost entirely since Sunday. Colonel Crawford was given the only spare bed, and four of us shared an empty room, on the bare wooden floor of which we placed our valises.

At 1 a.m. an alarm was raised; we hastily packed up, and "stood by" till 3 a.m., when orders came to march. On we went, through Berlancourt and Guiscard to Noyon, where I met the 1st Battalion Devonshire Regiment doing duty on the Lines of Communication; it afterwards formed part of my brigade.

In Noyon we evacuated by train our sick and wounded, of whom we got a goodly number each day. We crossed the River Oise and saw the arrangements made by our engineers for blowing up the bridge. During the retirement, as the last of our troops crossed the Oise, the Aisne, and the Marne, the bridges were invariably destroyed and thus our pursuers were delayed.

We found a most delightful resting-place among the orchards near La Pommeraye, just beyond Pontoise. Here we received our first mail from England, and what pleasure and excitement it occasioned! My brigade followed close upon the ambulance, and bivouacked in cornfields. I visited Brigadier-General Rolt, and then each of my four regi-

BRIDGE OVER THE OISE DESTROYED
DURING THE RETIREMENT.

"WE FOUND A DELIGHTFUL RESTING-PLACE
AMONG THE ORCHARDS."

ments in turn. Having asked for the officer commanding the Suffolk Regiment, imagine my surprise when a junior subaltern appeared, and my sorrow as I heard from him that he, the transport officer, and the quartermaster were the only surviving officers after our fights at Mons[1] and Le Cateau. Among the rank and file, too, this regiment's losses had been very heavy; in a few days it had been reduced from 1,000 to 180 men. I found the troops busily engaged in cooking a meal and making beds for themselves with the sheaves of corn. Tired though they necessarily were after having marched thirty miles in twenty-four hours, they were in excellent spirits, and were proud to tell of the stand made by their respective regiments. They spoke of the loss of their officers and pals, and expressed the desire for an early opportunity of avenging their deaths. "Give us a good feed and a good rest, sir, and we'll take on the whole blooming German Army," one man said to me. The lads, I'm thankful to say, had both that night. How they had fought and marched under the burning August sun, with so little sleep or rest, was well-nigh miraculous.

Under the star-lit sky, wrapped only in my great-coat, I slept the clock round! Rumours reached us the next day, August 29th, that the retirement was over, and that the Allied Forces would give battle to the advancing enemy on the line where they now stood. It was a glorious day, and my servant, Trooper Williams of the 11th Hussars, availed himself of the opportunity to have a washing day! The non-arrival of marching orders in the afternoon gave promise of my being able to hold services for my brigade on the morrow. Arrangements were made, therefore, by which all the units under my charge would have an opportunity of attending divine worship. The promise, however, was not to be fulfilled, for at 7.30 that evening we were again on the march. By 11.30 we had reached Carlepont, where Mr. Watkins and I slept in a hayloft.

On Sunday, August 30th, we moved off at 3 a.m. and trekked all the morning, crossing the Aisne at Attichy and pushing on to the village of Croutoy. Here we halted for some hours awaiting instructions, in accordance with which, about teatime, we retraced our steps and bivouacked by the river at Attichy. Those of us who could swim enjoyed a dip in the stream, and I again visited my regiments when they arrived and bivouacked near us.

Again our hopes of a stand were disappointed, and on Monday the

---

1. *The Great Retreat*, 1914 by Gordon George Stuart & Roger Ingpen, two views of the Great Retreat, is also published by Leonaur.

31st we were off early, doing one of our hardest marches, more than twenty miles, over indifferent roads, under a burning sun. We halted for the night at Crepy-en Valois. Mr. Watkins and I slept in a cart; we welcomed the friendly shelter which it afforded from the cold wind, but agreed that we had slept on softer beds!

Early on September 1st, at the time we were due to move off, some excitement was occasioned by the discovery of *Uhlans* in the woods on our left. A handful of gunners, acting as infantry, crept through the intervening mangold fields in extended order, and then searched the wood. They soon returned and reported having driven off the enemy; so we commenced our march. For the rest of the day we were unmolested, but there was some sharp fighting in the woods of Compiègne and Villers-Cotterets. At Nery "L" Battery R.H.A. was attacked by two German batteries and Maxims at close range. It put up a magnificent fight, but was soon reduced to one gun and three men. In a few minutes all would have been over, but the opportune arrival of some of our cavalry and infantry turned the tables on the enemy. "L" Battery was saved, and the twelve German guns were captured. The three men, Captain E. K. Bradbury, Sergeant-Major Dorrell, and Sergeant Nelson received the Victoria Cross for their bravery.

Having spent the night at Ognes, we marched on September 2nd, at 3.30 a.m., passed through Oissery and St. Soupplette, and reached Montge in the afternoon. The heat was again almost overpowering. We saw large numbers of French cavalry during the day, and very reassuring the sight of them was, for we knew they would be protecting our flank, around which the enemy was constantly doing his best to pass.

At 7 p.m. Major Fawcett, in charge of four ambulance waggons containing sick and wounded, left for Lagny. By the wish of Colonel Crawford, I accompanied him and drove, in a two-wheeled spring cart, a senior officer of the artillery who was suffering from a complete nervous breakdown. I remember the night so well; there was a brilliant moon, and we passed many street-barricades erected and guarded by French soldiers.

As there was little or no traffic we made quick progress, and at 10.30 called a halt in Annet-sur-Marne, where we were given refreshment in the house of Monsieur La Roche. Tidings of our arrival soon spread, and we were visited by the mayor, Monsieur Gabriel Chamon, who informed us with pride that he had fought in 1870, and much regretted not being able to do so now.

At midnight we reached Lagny, on the Marne,[2] parked in the station yard, and removed the sick and wounded to the waiting-rooms. Having ascertained that there would be no train for Paris till 4 a.m., I lay on a stretcher in an ambulance waggon and sought some sleep, but in vain, for the cold was intense. The Paris train arrived at 5 a.m. crowded with refugees, but we succeeded in getting all our sick and wounded aboard, and right glad we were to see them safely on their way to hospital. By the time we had had some coffee and visited the two bridges, which were mined ready for blowing up, the rest of our unit had arrived, and with them we pushed on to Mont Richet, a small village about five miles south of Meaux.

Friday, September 4th, was very hot, and thankful we were to be able to rest all day, seeking some shade in a field of "mealies." "*One man in his time plays many parts*"; today I filled the role of a barber. My subject was the Rev. O. S. Watkins, who placed himself in my hands with complete confidence, although the photograph suggests misgivings on his part. My work was voted so satisfactory that I was there and then appointed honorary barber to the officers' mess. At 10.30 p.m. we were off again, and, marching through Crécy and its dense forest, early on Saturday, September 5th, reached Tournan. We had some sleep during the day under an avenue of trees, and learned with joy that at last our retirement was ended.

During the past week we had often wondered whether we were going to find ourselves in Paris, participating in another siege. We were glad to be spared that experience, while we were disappointed not to see the city after being within fifteen miles of it.

Our retirement from Mons[3] will go down to history as one of the finest achievements of the British Army. Frederick the Great said that the most difficult of all the operations of war is a successful retreat. Ours was an unqualified success; the troops preserved their excellent discipline and morale; I estimate they must have covered at least 190 miles, pursued by a relentless foe at whom they frequently struck back, always inflicting heavier losses than they suffered; and, now that they learned that they were to cease to retire, they were as eager and confident as on the first day of battle.

---

2 *Stand & Fall* by Joe Cassells, is also published by Leonaur, a soldier's recollections of the 'Contemptible Little Army' and the Retreat from Mons to the Marne, 1914, a Highland Regimental Scout recounts his experience of the Retreat from Mons.
3. *Infantry Brigade: 1914* by Edward Gleichen, a relative of Queen Victoria and a divisional commander during the Great War, is also published by Leonaur..

"ONE MAN IN HIS TIME PLAYS MANY PARTS."

Chapter 7

The Battle of the Marne

The German Staff never made a greater mistake than in the first week of September by imagining that the British were demoralized and might, therefore, be regarded as a negligible quantity. They were soon to give Von Kluck a rude awakening and make him pay dearly for his mistake. On September 6th our commander-in-chief appealed to us to show now to the enemy our power and "to push on vigorously to the attack beside the 6th French Army." He expressed his confidence that the British, "by another manifestation of the magnificent spirit which they had shown in the past fortnight," would "fall on the enemy's flank with all their strength, and, in unison with our Allies, drive them back."

A splendid response was made to this appeal. The troops were in the highest possible spirits; they whistled and sang their "Tipperary" and other popular airs and cracked their jokes. "We'll soon pull old One O'clock's whiskers for him," I heard one man say; and many, as I greeted them, remarked, "We're going in the right direction now, sir."

At the very hour when our friends in the home-land were wending their way to the House of God for their early Sabbath morning sacramental worship, the British army was commencing its forward movement. Our thoughts were with them; it was inspiring to know that before many an altar that morning, in the Church's great intercession service, we and our cause would be remembered. We regretted that again we were unable, on the Lord's own day, to offer Him corporate worship; but we felt that if *laborare est orare*, then we too, by our efforts to drive back the apostles of hate, were offering the God of love an act of worship. "Good-morning, sir; no church again today. Well, never mind, I says me prayers as I marches along," one lad said to me; and I know his attitude was typical of the men generally, of whom it could truly be said *"they walked with God."* Their quiet confidence, their splendid heroism, were the outcome of strong faith in the God of all the earth.

The sun shone with blistering heat, and we welcomed the shade afforded by Crécy's forest, through which at first our route lay. I went on in advance of the Field Ambulance to take a sick officer to the headquarters of the 5th Division. My servant drove him in our spring cart, and I rode in front on my horse. We left him safely at Villeneuve, and I went off to do some foraging for fresh bread and eggs. Riding up the street, I saw a "Tommy" advance into the road with a broad smile on his face and glad I was to see one of my old Church orderlies from Dublin. "Is it eggs you're looking for, sir? Come along with me, and I'll put you on to some!" If anything is to be found you may trust "Thomas Atkins" to find it.

Having successfully accomplished my "shopping," my servant and I went off in search of the Field Ambulance, which we found parked for a midday rest near La Pilloneries. Our march today ended at Dammartin, near Mortcerf, where we bivouacked in the grounds of a beautiful *château*. Here an incident occurred which caused some amusement to those who witnessed it: in the darkness one of our officers fell into the moat, and, as he was dragged out covered with green slime and wet to the skin, he remarked, "Well, that's an experience." Someone described the mildness of his language as nothing less than "a miracle of grace." Poor fellow, we were really very sorry for him, and hung him out to dry in front of our camp fire! The Transport sergeant, whose duty it was to superintend the care of the horses, hearing the splash in the water, ran to the moat and exclaimed, "Oh, it's only a man; I thought it might be a 'orse!"

We had slept that night but a short time when we were aroused by two of our Infantry, who asked, "Have you any sentries? because we've just seen, in the next field, some suspicious figures who did not answer our challenge." We replied that we were a Field Ambulance, and, consequently, had no sentries. We assured them we were not in the least alarmed, and bade them return and shoot or capture the suspicious figures, should they prove to be enemies. Knowing, as we now do, how little respect the Germans have for the Red Cross, we were, perhaps, too optimistic. However, we were well protected, for next morning we heard that these self-same sentries had captured some stragglers of the enemy during the night.

Our march on Monday, September 7th, took us as far as Coulommiers, out of which the enemy had been driven by our troops at 5 a.m. that day. Near Voisins we passed the scenes of several German bivouacs, unmistakable from the large numbers of wine-bottles with which the ground was littered. Wherever these bivouacs were in close proximity to a village invariably we found on the ground tables, chairs, and bedding which the cultured foe had carried out from the ransacked houses of harmless villagers. Some of the inhabitants had remained; these now crept forth from their hiding-places, and, as they told of the dastardly deeds of the enemy, our blood boiled. The men, too, could see for themselves the many proofs of senseless and brutal devastation. Henceforward they had not only their own losses to avenge, but the wrongs of these innocent victims of the French countryside. They now realised that they were up against no ordinary foe, but Huns who must be crushed at all costs. Hence they pushed forward with new vigour and increased determination.

Early on September 8th we pushed on through Boissy and St. Germain till, in the village of Doue we came up with our batteries, which were in action. The bearer divisions of all three sections of the Field Ambulance went forward under Majors Goldsmith, Richards, and Fawcett. An empty cottage, prepared as a dressing-station, was very soon the scene of considerable activity. Hither the ambulance waggons bore the wounded, and, when they had discharged them, returned again and again to the field. By noon our infantry had progressed so far that it became necessary to form an advanced dressing-station, which was done at a farmhouse, Major Fawcett being left in charge. The wounded at the main dressing-station in Doue were evacuated to rail-head by some of our ambulances and supply lorries which, otherwise, were returning empty. In the meantime I had ridden on to do what I could at the advanced dressing-station.

Late in the afternoon the whole Field Ambulance re-formed here and we marched on after our victorious troops through St. Ouen. Here, in a cottage to which his regimental stretcher-bearers had carried him, we found Captain Whish, of the 1st East Surreys, mortally wounded. The doctor did everything possible for him, but it was seen that his case was hopeless. Those standing around having bared their heads, I commended his soul into the hands of his Creator, and he was then tenderly lifted into one of our ambulance waggons and watched by a nursing orderly. We continued our march, and in the darkness reached Rougeville.

Lieutenant G. D. Eccles, Medical Officer of the First East Surrey Regiment and Stretcher-Bearers

During the day our corps had encountered considerable opposition, but had driven back the enemy at all points with great loss, making many prisoners and taking several guns.

Arrived at the scene of our bivouac, I went in search of my friend Lieutenant-Colonel (now Brigadier-General) J. R. Longley, officer commanding the 1st East Surreys, to report to him the death of Captain Whish, and to ask that the pioneers of the regiment might dig a grave early in the morning.

About 4 a.m. on September 9th I met my friend Pioneer Sergeant Fisher, of the East Surreys, a regular communicant and a good soldier who has since won the D.C.M., and we selected a site for the grave in an orchard, where we laid the fallen officer to rest: representatives of the regiment who could be spared were present, and several villagers cast flowers upon the body, and promised to tend the grave. The pioneers erected a wooden cross, and I made a sketch of the location of the grave, which I sent to his relatives.

My sad task accomplished, I rode after the Field Ambulance and overtook it as it was descending the steep hill into Saacy on the Marne. Here we halted for some hours, and had a splendid view of the fierce engagement which was taking place on the north bank of the river, the crossing of which had been forced by our infantry some hours earlier in face of a terrific cannonade.

Soon after noon we were allowed to cross the Marne, and followed our fighting troops up a hill so steep that we had to seek the aid of the gunners' horses to get our waggons up it. We found ourselves in a wood with three of our batteries in close proximity to us, but they were so cleverly concealed that we and they enjoyed immunity from German shells. Along the crest of the opposite hill we could locate the enemy's batteries by the flashes of their guns and the bursting of our shells.

Our gunners did magnificent work, of which we found many proofs next day; in one case a whole German battery was destroyed; guns, carriages, and limbers lay in a confused heap, and only one German gunner, out of about ninety men, survived to tell the tale. By nightfall our troops had won a great victory, and were encamped several miles north of the Marne, with the enemy in full retreat.[1]

All day long our stretcher-bearers worked hard and with a fine disregard for danger. I was thrilled with admiration as I watched their

---

1. *1914: the Marne and the Aisne*, two accounts, by H. W. Carless-Davis and A. Neville Hilditc, is also published by Leonaur.

British and German wounded being sent to hospital after the Battle of the Marne

devotion to duty. They would come into the wood where the Field Ambulance had its dressing-station in comparative shelter, deposit their bleeding burdens, give us a word or two about the progress of the fight, wipe the sweat from their brows, and then willingly and eagerly return to pursue their work of mercy where the bullets were falling like rain. If there are degrees of bravery, then, surely, theirs was bravery of the highest order.

At the dressing-station we were fully occupied all the afternoon and long after dusk. When the bearers' work was completed I mounted my horse and took a convoy of wounded to a neighbouring village, from whence they were removed in motors to rail-head. Then I returned with my commando to the Field Ambulance, and we all lay down after our exhausting day to seek some rest; of sleep we had little, for it rained heavily.

At dawn next morning the Rev. O. S. Watkins and I decided to go over the field in different directions and to bury any dead whom we found, irrespective of their religious denominations. Through the wet cornfields I rode accompanied by three or four men of the Royal Army Medical Corps, and whenever we found a fallen comrade we bore his body to a corner of the field, to secure as far as possible its never being disturbed, and there we dug a shallow grave. Often, of course, more than one, sometimes three or four, and in one case eighteen men and two officers did I bury in one grave. Always I carefully located the grave by a rough sketch, and kept a record of the names and regiments of those whom I buried. Whenever possible I made a rude cross, by tying two sticks together with string, and set it over the grave.

Once or twice I came upon burying parties from the regiments, and one said to me, "Please, sir, we have just buried two chaps over there: maybe you would come and say a prayer over them." While one of the party held my horse, I said parts of our beautiful Service for the Burial of the Dead, and it always seemed to comfort those who were mourning their pals. What a multitude of thoughts passed through my mind as I laid the brave lads to rest; I thought of the splendid fight they had put up, of the pain and agony which it was evident some of them had endured, of their mothers and wives who would look upon their loved ones no more in this life. Whenever I could find the address of any such I invariably wrote them a word of sympathy, and in reply have received some treasured expressions of gratitude, and often the promise of their prayers. Brave women; God comfort and bless them.

In one part of the field I saw striking evidence of the fierceness of yesterday's encounter. I came across a small wood from which we collected twenty of our dead, and in another wood, separated from the former by a field only eighty yards in width, we found many German dead. Imagine what it must have been like while opposing forces were blazing away at one another with hundreds of rifles at such close range. The marvel is that so few were killed. I also saw a dummy battery with which, for a while, the enemy had drawn the fire from our guns. The real one had eventually been discovered, and we saw the results of our gunners' good marksmanship.

Soon after noon the Rev. O. S. Watkins and I met, and, by comparing notes, concluded we had covered the whole of the ground over which our brigade had fought. As a matter of fact, I buried a considerable number belonging to another brigade of our division as well.

We hurried away, for our Field Ambulance had gone on some hours ago. We had not ridden far when we came upon Lieutenant Grenfell, our quartermaster, with part of our transport in difficulties. A wheel of one of the waggons had sunk deeply into a hole in the road and was defying all efforts to get it out. As the waggon contained rations, the quartermaster was getting anxious. Most opportunely some gunners, whom I knew, were passing with their ammunition waggons. In their hearing I said, "If anybody can get the waggon out the gunners will," immediately there came the cheery response, "We'll have a try, sir."

No sooner said than done: the waggon was hauled out and sent on its way. These same gunners had yesterday helped us up a hill, now out of a hole, and a few miles farther on some of them dismounted and dug a grave by the roadside in which I buried a sergeant of the West Kents who had been killed accidentally as the regiment marched along. Not without reason, I knew, have the Gunners as part of their regimental motto the word *"ubique"*; they seemed to be everywhere and able to do anything.

As we rode on I heard that a friend of mine. Captain the Hon. A. R. Hewitt, of the 1st East Surreys, had been severely wounded, and that Lieutenant Danks, one of our doctors, who had remained with him in a cottage, had been taken prisoner. The former was too ill to be moved, so the Germans took his doctor! I learned, too, with great pleasure of the conspicuous bravery of my friend, Sergeant-Major Hyson (now Quartermaster) of the 1st East Surreys, in rescuing wounded under fire. For his conduct on this occasion he has since received both the D.C.M. and the Military Cross.

The Battle of the Marne, or the Battle of the Rivers[2] as it is sometimes called, which had commenced on the morning of the 6th was now on the 10th really over. The Allies had scored a great victory, large numbers of prisoners and guns, as well as a vast quantity of stores, falling into their hands. Von Kluck paid dearly for his mistake in placing such a low estimate upon the fighting powers of the British Force. Five Divisions of British Infantry drove before them a greater number of the enemy in spite of their being on the defensive and often in strong positions on the rivers. The Germans were now in full retreat to the Aisne, and the operations during the next two days partook of the nature of a drive. The British pursued as relentlessly as they had before been pursued: at last "Tommy" was "getting a little of his own back."

---

2. *The Western Front, 1914 Trilogy* by Edmund Dane is also published by Leonaur. (Contains *Hacking Through Belgium, Battle of the Rivers* and *Battles in Flanders*).

CHAPTER 8

The Battle of the Aisne

During the next two days we followed hard upon the Germans, who had made off in a north-easterly direction. Unfortunately, the weather now changed from almost tropical heat to heavy rain and cold winds. The roads soon became a sea of mud, and our transport was often in difficulties. Marching and riding were most unpleasant, but even those who were drenched to the skin maintained a wonderful cheerfulness. If we were having an unpleasant time ourselves we knew the Germans must be having a much worse; they dared not halt, for we were close on their heels; they were dejected by their defeat at the Marne, our troops were victorious, and neither rain nor mud could damp their enthusiasm. They pushed the enemy hard, and many were the signs we saw of the hastiness of his retreat.

Their unburied dead lay by the roadside and in the fields; in the hedgerows lay articles of equipment abandoned by desperate men to expedite their flight from the British. Many prisoners fell into our hands, some surrendering even to our Field Ambulance. And, as the enemy fled, the Allied cavalry pursued and cut them up, and our artillery wrought awful havoc among their battalions and convoys. Thus the *Kaiser's* hosts, which were to shatter France and march triumphantly into Paris, fled precipitately across the plain of Châlons to the banks of the Aisne, where their engineers had for many days been preparing the defences of a position which is one of great natural strength.

Friday, September 11th, found the Field Ambulance at Billy-sur-Ourcq, where we spent a wet night in the fields. Our brigade found billets in the village, and I'm afraid, as we lay awake and thought of them, we came very near to breaking the tenth commandment. I crawled under a waggon, where I rested if I could not sleep; it was far too wet and cold to get much of the latter. From 5 a.m. to dusk on the next day we marched in a pouring rain and were very thankful to secure billets in the village of Chacrise. The sons of our host and hostess were away fighting in the ranks of the French Army, and doubtless this fact made them take the more cheerfully the crowding of eight or ten of us into their small cottage. They did everything they possibly could to secure our comfort.

One incident of our stay here I must note. Late in the evening, as we marched, there had been brought to us Trooper Marsh, of the 4th Hussars, severely wounded in the abdomen. He had been entrusted with an important message, and, while in the act of carrying it, had been shot by the enemy. Bleeding though he was, and faint, he had clung to his saddle and faithfully discharged his duty; but, of course, by so doing had considerably aggravated his wound. His case was seen to be very serious, and I was called to see him as he lay in one of our ambulance waggons. "Thank God, sir, I did my duty," the brave fellow said to me, "and, having done that, I am quite ready to die, if it's God's will." He had sacrificed himself for his chums, and "*greater love hath no man than this.*" Soon afterwards he was borne into our cottage for an operation which, the doctors said, was his only hope.

In spite of the cramped space and other difficulties, the operation, a most delicate one, was successfully performed; but the young hero died a few hours afterwards, in spite of every care and attention. Next morning I remained behind to bury him. I called upon the mayor, and he directed some of the villagers to prepare a grave in the cemetery. I remember I had some difficulty in explaining that no coffin was required, for, on active service, the best we can do for our fallen comrades is to sew their bodies into a blanket. In the presence of a few villagers I laid the trooper to rest at 6.30 a.m. and then rode after the Field Ambulance, which I overtook as it was descending the steep hill into Serches, a pretty village nestling at the head of a valley which runs at right angles to, and, at a point three miles farther north, joins the valley of the Aisne.

The Germans had taken up a strong position on the north bank of the Aisne, and had destroyed all the bridges behind them. The British Force had reached the south bank on September 12th, and now occupied a front of some fifteen miles, extending from Soissons eastward to Villers. Early on the morning of the 13th the Battle of the Aisne commenced, the whole British Force advancing to force the passage of the river. The enemy's position was such as to make it impossible

HORSES AND AMMUNITION BEING FERRIED ACROSS THE AISNE.

PONTOON BRIDGE OVER THE AISNE NEAR ST. MARGUERITE.

to accurately gauge his strength, but there is no doubt that there were overwhelming numbers opposed to us, with a preponderance of Artillery skilfully concealed. In spite of this, by nightfall our troops had secured a footing upon the north bank at various points along the whole of our front. The British had forced difficult river-crossings before at the Modder and Tugela, but never so quickly, nor against stronger opposition. Their success was due very largely to the daring work of the Royal Engineers, who constructed rafts, built pontoon bridges, and repaired, under heavy fire, those which had been destroyed by the Germans.

Captain Johnston, R.E., attached to our division, worked with his own hands two rafts at Missy, where our brigade crossed, and for this service was awarded the V.C.

Our stretcher-bearers, in charge of Majors Goldsmith, Richards and Fawcett, had gone out from the Field Ambulance at Serches early in the morning, following close upon our brigade as it advanced to the attack. Late in the evening an advanced dressing-station was formed at the farm Rapreux, about five hundred yards south of the river, and the whole Field Ambulance moved forward two miles and established itself in the village of Jury.

All night long the engineers worked incessantly at their pontoon bridges, and the stretcher-bearers passed to and fro between the advanced dressing-station and the firing line. They were accompanied in turn by Majors Richards and Fawcett, of whose devotion and bravery it is impossible to speak too highly. These two officers and their stretcher-bearers continued this devoted work during the whole time we remained in this locality. When the enemy retired next day to the heights and a regimental aid-post was established in a farm near St. Marguerite their work became even more arduous, for the wounded had then to be carried a distance of quite a mile and a half across an open plain, consisting of ploughed fields sodden with the heavy rain, which was frequently swept by shrapnel.

Equally good work was done, though under less trying conditions, at the headquarters of the Field Ambulance in Jury. Colonel Crawford gave himself no rest in superintending the many excellent arrangements made for the reception, the treatment and the evacuation of the wounded. During these days many men owed their lives to the surgical skill of Captain Lindsay, and Lieutenants Clark and Tasker. On one occasion they worked in the operating theatre, a room in a farmhouse, from 7 p.m. until 2 a.m. incessantly. One night we were especially busy, the ambulance waggons bringing us in as many as a hundred and fifty wounded. As they lay on straw in the rooms of the farm-house, in barns and in outhouses, I went around and did what I could, taking a message from one, writing a card for another, giving drinks of Bovril, helping some to move into a more comfortable position, saying a word of cheer to all, and having prayers with the most serious cases.

The fortitude of these wounded was magnificent, not a word of complaint did one of them utter, though many were suffering from ghastly injuries. This has invariably been my experience, and one of our doctors bears the same testimony, he says:

> Believe me, the Victoria Cross is won over and over again in a single day. They are brave! What if you were to see how the wounded act after the excitement of battle! They suffer their wounds, great and small, without a murmur; they get their wounds dressed, take chloroform, give consent to have their limbs amputated, just as if they were going to have their hair cut. They are gloriously brave.

As I went my rounds I was told a wounded officer would like to see me, and among other things he said to me was this: "Remember, *padre*, I want to wait till all the men have been attended to before they operate on me." This splendid unselfishness is one of the characteristics of the British officer which endear him to "Tommy." I gave him a drink, covered him with blankets, and then he said, "Don't let me keep you, for others will need you." He waited till the very last, though his wound was a most serious one, and I was very glad to hear, some weeks afterwards, that he had made a marvellous recovery. "Tommy" always had a great admiration for his officers, but this campaign has increased it. "Our officers are grand," one man said to me, "if there is dangerous work to do, they wants to do it and they always takes more than their share of the risks."

I am reminded of a night when I was talking to a sergeant as he lay on a stretcher badly wounded. He was making many anxious inquiries for the officer who had been wounded as they fought together, and, at that very moment, the wounded officer was carried in and placed on the floor beside the sergeant, whose face was swathed in bandages which covered his eyes. The latter heard the officer's name mentioned, and asked, "Are you there, sir?" stretching out his hand to clasp that of his officer. "Are you all right, sir?" The anxious inquiries,

ADVANCED DRESSING-STATION
500 YARDS SOUTH OF THE AISNE.

A FARM, NORTH OF THE AISNE,
USED AS A REGIMENTAL AID-POST.

the clasp of the hands, were eloquent tributes to the devotion of the soldier to his officer. This is a typical instance; and as we watched the scene our eyes were dimmed with tears. With such a splendid spirit of good comradeship existing between officers and men, it is not to be wondered at that the men need no driving, like the German soldiers, but will follow anywhere, through anything, those whom they love, admire, and trust.

Whenever I could be spared from the Field Ambulance I rode around to visit the outlying batteries, the advanced dressing-station, and the regimental aid-post. To reach the last-named, I crossed a pontoon bridge and then over the open plain where I knew I was in full view of the enemy. I never hesitated to do this because I felt that a single horseman wasn't worth firing at, or that, if the enemy thought otherwise, the chances of his hitting me were very small. Evidently my first conclusion was justified, for I enjoyed my rides unmolested. The regimental aid-post, a farm used also by General Rolt as his headquarters, was a "warm spot." It could be approached only from the back with any degree of safety; the front entrance was covered by the enemy's snipers. Here I found the regimental medical officers busy rendering first aid to the wounded and then handing them over to the stretcher-bearers from the Field Ambulance.

In the corner of an orchard I saw the graves of an officer and two or three men who had been buried on a night when I had been too occupied with my ministrations to the wounded to get over there to conduct the service. One of the regimental doctors had, on this occasion, read the prayers over the graves. I buried our dead whenever possible, but on the occasions when my duty to them and to the living clashed, I felt it was more important that I should be with the latter. Now that each brigade has two Church of England chaplains this difficulty has, of course, been removed.

On my way back, taking a slightly different route, I came upon two of my regiments, the Suffolks and the Cornwalls, in their shelter trenches. Suddenly heads appeared from holes in the ground, and I was greeted with "Good-morning, sir; come in and see our 'appy 'ome." Having dismounted and tied my horse to a tree, I accepted the invitation. The "home" was, indeed, a happy one, for a cheerier lot of fellows I've never met. They had plenty to eat and smoke, so were perfectly content. The floor of their "home" was mud, the roof leaked, but these things mattered not. They had marched and fought in the soaking rain for days, they were now living an unnatural existence more like moles or rabbits than men, and yet never a word of complaint did I hear. They were cheerfulness personified. Truly "Tommy Atkins" is a marvel. They welcomed me most heartily, and as I rode away they shouted, "Goodbye, sir; take care of yourself."

Another day I accompanied the Rev. O. S. Watkins when he rode off to visit the 13th Brigade, for the Wesleyans in which he was responsible as well as for those in the 14th and 15th. I did so the more gladly because there was the prospect of my meeting some of my old Dublin friends. We climbed a steep hill, at the top of which we found a squadron of the 19th Hussars billeted in a large farm. As a matter of fact, they occupied chiefly some natural caves in the rocks, which were entered from the farmyard; the French peasants are said to have used them as hiding-places in their last great war. Our road to Sermoise lay now on the sky-line, and we had a splendid view of the German position. Suddenly from his observation post an artillery officer called to us, "You're two brave men; but don't stop, or you'll give us away."

We shouted a cheery reply, and continued to trot our horses as we had been doing when he addressed us. Alas, only a few days later the enemy spotted this observation-post, and one of his shells killed two and wounded several of our gunners here. Having safely crossed the plateau, we descended the steep hill into Sermoise. We found part of the 13th Brigade dwelling in caves and dugouts on the hill-side. In the village, occupying the only house which was undamaged by shell-fire, we visited my friend Lieutenant Helm, the medical officer of the Yorkshire Light Infantry, whom I had last seen on the other side of a tennis-net in Dublin. His dwelling owed its safety to the shelter afforded by a higher building, the church, which had been very badly damaged. This was a "warm" spot, but he was to occupy "warmer ones" later on. For his conspicuous bravery he has been mentioned in *Despatches*, and awarded the Military Cross. We saw the whole countryside studded with enormous holes made by the shells from the German big siege-guns, to which, on the Aisne, we had our first introduction, and for which "Tommy" soon found the nicknames of "Black Maria" and "Jack Johnson."

By September 18th the worst of the fighting was over, and the Battle of the Aisne, in the strict sense of the word, ended, for the Allies abandoned the idea of carrying the German position by a frontal attack. The fighting of the past five days had unmasked the enemy's strength, and proved that he was not merely fighting a delaying action, preparatory to a further retirement to the Sambre, but was making a serious stand in a strong position of his own choosing. The only thing to be done was to dig ourselves in and hold the enemy while the French developed a flanking movement on our left. The Battle of the Aisne now became a siege.

September 20th I shall always remember as the first Sunday, in this campaign, on which I was able to hold divine services. I celebrated the Holy Communion at 7.30 a.m. in one of the farm buildings on the floor of which clean straw had been laid. A good number of officers and men of various units attended. At the door knelt our hostess, the fanner's wife, a reverent, though necessarily a silent, worshipper. For my own brigade I could, on this Sunday, do nothing, as they were in the trenches, but, with some hymnbooks in my saddle-bags, I rode around to, and had brief services with, some of the outlying units. In the evening the Rev. O. S. Watkins and I conducted a united service, of which one of the officers present wrote home the following description:

> In the evening we had another service in a barn, conducted by the chaplain and the Wesleyan Minister. A great crowd of officers and men collected. The scene was very impressive, with the room lit with only camp candles, the soldiers rough and dirty with the work of war, some of them just returned from the trenches, and others going there the same night—some who in all probability would be dead before another night came along. The men sang heartily, but when the prayer for the dear ones at home was being offered there were few dry eyes among those brave men who faced death daily; and all through the service we could hear the roar of the cannon sending forth their messages of death and sorrow. It was terrible in its impressiveness.

The arrival of the 6th Division from England enabled a system of regular relief from the trenches to be established, and the Field Ambulance was moved back to Serches, that the whole of the village of Jury might be available for the resting brigade. When the time came for my own brigade to come back into reserve my days were fully occupied in visiting my regiments and holding informal meetings and services for them. On Sunday, September 27th, for the first time I got the whole of my brigade together for a parade service. It was a novel experience for me to see my congregation with rifles as well as sidearms. I have never heard the hymns, "Jesu, lover of my soul," "Oft in danger," and "O God, our help in ages past," sung more heartily.

On the hill, not half a mile from us, the Germans were bursting their shrapnel with disastrous results, of which I have already spoken, to some of our gunners near their observation-post. Captain T. Lindsay and our stretcher-bearers very gallantly removed the wounded under a heavy fire. Tidings of the disaster reached me, and I rode up, immediately after my service, to make arrangements for the burial of the dead, but the officer in charge of the battery said it would not be possible to perform this duty till after dusk because the place where the bodies lay was constantly being shelled. I promised to go up again after my evening service. The early celebration and morning service which I had arranged had to be cancelled at the last moment in consequence of my brigade being called out to assist in repelling a threatened attack by the enemy. However, the parade service was held in the afternoon instead of the morning, and in the evening I conducted a voluntary service which was well attended.

For us at Serches the monotony of the remaining days on the Aisne was relieved by camp-fire concerts arranged by Sergeant Plume, and the spectacular fights between our aeroplanes and the German Taubes, of which we saw one brought down and others go limping home. One day I joined our mess president in a ride to Soissons, whither he went to replenish our store of provisions. We saw the terrible havoc wrought by the enemy's guns upon the beautiful twelfth-century cathedral and the ancient Abbey of St. Jean des Vignes; some of the streets were actually blocked by the debris from demolished houses. Many of the townspeople had remained during the bombardment, others were now returning, and business was being resumed.

The men in the trenches very soon found ways and means of relieving the tedium of their new kind of existence. In many places their trenches were separated from those of the Germans by not more than 60 yards, and the occupants would shout their jibes and jokes one to another. I have been told how, at first, in response to our men's call of "Waiter," several heads would appear above the parapet of the opposite trench. I say at first advisedly, for the Germans quickly learned that what "Tommy" sought was not a drink but a target. In our quarter the opposing forces would mark or signal each other's shots as if they were on a rifle-range.

In two cases the Cornwalls saw Germans fall hit when the bull's-eye was signalled. Often the two sides would unite in singing the same songs or hymns, and the Germans were always glad to hear the latest football results. Tobacco and cigarettes were flung from one side to the other in exchange for food, and news of the latest success by land or sea was invariably shouted for the information of their opponents. These truces never impaired the constant vigilance, and neither side dare take great liberties with the other; but in these and other ways the tedium of trench life was relieved and the days were helped along.

And then the day came when the British troops marched away from the Aisne, where, under the trying conditions of heavy rain and cold which had prevailed most of the time, subjected by day and night to Infantry attacks by superior numbers and the fire of guns of a calibre never used before in field operations, they had stood their ground, and "once more demonstrated the splendid spirit, gallantry, and devotion which animates the officers and men of His Majesty's Forces." Our losses in killed, wounded, and missing of 561 officers and 12,980 men testify to the severity of the struggle in which we had been engaged. The stale-mate had become chronic, and less seasoned troops might be trusted to hold the position.

The Allies' line was daily stretching farther north, and, if it was eventually to reach the sea, it would be advantageous that we should again be on its left where we could draw our supplies through the Channel ports which were so near home. A still more weighty reason for our transference lay in the discovery of a new German offensive aimed especially at the British, and which had as its objective Calais and other Channel ports. It was most fitting that we should be there to meet it. The story of the part we played in the race for the sea, in the closing of the door to Calais, and in holding it against the German assaults will be told in subsequent chapters.

Chapter 9

The Race for the Sea

In the evening of October 1st I had walked over to Couvrelles, where the 13th Field Ambulance was billeted, to visit my friend the Rev. T. S. Goudge, C.F., and upon my return to Serches at 7.30 I found the unit, to which I was attached, ready to march off. This was a great surprise, because, when I had left two hours earlier, there had been no intimation of a possible move. What could it mean? Were we advancing or retiring? The former possibly, the latter we would not believe. Soon we were informed that neither the one nor the other was happening. Were we, then, to be given the rest spoken of frequently by many and even dreamed of by not a few? The arrival of other regiments to relieve us lent colour to the last conjecture, and, as I watched my regiments passing through the village on their return from the trenches, I the more heartily wished it might be even as we hoped, for the men badly needed rest and sleep after their almost ceaseless vigil on the Aisne. We now know that before us there was not much rest, but that we were then beginning the race for the sea which involved long marches, a railway journey, and then still more marches.

The Rev. O. S. Watkins, Lieutenant Grenfell and I volunteered to form the billeting party, and rode off in the darkness to Nanteuil, where we were told to report to the brigade billeting officer, Captain Dorling. By him we were assigned a large farm, near the little Norman church, as our billet. All the French farms we saw seemed to be built on much the same plan. The yard has on one side of it the dwelling-house, the other three sides are formed by barns and sheds for the cattle, carts, and implements. The entrance is usually by heavy iron gates or high wooden doors; on this occasion we were confronted by the latter and found them securely fastened on the inside.

Our repeated shoutings and hangings having failed to arouse the occupants of the house, the Rev. O. S. Watkins climbed over the doors, like some professional burglar, and opened them from the inside. Luckily for him the ferocious dog was chained up! Very soon the farmer appeared on the scene and we explained the object of our coming. He seemed anything but pleased to see us. Perhaps in the darkness, and from the method of our entrance, he judged us to be Germans; but I don't really think this could have been so, because he, his wife and daughters, were just as disagreeable and disobliging next day, when any doubts they may have had about our nationality must have been removed. No, they were just a churlish, ungrateful lot, the like of whom we never met again. Their behaviour was the more noticeable because it was in such striking contrast to that generally shown us by those in whose houses we found shelter.

The sick and wounded whom the Field Ambulance brought along were placed in the little church, and the 1st Battalion of the Devonshire Regiment, which had joined my brigade the day before in relief of the Suffolk Regiment, bivouacked in the fields around the farm. My service in the 4th Volunteer Battalion of this fine old regiment from 1893 to 1904 had given me a peculiar interest in it, and made me welcome the more heartily its 1st Battalion to my brigade.

We now commenced to observe a new order of things, marching by night and resting by day. Waggons and guns, etc., were secreted under trees, and the men were bidden to keep to their billets or to hide themselves whenever an aeroplane was sighted. It was, we were told, of the very essence of the movement in which we were now engaged that it should not be discovered by the enemy. This helped us to a solution, and we concluded that we were being taken around to the enemy's flank. In this conjecture we were quite correct; now the only question was, should we be in time to cut off the Germans from the sea?

Having rested all day, at 6.30 p.m. we, the billeting party constituted as before, met representatives from the other units of the brigade, and rode off due west. On this and succeeding nights we had the benefit of a full moon and perfect weather. We passed through the villages of Muret, Droizy, Hartennes, Tigny and Villers-Helon; most of these places possessed a church of exceptional architectural beauty, and in many of them we met French soldiers, as we were now intersecting our Ally's lines of communication. Our route next took us through a very pretty neighbourhood, beautifully wooded, with picturesque villas, lovely gardens, and orchards. Descending a steep hill, we found ourselves in the old-world town of Longpont, with its city-gate, fine *château*, and ruined twelfth-century abbey, all objects of great interest.

Here the billeting officer awaited us; the gunners got the *château*, the Infantry found accommodation in the town, but the Field Ambulance had to be contented with an avenue of trees for its bivouac. Hither we repaired about 11.30 p.m., tied our horses to trees, gave them a feed, collected sticks, made a brew of tea, and dined off "bully" beef and biscuits. We sat around the fire and yarned till 1.30 a.m., when the Field Ambulance arrived, all very tired after their eighteen-miles march. I'm afraid the billeting party was not in very high favour on this occasion!

We who had been living in the constant din of battle, with the enemy's shells bursting over our billets, and our own batteries around us shaking the earth and filling the air with a deafening roar, thoroughly appreciated the restful quiet of these days. Had we not occasionally heard the distant rumble of the French guns it would have been difficult to realise we were on active service, and as we passed through the beautiful country we could now enjoy it to the full, for there was no foe at our heels. We knew not what experiences lay before us; that there was work, and strenuous work, to be done we felt certain; but no anxious forebodings marred the enjoyment of these peaceful days which did so much to reinvigorate the troops, upon whom a great demand was to be made a week later in front of La Bassée.

I spent Saturday, October 3rd, in visiting the men of the Devonshire Regiment in their billets, and in viewing the ruins of the one-time magnificent abbey. At 6 p.m. I again accompanied the billeting party, and our ride through Corey, Fleury, and the forest de Retz was the most pleasant of many delightful ones we had. The effect of the moon shining through the trees was grand. These rides were the more enjoyable because, being a small party, we could vary our pace, as and when we liked, to the mutual advantage of man and beast. A column of mixed troops on the march must necessarily observe the pace of the infantry, and this is very trying for those who are mounted; and the clouds of dust raised by wheels and the tramp of many feet poison the air and detract from the enjoyment of even the most beautiful scenery.

In Villers-Cotterets, the scene of some spirited fighting during the great retirement, we called a halt. We watered our horses and gave them a nose-bag feed in the public square, and refreshed ourselves with coffee. The splendid condition of our mounts and the fitness of

City gate at Longpont.

Ruins of Abbey at Longpont.

our troops filled the townspeople with admiration; and I remember a sergeant of the French Aviation Corps showing me, with great pride, a Mauser pistol which he had taken from the person of a German officer whom he had shot down in flight. The town was full of French troops, and many were the friendly and enthusiastic greetings which they exchanged with us.

Through the town, out on to the moonlit road bounded (as one so often finds the roads in this country) on cither side by tall trees, on through Largny and Vez we rode to Fresnoy la Rivière, where we met Captain Dorling, who assigned us as our billet a farm in the hamlet of Rocquigny, about a mile and a half farther on Thither we rode, and, as it was now past 11 o'clock, we found the occupants had retired for the night. Our hangings at the iron gate soon brought to one of the bedroom windows a man, who, at the announcement of our mission, said he welcomed us and would have great pleasure in offering us hospitality. What a different reception from that accorded us at the last farm in which we had stayed!

Here the occupants, a postman and his wife, relatives left in charge by the farmer who was absent fighting in the French Army, could not do enough for us. They were not in the least perturbed when we broke it to them gently that twelve officers, two hundred and fifty men, and an unknown number of sick must find accommodation there. *Madame*, who wished to prepare beds for the officers, actually wept with disappointment when we informed her that we had our own valises and merely required floor-space on which to place them. Was there nothing she could do? she asked; yes, she might give us some refreshment, we told her. Again she was perfectly happy, and soon set before us delicious coffee, butter, and home-made bread.

The hours of waiting for the Field Ambulance passed very pleasantly in conversation with our host and hostess. Among other things, they told us that the Germans had occupied the farm on the night of August 31st. We remembered that on this selfsame night we had, during the great retirement, bivouacked at Crépy only three miles away! I have already mentioned the fact of our being harassed by *Uhlans* as we were leaving Crépy on the morning of September 1st.

It was 4 a.m. on Sunday, October 4th, before the Field Ambulance and infantry arrived after their march of twenty-two miles. Under the circumstances an early celebration was out of the question, and the troops could not be massed in the open for a parade service. The best I could do was to hold a voluntary service at dusk in the shelter of the farm buildings; the troops turned up well to this.

Two days later we continued our trek westwards through Saintimes, Verberie, and Pontpoint to Pont St. Maxence, an old-world town on the Oise, which we crossed by a pontoon bridge constructed by the French, who had destroyed the fine stone one during their retirement. At the railway-station our march ended, and we were informed that in a few hours we were to entrain for a destination known only to the Staff. Never shall I forget the long wait in the station yard that bitterly cold night; we dozed before a huge log fire, we walked about, we helped to man-haul our waggons on to the trucks: at last, dirty and tired, we got away about 8 a.m. on our ten-hours railway journey. Of this I don't remember much, because I slept most of the time, but I know we went through Clermont and Amiens.

I believe the original intention had been to take us much farther north, but a change in the military situation made it necessary to detrain at Abbeville, at the mouth of the Somme, and only forty-five miles from Boulogne. Farther north the Belgian Army and British Marines were heroically holding on to Antwerp and engaging the attention of large forces of the enemy, while the Allies hurried up troops from the south. The Seventh Division, under Major-General Capper, and the Third Cavalry Division, commanded by Major-General the Hon. Julian Byng, were landing at Zeebrugge and Ostend and were soon covering the retreat of the brave defenders of Antwerp.

The night of October 7th was spent by us in the village of Montfliers, where there is a beautiful little church built to contain a figure of the Virgin and Child which is said to have been hidden in the trunk of a tree still standing close by. Next day we rode through Vauchelles, St. Riquier, with its fine abbey, Oneux, Yvrench, and Vitz-Villeroy to the hamlet of Neuville, which we found bolted and barred against us, and in which we secured billets only after great difficulty in consequence of our being, at first, mistaken for Germans. It was a grateful countryside through which we had ridden, and once again we heard those shouts of welcome with which we had been received in the early days of the campaign. Many of the villagers stayed up all night to preside at tables, which they placed in the streets, spread with cakes, bread and butter, chocolate, apples, tea, and coffee. These were pressed upon the troops with lavish hospitality as they marched through. Again the British were acclaimed as deliverers, for bands of German cavalry had been seen in the neighbourhood.

A day's rest, after this twenty-five miles march, was much appreciated, and then we moved on through La Ponchel, Genne-Ivergny, Willeman, Oeuf, Siracourt St. Pol, and Brias to Dieval. The infantry and the dismounted personnel of the Field Ambulance were conveyed in motor lorries, and the distance covered that day was quite thirty miles. The heat was intense, and the dust blew in clouds; we reached our billets looking like millers!

The nature of the country through which we passed on Sunday, October 11th, on the last day of our trek to the north underwent a complete change. Smiling hillsides now gave place to a flat, uninteresting neighbourhood intersected by dykes and canals; factory chimneys and the head-gear of collieries disfigured the landscape; the pretty cottages covered with creepers were left behind, and now one passed nothing but rows of ugly dwellings. Except for the absence of hills, we might have been in Yorkshire. Camblain, Chatelaine, Marles and Lapugnoy were all of this nature. We halted for the night at Chocques, three miles west of Bethune, and established ourselves, by the *maire's* permission, in a fine *château* near the railway. The occupants were away, but the caretaker did everything possible for our comfort. A glorious fire soon blazed in the drawing-room, where the discovery of a grand-piano rejoiced the heart of Captain Bell. We had come through a somewhat depressing neighbourhood, it had commenced to rain as we arrived in the darkness, we were tired and none too cheerful. The music and the warmth restored our good spirits, and oh—the joy of sleeping on a thick, soft carpet after bare boards and stone floors!

We were told that on the morrow our brigade would probably be engaging the enemy; that during this day our Second Cavalry Division, under General Gough, had come in contact with the enemy's cavalry on the north of the Bethune-Aire canal and driven them from the forest of Nieppe. The enemy cavalry were merely a screen for large forces of infantry and artillery which were advancing from the east in an attempt to turn the Allied left, which rested upon the main road from Bethune to Lille, and, if possible, to force a way through to Calais. The British were just in time to defeat both these objects; they had won the race by a narrow margin. Our Second Corps was even now linking up with the French, the Third Corps was detraining at St. Omer farther north-west of us, and the First Corps was working up from the Aisne. In a few days, holding the line from La Bassée northwards in the order mentioned, the three British Corps, with the gallant little Belgian Army on their left, would close all the roads to Calais and the Channel ports.

The transference of the British Force from the Aisne to Flanders without friction or mishap was a brilliant piece of transport work which reflects the highest possible credit alike upon those who conceived it and upon those who carried it through. That a "delicate" operation of this nature was performed so successfully is speaking testimony to the excellent feeling which exists between the French and British Armies. The whole thing was a great triumph for every one concerned therein.

CHAPTER 10

The Second Corps Bars the Way to Calais at La Bassée

The task assigned to General Smith-Dorrien at this time was to seize the Aire-Bethune canal, pivot on the latter place, and then to march due east, get astride the La-Bassée-Lille road near Fournes, and so to threaten the flank and rear of the enemy's position. From October 12th to 18th the Second Corps was engaged in this offensive movement, but the arrival of large reinforcements for the enemy compelled it to act on the defensive from the 19th till the end of the month, when it was relieved.

The Field Ambulance followed close upon the 14th Brigade when, on the morning of October 12th, it won its way across the canal. We met about 2,000 French cavalry, which had been engaging the enemy on our right while our division connected with the French left. With their plumes of varied colours, their cuirasses of polished steel, and their coats of red and blue, they presented a very imposing appearance. The thick mist of early morning developed into a heavy rain, the roads were narrow and deep with mud, the fields were marshy and intersected by deep ditches, the Germans were strongly entrenched and well served by their artillery; but in the face of every difficulty the Second Corps made good progress. Doors and planks were flung across the ditches, and over these the British rushed at their foe with the bayonet, and that night our brigade occupied his abandoned trenches. The enemy was pushed farther and farther back on succeeding days till on the 17th the left of the Second Corps rested in the village of Herlies only a mile and a half from Fournes.

During the heavy fighting in this advance the 3rd Division lost its commander, Major-General Hubert Hamilton, who was struck by a shrapnel bullet as he was directing operations on our left. He was buried in the churchyard of Lacouture by the Rev. E. G. F. Macpherson, C.M.G., C.F., and one who was present has given the following graphic description of the solemn service:—

> Just at the moment when the priest was saying the last prayers the guns began to roar again, and projectiles whistled over the heads of the mourners. The German attack was directed from a distance of a few hundred yards. The moment was well chosen, for the volleys fired by the troops of the Allies in honour of the dead, gloriously fallen for the common cause, were at the same time volleys of vengeance. Crackling reports of rifles continued round the ruined church, but the voice of the priest, reciting the last words of the *Requiem*, lost nothing of its calm and clearness.

As the brigade advanced so the Field Ambulance was pushed forward first to le Touret, then to Richebourg l'Avoue, and finally an advanced dressing-station was established in a house half a mile from Neuve Chapelle. The dead cattle which we saw lying on the road and in the fields, the trees decapitated, and houses demolished by shell-fire, the marks of rifle-bullets upon walls and doors, and the graves of friend and foe dotted about were speaking testimony to the severity of the fighting in which our troops had been engaged. Among the graves of Germans I found one of a doctor which bore upon a cross this inscription:—

> Leutnant A. R. Dr. Riese—14 Oct. 1914
> Kurmärk Dragoner Reg. No. 14.

and another, over which was written:—

> *Hier ruhtin Gott*
> *1 Ulan 2 Husaren*
> *gef alien 13.10.14*
> *Ruhe Sanft.*

During these days it was my sad duty to lay to rest the bodies of many of our comrades. At the headquarters of the Field Ambulance in Richebourg l'Avoue I chose a corner of a very pretty garden for a cemetery. I buried many here, at the advanced dressing-station, and behind the trenches. One Sunday morning the gunners carried the body of Lieutenant Pollard, R.F.A., to the churchyard at Lacouture and we buried him near General Hamilton. One of the saddest funeral services I took was that over the grave of Sergeant Willie Macdonald, 2nd K.O.Y.L.I. He and his brother were killed on the same day; both had displayed conspicuous bravery, and been recommended for rewards. Willie was brought back to the Field Ambulance in a comatose condition and died soon afterwards. A few of his comrades from the regiment were present at the grave, over which, in spite of a lump in our throats, we managed to sing the beautiful hymn "On the resurrection morning." He had been a member of my voluntary choir in Dublin, and we all felt, therefore, it was fitting to pay him this small tribute.

One morning I received a telephone message to go out to Lorgies to bury two officers of the Duke of Cornwall's Light Infantry. I went off at once, but, arrived at brigade headquarters, the acting-brigadier would allow me to proceed no farther because, he said, I should be courting almost certain death. Having given me permission to go out after dusk, I did so in company with our bearers, whom I joined near Neuve Chapelle. The darkness was intense, the mud awful, and shells from our Howitzers flew over our heads with weird shrieks. Numerous sentries challenged us as they stood in the shelter of some dismantled buildings. No smoking was allowed, lest the striking of a match might draw the enemy's fire. Lorgies was but a heap of smoking ruins, the outer walls alone of the church remained, and the light from blazing corn-stacks and burning dwellings revealed to us the awful devastation of the place. Silent figures moved about carrying rations and ammunition, and the regimental stretcher-bearers passed to and from the trenches on their hazardous work of bringing in the wounded.

One house alone in a long row of dwellings still boasted a roof, and here we found Lieutenant G. D. Eccles, the medical officer of the 1st East Surrey Regiment, busy with the wounded. He looked very weary after his almost ceaseless vigil and constant labours, but cheerfully he addressed me with, "Good evening, *padre*, glad to see you; what do you think of our quarters? We had a bullet through the back window this afternoon, which passed through a door and landed on the mantelpiece there. In front the road has been shelled most of the day. However, we are fairly safe now as long as we show no light at the back." With admiration I watched him a while as he went about his work, deftly bandaging the wounded and saying a cheery word to all. I found Lieutenant J. B. Matthews, medical officer of the D. C.L.I, similarly engaged in a ruined house nearer the church.

"The C.O. would like to see you, *padre*," he said to me; "you'll find his headquarters down that road by the burning farm." Following his directions, I found myself in some of our reserve trenches, where the men bade me exercise care because the Germans were less than a hundred yards distant; and, finally, I discovered the C.O., who thanked me for coming and bade the adjutant show me where the graves had been prepared for Captain Passy and Lieutenant Elliott. In the middle of the service heavy riflefire commenced, and the bullets whistled about us; but I went on with the prayers, and most fortunately none of us were hit. By this time our ambulance waggons, which had been compelled to make a second journey, were having the last of the wounded, of whom there were more than a hundred, placed in them, so, after bidding Eccles and Matthews goodnight, I returned with our bearers, and reached my quarters about 1.30 a.m. to find good thoughtful Major Fawcett waiting up to give me some hot tea.

For the regimental medical officers especially I have a great admiration based upon first-hand knowledge of them and their work acquired on many visits to their aid-posts such as the one just described. The heavy casualties among them testify to the dangers they face in their devotion to duty. Not the least trying feature of their work is its isolation; then they are on duty practically day and night, and can only snatch brief and uncertain intervals for sleep in a building out of which they may be shelled at any moment, Captain T. W. Browne (Manchesters), Lieutenant G. D. Eccles (Surreys), Lieutenant J. B. Matthews (D. C.L.I.) and Lieutenant N. F. Hallows (Devons), medical officers in my own brigade, I count among the bravest of the brave.

Then there was Lieutenant Helm, medical officer to the K.O.Y.L.I., who, about this time, had a most trying experience. The farmhouse he was occupying as his aid-post was demolished by shell-fire. He stuck to his patients, took them into the cellar, and was afterwards imprisoned there by the bursting of another shell which killed those whom he was devotedly tending. He was afterwards dug out, though with great difficulty; but what an awful experience! This is but one example, of many which might be given, of the devotion to duty shown under great dangers and difficulties, by the brave men of whom the regiments affectionately speak as their "doctor."

While we were in the neighbourhood of La Bassée a good many German wounded passed through our hands, and they invariably seemed surprised at the kind treatment they received. I suppose they had been taught to expect otherwise. As I gave a cigarette to one who lay on a stretcher, he looked up and said with a smile, "English very good." Unfortunately our wounded were not always treated so well, as the following stories prove. One, who had had part of his face blown away, was sitting in his trench when some of the enemy gained temporary possession of it. One of them, seeing him, took up a clod of earth, and, exclaiming "You English dog," threw it in the poor man's face. Another was bidden, by a German more humane than the rest, to lie down at the bottom of the trench and feign death lest he might be shot. I have these stories on the authority of one of our stretcher-bearers, who, when the trench had been regained, helped to bring in these two wounded, from whom he heard the facts.

How splendid our own wounded always were! There was the man with his jaw blown away who, unable to speak in consequence, made signs that he wished to write. When paper and pencil were brought it was no selfish request he had to make, no message even for loved ones at home he had to send, he simply wrote, "My captain is a brave man, and deserves the V.C." Another, who had one side of his forearm torn away by shrapnel, in answer to my inquiry as to how he felt replied, "I'm all right, sir, 'cept for a bit of rheumatic in me leg." Then there was the officer of the Dorsets who, as he was being carried away from the field on a waterproof sheet by four men, sat up and shouted "Stick it, Dorsets." The wounded were invariably cheery, but one night they were particularly so.

I soon discovered that this was accounted for by the fact of their having got into the enemy with the bayonet. "Tommy" dearly loves a hand-to-hand scrap. These were Lancashire lads who had driven the Germans out of Violaines and helped to hold the right of our line against one of those many fierce counter-attacks which the enemy was now launching against it. A few days later Second Lieutenant Leach and Sergeant Hogan of this splendid Regiment, the 2nd Manchesters, did a superb bit of work at Festubert, recapturing a trench by themselves, killing eight of the enemy, and making sixteen prisoners. For this they have both been awarded the V.C.

About this time my brigade lost its commander, Brigadier-General S. P. Rolt, C.B. The strain of the last few weeks especially had told heavily upon him, and he was now stricken down by a severe attack of influenza which necessitated his being invalided. All ranks bade good-bye to him with great regret. He was succeeded by Brigadier-General F. S. Maude, C.M.G., D.S.O., a very keen soldier and capable leader whose excellent work has since won for him the C.B. and promotion to the rank of Major-General.

My ministrations to the wounded, of whom, consequent upon the severity of the fighting, we had great numbers here, occupied the greater part of my time, but whenever I could be spared from the Field Ambulance I visited such troops as I could reach. These duties, added to the censoring of letters, correspondence with the relatives of the fallen, funeral and other services, and the distribution to the troops of gifts sent by friends at home, kept me busy. Through the medium of Lady Arnott and Mrs. Westby, members of an Association of Irish ladies formed for the purpose, I, as well as others, received large consignments of tobacco, cigarettes, writing materials, tooth-brushes and powder, soap, and other most acceptable articles. The distribution of these opened up many an opportunity for quiet talks to the men on more serious and important subjects. If only the many kind friends who send out gifts for the brave men at the front could see the pleasure which they afford to the recipients, they would be amply repaid.

Few of us will ever forget the anxious days spent before La Bassée. There were no regiments in reserve, and the question we frequently asked ourselves was, would our men, weary after thirteen days in the trenches and sadly depleted in numbers, be able to hold on against the enemy, who, with superior numbers, was launching against our line, with ever-increasing vehemence, constant attacks in his determination to hack a way through? Would not mind and body fail under such an awful strain? It was the most terrible ordeal, the greatest test of endurance, which these troops had, so far, been called upon to undergo; but their indomitable pluck triumphed. The Second Corps held on to its position with grim determination, and, by so doing, prevented the German advance upon Calais by the La Bassée gate.

This achievement must rank as one of the finest in the campaign. But the cost had been great, the losses were enormous, and the remnants of the Corps were exhausted. This was the situation when, on October 24th, supports arrived in the shape of the Lahore Division of the Indian Corps. How we welcomed them! Before us there passed Sikhs, Pathans, Baluchis, and the little Gurkhas from the Eastern Himalaya, hillsmen who could shoot marvellously and wield the ruthless kukri with unerring accuracy. They seemed intensely eager to get to grips with the enemy, pointing in his direction, scowling as they muttered the word "Jarmans," and drawing their hands across their throats, with a gesture of disgust, to show what the Huns might expect from them. They soon struck terror into the Germans who, they knew, had

Major-General F. S. Maude,
C.B., C.M.G., D.S.O.

spoken of them as "niggers."

Of their ultimate objective these warriors from our Eastern Empire stood in no doubt, as the following story proves. A Gurkha lost his way in Marseilles and those who found him received, in reply to their many questions, the oft-repeated answer, "Berleen, Berleen, Berleen." May they not be disappointed of their goal! The initiative and resourcefulness of these new troops soon made a most favourable impression, and, in spite of the unfamiliar type of warfare and the trying climate of a European winter, they have continued to be a most valuable asset of the British Expeditionary Force.

The arrival of the Meerut Division on October 30th made it possible to withdraw the Second Corps partially into reserve. The men of my own brigade had been in the trenches for twenty days consecutively, they were necessarily exhausted by lack of sleep and almost continuous fighting, and yet, believe me, they marched back in the rain, to their badly needed rest, whistling and singing! Such men command the highest admiration. The Germans must have had a special grudge against this brigade, for that very night to the village of Lacouture, where we had hoped to enjoy a peaceful rest, a "Jack Johnson" pursued us. The East Surreys were the sufferers on this occasion, having one man killed and several wounded. We moved farther back next day and found a most comfortable billet, which we would feign have occupied for the remainder of our rest period; but we were shelled out of this at 2 o'clock on a Sunday morning. Some spy must have given us away; we did hear that one had been caught in the church tower signalling to the enemy by means of the hands of the clock: such things were done.

With the whole of my brigade out of the trenches I had looked forward with pleasure to a busy Sunday; but, alas! *"the best-laid schemes o' mice an' men gang aft a-gley."* The early celebration was held at headquarters, but when I turned up to take the first parade service I found the brigade, acting on sudden orders, moving off to another area. I arranged to go over there to hold evening services for the regiments; but again I was to be disappointed, for we were all on the march by teatime. My programmes for Sunday work were so frequently disturbed in this way that probable moves came to be associated with them, and often I have had it said to me, "Now, *padre*, don't fix up services for next Sunday, or we shall be moved! "

Having for one week acted as part of the corps reserve to the Meerut Division, my brigade took over part of the line near Laventie to give some relief to the Lahore Division. The Field Ambulance was billeted in a farm near Estaires, to which the late Lord Roberts came at this time on his visit to the Indian troops. The advanced dressing-station, in charge of Major Fawcett, was a very "unhealthy" spot; the fields all around, and the road leading to it, were studded with "Jack Johnson" holes during his tenure of it. But this brave officer and his assistants remained at their posts, and, most fortunately, suffered no casualties.

The work of collecting the wounded from this point was rendered more hazardous by German snipers. The usual procedure of these men is to leave their lines with a big supply of ammunition, and then, under cover of darkness, to get through our own and hide themselves in some building, or even in a tree. They sleep by day, and with the return of darkness recommence their lowdown game of potting at the road or path used by our stretcher-bearers and others on their way to the trenches, whenever they hear upon it the noise of any movement. Their rifles are, of course, in most cases previously trained upon the road in the daylight and then securely fastened in position; so all the snipers have to do in the darkness is to pull the trigger and reload when necessary.

We at headquarters, too, came under the fire of the enemy's guns. One night we were awakened by the sound of shells bursting around our farm. The farmer and his wife were for a hurried flight, but contented themselves with the cellar when we assured them that the bombardment would soon cease. We found that many of the shells had gone to earth without exploding; one, however, had burst only five yards from the door of a cottage, very near us, in which some of our men were sleeping. The windows and door were smashed, but no further damage was done. Truly "*a miss is as good as a mile*," but one doesn't care to contemplate what the results of hits would have been.

On another occasion I myself had a narrow escape when out riding. Five shells fell in the garden of a house which I had left only a few minutes earlier, and, on my homeward journey, others exploded quite near to the road, causing my horse to take fright.

The desolation in this part of the country was appalling: farms burnt to the ground, with the remnants of waggons and implements and the charred remains of animals lying about; other dwellings battered beyond the possibility of repair; factories and mills, the source of livelihood for thousands, razed to the ground; gardens and vineyards hopelessly trampled; the churches heaps of ruins. It was inevitable these last should suffer, because their towers and spires are the only landmarks in this monotonously flat district; and it is not just to attribute it, in every case, to wanton destruction. I often wondered whether these churches would ever be rebuilt. The French, with whom I discussed the subject, invariably expressed the opinion that they would, and predicted that the war would result in a great religious revival in their country.

In districts out of which we had driven the enemy we often witnessed heartrending scenes as the inhabitants returned only to find their homes pillaged or destroyed. On one occasion we were billeted in the house of a wealthy mill-owner. His cotton-mill, which had given employment to most of the villagers, had been completely destroyed. For several days his house had been occupied by a German general and his staff; the condition in which we found it almost defies description. Broken wine-bottles, crockery and ornaments, remnants of food, and the contents of cupboards were strewn about the floors. The beds had been slept in by officers who did not think it desirable to take off their muddy boots. The chests of drawers were emptied; some of their contents we found in the German trenches, many lay trampled upon the floor. Imagine the owner's grief when he returned to find his home in this condition! If a German general countenanced such wanton destruction, can similar and even far worse crimes committed by the rank and file be wondered at?

On the Sunday within the octave of All Saints the celebrations of the Holy Communion were well attended. This Festival appeals to men on active service with additional force, and, as we prayed "*We also bless Thy holy name for all Thy servants departed this life in Thy faith and fear,*" our thoughts very naturally were first with our comrades who, laying down their lives for the brethren, had died in God's "faith and fear" as true saints of His. Among other services I remember a very hearty one held for the Manchester Regiment in a barn near the reserve trenches. The general, from whom I always received the greatest possible encouragement in my work, came over from headquarters and read the lesson. I have very happy memories of services such as these and of others held in billets and in the fields. Rarely was it possible to have any instrumental music, but the singing was none the less hearty in consequence; I sometimes thought it was more so. A great earnestness seemed to pervade one's congregations; how could it well have been otherwise, surrounded as we were by death and destruction?

The services which, perhaps, impressed me as much as any were those conducted for the men in the billets. They would crowd in and sit upon the floor, and one was able to give them a straight heart-to-heart talk in a way that is not possible at a more formal service. It was then that the men would unburden themselves, produce from their pockets a New Testament, or some small book of devotions, from which they said they had derived much comfort and help, and speak of their Sunday school and choirboy days, and of the old church at home. The soldier may sometimes display a rough exterior, but his heart is a heart of gold, and I have found few upon whom religion has not taken a strong hold, though, ordinarily, they do not speak of it.

The work of evacuating the sick and wounded was from now onwards considerably expedited by the employment of motor ambulances. The majority were supplied by the British Red Cross Society, but in not a few instances private owners had had their cars converted for the purpose, had lent them for the work, and now drove them themselves. The introduction of these vehicles has resulted in the journey from the Field Ambulance to the Clearing Hospital being performed both more quickly and comfortably. To the wounded no better service has been rendered by voluntary agency. The excellent Society to which I have just referred is doing another good work by supplying substantial wooden crosses and placing them upon graves which have no mark of a permanent nature.

When, at the end of October, the troops of the Second Corps had gone into reserve, they received from Field Marshal Sir John French a message in which he expressed his admiration of their tenacious stand before La Bassée, and spoke of their courage and endurance as being "beyond all praise." At the same time he stated he was about to make another "call" upon them, and knew he would not do so in vain. The "call" came to eleven battalions of our corps on November 5th, when they were hurried away to strengthen the line further north in relief of the Seventh Division which, in the desperate fighting east of Ypres, had been reduced from 12,000 men to 2,336. There, insufficiently rested though they were after their trying experiences in the southern part of the line, they rendered conspicuous service and gallantly maintained their positions against the violent assaults of the enemy. To my own brigade there came now the "cal" of which the commander-in-chief had spoken, and on November 15th it marched straight from the trenches near Laventie to participate in the final stages of the first great Battle of Ypres which lasted for three weeks, and ended in a decisive victory for the Allies.

CHAPTER 11

The Winter Campaign 1914—1915

Again we cross the Belgian frontier, but under very different conditions from last time. Then the enemy was at our heels, but now, having been foiled in his attempts in turn upon Paris and Calais, he was tied down to his trenches, where he has been compelled to remain ever since. The latest attempt made at this time at Ypres, with vastly superior numbers, ended in a dismal failure; his losses, estimated at three times as many as our own, were appalling, and he achieved nothing. To have held our positions against forces which outnumbered us by five to one, and indeed by as many as eight to one in some parts of our line, is a victory the greatness of which is not, I fear, generally appreciated. Judging from innumerable remarks which I have heard made by gloomy critics, it would seem that it is only by an advance that so many measure success. The advance will come, of this I feel confident, but, in the meantime, we score a great success each time the enemy makes a futile attack and, in so doing, loses more heavily than we; we become relatively stronger, and do much to ensure that, when we assume the offensive, the enemy will have been so weakened that we shall push him back not a few miles only, but as far as it suits our purpose.

The weather was now about as bad as it could be: a piercing east wind, snow, and then a deluge of rain welcomed us as we crossed the frontier. The troops, however, were in excellent spirits; a good night's rest near Meteren, a wash, and a shave had worked a transformation. It was difficult to believe that these were the same men who yesterday had come out of the trenches plastered with mud and weary from lack of sleep. His powers of recuperation are not the least wonderful characteristic of the British soldier.

Through the town of Bailleul we reached the little Belgian village of Dranoutre, where the Field Ambulance found quarters in the school. An *estaminet* was utilised as a dressing-station and operating theatre, and accommodation for the sick and wounded was provided in the church. Straw was laid upon the floor of the north aisle and there the wounded were carried to await the motor ambulances which would convey them to hospital. And all the time the services of the sanctuary went on as usual.

Many of our comrades lie in the northwest corner of the churchyard, and on Christmas Day I buried Lieutenant H. R. Farrar, Sergeant H. Williams, and Private G. Robinson, all of the 2nd Manchesters, near the south transept, at the end of which there is a beautiful calvary.

The village had been untouched by shot or shell, but there was just the possibility that it might receive attention from the enemy's long-range guns. The Field Ambulance, therefore, was ordered to construct a "dugout," or, as "Tommy" facetiously calls it, "funk-hole," sufficiently large to shelter its personnel of 250 men. Under the superintendence of Captain Lindsay the men of the R.A.M.C. expeditiously performed the work, proving themselves as skilful in using picks and shovels as in handling the wounded. None of us, however, regretted that there was no need to occupy the "funk-hole," for it was dirty and very wet, and couldn't exactly be called comfortable!

Our brigade now held a somewhat extended line, the roads leading to which from Dranoutre were few, indirect, and very bad. The journeys each night to collect the wounded were, in consequence, long and arduous. I will try to describe one which is vividly impressed on my memory. A telephone message had come saying that my services were required at the aid-post of the Manchester Regiment. At 9.15 p.m. I joined two of our medical officers and three squads of bearers, who, with three horsed ambulance waggons, were just setting off for the same destination. It rained heavily, and *"there was a thick darkness"* which considerably increased the difficulties of those who drove the waggons. The centre of the road was paved to little more than the width of the wheel-track, and the slightest deviation involved the waggons in difficulties. The wheels would sink down into the deep mud, and it required great efforts to lift them on to the paved track again.

All went well till we reached the village of Neuve Eglise and met ammunition and ration waggons returning, when, of course, there was nothing for it but to pull into the mud and wait till the road was clear. Later on we met troops returning from the trenches, from which they

WOUNDED SOLDIERS IN THE CHURCH AT DRANOUTRE.

THE GRAVES OF LIEUTENANT FARRAR,
SERGEANT WILLIAMS, AND PRIVATE ROBINSON.

had just been relieved. Poor beggars, plastered with dirt and drenched to the skin, how we pitied them as they stumbled along in the darkness and floundered in the mud!

As we neared our destination, the village of Wulverghem, the bursting of star-shells illuminated the sky and a terrific fusillade from rifles, maxims, and field-guns disturbed the silence of the night. We halted for a while behind the shelter of some buildings, for this bit of road was none too "healthy" during an attack. We were soon able to proceed, and safely reached the farm which Captain Browne, the medical officer of the 2nd Manchesters, was using as his aid-post. "Glad to see you," Browne said; "we've had an awful time today. Poor Nicholson has been killed, we've got him here, and two men also, for you to bury. Now I hear they have another dead officer in the trenches, and probably more men, but it will take some time to get them all brought down. Can you wait?" Having told him that I would, and seen the wounded sent away in two of our ambulance waggons in charge of a medical officer, I sat down with Browne till the graves had been dug and all the dead brought down from the trenches. "We've had an awful business getting the wounded in tonight," he said. "One of their beastly snipers has potted at my bearers every time they went up to the trenches. Listen; you can hear him now." Yes, I could distinctly hear the crack of a single rifle, and it was repeated at intervals during the whole time I remained there, from 11 p.m. till 5 a.m., when, with the breaking of dawn, I suppose the sniper crept away to his lair to await the return of darkness.

At frequent intervals Browne would go to the door, look out into the darkness, and listen for the return of his stretcher-bearers. Brave fellows these! Bandsmen most of them in peace time, on active service their work is to carry the wounded from the firing line to the regimental aid-post. Only those who have seen it can fully appreciate the arduous and hazardous nature of the work performed by these devoted men.

A few days later, near this very village of Wulverghem, a regimental stretcher-bearer in my brigade, Bandsman Rendle of the 1st Duke of Cornwall's Light Infantry, won the Victoria Cross for his conspicuous bravery. The parapet of a trench had been blown away and wounded men were lying in the open exposed to shell and rifle fire. With a splendid courage and scorn of death, Rendle went to their rescue and carried them one by one to a place of shelter. With none of the excitement which stimulates combatants, but facing the dangers of fighting all the same, stretcher-bearers, both regimental and those attached to Field Ambulances, have done some of the bravest deeds of the war. In their case especially do I share the regrets expressed by Field-Marshal Sir John French, "that circumstances have prevented any account of many splendid instances of courage and endurance coming regularly to the knowledge of the public."

At last, after one of his many visits to the door, Browne came in and announced, "The bearers have just brought in young Caulfield's body. Poor boy, it's awfully sad about him. Only a few days ago he transferred from the Army Service Corps to the Manchesters because he wanted to do some fighting." It was now about 1.30 a.m., and as we sat and talked we were joined by the second medical officer of the Field Ambulance, who, with two squads of bearers, had made a perilous journey to the aid-post of another regiment. Having left the third ambulance waggon with us, they had made their way in the darkness across ploughed fields and dykes and then carried two seriously wounded men a distance of over a mile. At one place a broad dyke had to be negotiated by means of a tree which had fallen across it. But this difficulty, like many others, was surmounted by the undaunted bearers. The medical officer had fallen into a "Jack Johnson" hole, and now appeared before us smothered in liquid mud. Quietly and unobtrusively, but with splendid courage and patient endurance, this work of collecting the wounded goes on night after night.

After a few moments' conversation, during which the two wounded men were transferred to the waiting ambulance, we bade the medical officer goodbye and went out to the little cemetery to give instructions about the preparation of the graves. The work of digging these had necessarily to be performed in the darkness, because the showing of a light might have drawn the enemy's fire.

About 4.30 a.m. Browne announced, "Everything is ready at last, *padre*; there are two officers and four men for you to bury; all Manchesters." I accompanied him to a barn where our fallen comrades lay. Picture the scene if you can. The medical officer walks by my side, the six stretchers, each carried by two men, follow, and, as we wend our way through the farmyard between waggons and machinery, there fall upon the stillness of the night the glorious words, "*I am the resurrection and the life, saith the Lord.*" Having groped our way to the graves, the bearers reverently lift the lifeless forms from the stretchers and at once lower them into the ground. Then the prayer of committal and the rest of the Church's beautiful form of service for the burial of the dead are recited from memory. What a multitude of thoughts rushed through our minds as we stood a while beside the open graves! On the morrow loving hands would place above them wooden crosses, and successive Regiments will keep the mounds green.

My sad task accomplished, as the first streaks of dawn appeared in the sky, I said goodbye to Browne and set out on my solitary four-miles tramp to Dranoutre. The only living souls I saw during the first two miles were the sentries, one of whom appeared with startling suddenness from apparently nowhere, and, with his bayonet at my breast, made many inquiries as to my identity.

Having reached "home" about 6 a.m. I lay down fully dressed, for I had to be up again by 8 o'clock to visit the sick and wounded before the motor ambulances bore them away to hospital.

While the fighting on our front was now much less desperate, the troops were subjected to a trial of another nature arising from the severity of the weather. The snow, hard frost and periods of almost continuous rain, combined with the necessity for standing many hours waist-deep in mud and water, imposed a very searching test upon the men's physique and powers of endurance. Fur coats were served out to them by the authorities, and warm clothing was provided in abundance by generous friends at home. Their rations, which were always good, were increased to a scale never known before. Braziers were supplied for the trenches, which were kept as dry as possible by the resourcefulness of the Royal Engineers. But, in spite of every expedient being adopted which science could suggest, many of the troops suffered severely, the most common forms of sickness being rheumatism and frost-bite.

The health of the troops generally was, however, surprisingly good, the sick-rate being no more than 3 *per cent*. This excellent result is due very largely to the untiring zeal, skill, and devotion with which the Royal Army Medical Corps performed its work. Colonel Crawford and the other medical officers of the Field Ambulance, as well as those in charge of regiments, spared neither time nor labour to keep the men fit. Great attention was paid to sanitation, and in this sphere Lieutenant Cooper, R.A.M.C., a graduate of the Lister Institute, assisted by his "sanitary squad," toiled unceasingly with skill and energy. Similar good work was done throughout the army, with the result that the troops were kept free from any epidemic. The regular periods of rest, which the arrival of additional regiments now enabled the troops to be given, was another contributing factor to their health.

Beyond the reach of the German guns they could now have adequate and undisturbed sleep; and excellent arrangements were made by which all could have a hot bath, combined with a complete change of underclothing. Not a little credit is due to those, too, who helped, by the organisation of games and entertainments, to maintain the excellent spirits of the troops. In my own brigade an Association Football League was formed, the four regiments, the Field Ambulance, and the attached company of the Divisional Train each entering a team. An appeal to friends at home brought a liberal supply of footballs, and hop-poles served as goal-posts. One of the competing teams always wore broad red sashes as a distinguishing mark. Many of the matches were necessarily played under very unfavourable conditions; often it rained heavily, and much of the ground was under water. The "gates" were invariably good; sometimes whole regiments would combine a route-march with attendance and come on to the ground, under arms, to encourage their teams.

The general "kicked off" at the first match, and was always present when his duties would allow. It had been decided that each team should play each of the others twice, but unforeseen circumstances intervened, and the competition concluded with the completion of the first round, in which points were gained as follows. 1st D. C.L.I., 10; 1st Devons, 8; 14th Field Ambulance, 6; 1st East Surreys, 4; 2nd Manchesters, 2; 3rd Co. 5th Divisional Train, 2. The competition excited keen interest, afforded great pleasure to players and spectators, and did much to divert the men's thoughts into more cheerful channels.

Perhaps even greater pleasure was afforded by the entertainments which it was now possible to organise. Thanks to the efforts of Sergeant Plume, R.A.M.C, the personnel of the Field Ambulance had often enjoyed a "sing-song." This energetic non-commissioned officer now made himself very largely responsible for two entertainments each week, to which it was possible to invite each night four hundred and fifty men from the brigade and attached units. In one village in which we were billeted for three or four months an excellent room with permanent stage and proscenium was available. At first the R.A.M.C. contributed the programmes almost entirely, but later on the various units made themselves responsible in turn. The friendly competition among them to produce the best "show" was very keen.

Several most amusing farces, from the pen of Sergeant Plume, were performed by himself and the talented dramatic party of the Field Ambulance, who also gave a very laughable production of Harry

Men of the 14th Infantry Brigade playing football.

Some members of the 11th Field Ambulance Dramatic Party.

Tate's motoring scene. A mouth-organ band, composed of men from the same corps, rendered selections of music with great precision under the conductorship of Private Vick, R.A.M.C, who had trained them. Privates Wright and Prager of the East Surreys were inimitable in their duets and patter; while Lieutenant Martin Row, with his amusing stories, and Lieutenant Grenfell by his recitations, gave great pleasure to their audiences. These are but a few of the many excellent items contributed at these entertainments. The preparation of the programmes helped to occupy the performers in their spare time with healthy diversion. "Tommy" displayed great resourcefulness in securing his "props"; apparently he could make anything from a footlight to a motorcar out of empty biscuit tins.

The pleasure afforded to the crowded audiences by these entertainments, and the beneficial effect they had upon the spirits of the troops, it would be impossible to assess. The "Tommy" who was heard to say, "I wouldn't have missed the show for a tanner," probably represented the appreciation of his fellows; while the officer who said, "These concerts are jolly good things; my men always return from them very happy, whistling and singing," did, I know, voice the approval of other commanding officers.

At the end of November, when the long and arduous Battle of Ypres-Armentières had ended in a great victory for the Allies, His Majesty the King arrived in the field to visit his army. He carried out numerous inspections, and presented V.C.'s, D.S.O.'s. and D.C.M.'s, being everywhere received with tremendous enthusiasm by the troops, to whom his visit was the greatest possible encouragement.

From now onwards to the time when, some four months later, the enemy made his second attempt at Ypres there was nothing in the nature of a general engagement on the front of the Second Corps; but German guns and snipers continued to take their toll, and there were few days on which I was not called upon to minister to the wounded and the dying.

During these months my work varied little, and consisted largely of a repetition of that of which I have already written. The addition of a fifth battalion, the 5th Cheshires, to my brigade, coupled with the fact that there were now always two, and often three, of my regiments in reserve, gave me greater opportunities for personal visitation. Week-night meetings for Bible study and intercessory prayer were tried with considerable success. My Sundays now were especially full days; an average one would include an early celebration, two parade services, and evensong in the village in which we were billeted. In the intervals, having filled my saddle-bags with hymn-books, I rode around to outlying units, and had short services in barns, and more often still in the fields. It was not unusual in this way to get in as many as six or seven services during the day.

Of the Christmas Festival I have very happy memories. In the early morning of Christmas Day, while it was still dark, I went to a farm-house situated under Mount Kemmel, where, in the kitchen, a celebration of the Holy Communion was attended by about fifty gunners, many of whom had walked nearly two miles in order to be present. At the second celebration, held in a room at brigade head-quarters, the communicants overflowed into the passage and into the room on the other side. Men came in straight from the trenches, fully armed and plastered with mud, eager to worship at the manger throne. I was reminded of those who, saying one to another *"Let us now go even unto Bethlehem, and see this thing which is come to pass,"* hastened away from the fields to do homage to the newborn King. The other celebrations were equally well attended. Two parade services, necessarily shorter even than usual because of the intense cold, were held in the snow-clad fields. As we sang the old favourite hymn, "While shepherds watched their flocks by night," we could realise, as perhaps we had never done before, the loving condescension of the announcement of the Saviour's birth first to simple men doing their humble duty out in the fields.

Everything possible under the circumstances was done to celebrate the festive season in the time-honoured way. On Christmas Eve the various billets in the village received a most welcome visit from a party of carol singers organised by Corporal Burdett. On the day itself every member of the British Expeditionary Force received a much-treasured card from their Majesties the King and Queen, bearing autographed portraits of themselves and conveying their good wishes. From Her Royal Highness the Princess Mary there came a very thoughtful and much-prized gift in the form of a brass tobacco box, tobacco, and cigarettes. Plum-puddings and other appropriate fare arrived in abundance, and in the evening we did our best to be mirthful and happy.

The spirit of Christmas spread even to the men in the trenches, and in many places informal truces were arranged. The opposing forces left their trenches and fraternised on the intervening ground, exchanging gifts and good wishes! For his enemy individually "Tommy" has no hatred; he only wants to meet and beat him on a purely sporting basis. He is goodness itself to German wounded and prisoners, to whom I have seen him give the last of his precious "Woodbines." One was not, therefore, surprised to find him prepared to shake hands with his foe on Christmas Day. It was good to know that some at least of the regiments opposed to us were untainted by that childish venom of hate which the enemy as a whole evidently regards as the proper spirit in which to fight. Both sides were equally glad to avail themselves of the opportunity afforded by the truce to improve their trenches and to bury their dead.

"*A day of comparative quiet along our whole front.*" In some such words ran the official report of a day, March 5th, which brought a sad disaster to the 14th Field Ambulance. For two months we had been stationed in a village which the Germans shelled at intervals. Little harm was done as long as they confined themselves to shrapnel, but as time went on they bombarded the village with high explosive shells, which knocked the houses down like packs of cards and caused many casualties among the troops and civilians. I had paid my morning visit to the sick and wounded, and the worst cases among these had been sent to hospital by motor-ambulances, when, without the slightest warning, a six-inch shell came through the roof of our dressing-station and burst in the middle of the building. Captain Bell and Lieutenant Clarke, R.A.M.C., as well as several patients and orderlies, were wounded. One orderly and three patients were killed.

There were many in the building at the time, and the wonder is that any escaped. At the moment, I was on the outskirts of the village superintending the preparation of a field for a football match. Seeing the shell burst in the dressing-station, I immediately ran there to do what I could to help with the wounded. However, before I could get there a second shell burst in the yard by one of the doors leading into the dressing-station, mortally wounding Major F. G. Richards, who was superintending the removal of the wounded. We carried him to a cottage on the edge of the village, where everything that love and skill could suggest was done for him by Lieutenants G. D. Ferguson and R. Hay, R.A.M.C.

"Dear old Richards," as we who knew him so well always called him, was one of the best; with the heart of a child and the bravery of a lion, he was both a good soldier and a fine Christian. He made no display of his religion, but his life was rich in its best fruits. Sympathetic with his patients, most conscientious in the discharge of his duty, a strong disciplinarian, and yet absolutely just to those serving under

DRESSING-STATION OF 11TH FIELD AMBULANCE BEFORE BOMBARDMENT.

AFTER

him, unselfish, thoughtful, and courteous, it was little wonder he was a universal favourite. A private, with tears in his eyes, said to me, "We all loved him, sir," and this remark does indeed sum up the feelings we all entertained for him. I had known him well for ten years, we were great "pals," and even now, after an interval of four months, I find it hard to realise we shall not meet again in this life. He was conscious almost to the end, and often murmured his thanks to the doctors and orderlies. About an hour after receiving his injuries, he died very peaceably in the faith and love of God whom he had served so well. We carried him that night to the churchyard, and buried him with four others who had met their deaths in the same disaster. As part of the inscription which the cross over his grave bears, I chose the words "*Faithful unto death*," for if any one ever earned them he did. For lives like his we thank God, and, though his body rests in Belgian soil, his memory lives and his good works will not be forgotten. R. I. P.

A few days later a letter appeared in a London paper in which the writer quoted this disaster to the 14th Field Ambulance as an instance of the enemy's disregard of the Red Cross flag. Knowing all the facts, I must acquit them of the charge of having, in this case, deliberately fired upon the wounded and non-combatants. They probably knew fighting troops were quartered in the village, or they may have been searching for one of our batteries near us which frequently gave them trouble. In any case, it would be quite impossible for the German gunners to see our hospital flag.

******

Now my story is done. It has been written in response to many requests, and claims to be nothing more than a faithful account of the life lived and the work done in "the fighting line" by one priest of the Church of England, who is fully conscious of his many failures as well as of the fact that his experiences were in no way exceptional ones. Of the work done by the chaplains generally it would have been presumptuous for me to have spoken. One who is qualified, however, to judge of that work has borne generous tribute to it. Field-Marshal Sir John French, in his 5th Despatch, said:

> I cannot speak too highly of the devoted manner in which all chaplains, whether with the troops in the trenches or in attendance on the sick and wounded in casualty-clearing stations and hospitals on the line of communications, have worked throughout the campaign.

Further, of the chaplains he said: "The number with the forces in the field at the commencement of the war was comparatively small," and expressed the hope "that the further increase of personnel may be found possible."

This hope, which I know was shared by the Church generally, has been realised, and there are now seven chaplains to each division where before there were only three. Will the Church now pray unceasingly that "the labourers" sent may be given wisdom, love, and strength to gather in the rich harvest which undoubtedly is ripening among the souls of men in our army? On behalf of myself and brother chaplains I feel confident I shall not ask in vain,

Brethren, pray for us.

Appendix

Names of officers, warrant officers, non-commissioned officers and men of the 14th Infantry Brigade and attached units to whom decorations and medals have been awarded for distinguished service and acts of gallantry and devotion to duty during the present campaign.

V.C.

Lieut. G. R. Roupell } 1st E. Surrey Regt.
Lance-Corpl. E. Dwyer

Bandsman T. Rendle, 1st D.C.L.I.

2nd Lieut. J. E. Leach } 2nd Manchester Regt.
Sergt. J. Hogan

C.B.

Brig.-Gen. F. S. Maude.
Lieut.-Col. H. L. James, 2nd Manchester Regt.
Lieut.-Col. M. N. Turner, 1st D.C.L.I.

C.M.G.

Lieut.-Col. E. G. Williams, 1st Devon Regt.
Lieut.-Col. G. S. Crawford, R.A.M.C.
Major H. T. Cantan, 1st D.C.L.I.
Major R. S. Weston, 2nd Manchester Regt.

D.S.O.

Staff Captain G. F. Phillips.
Lieut. R. E. Hancock, 1st Devon Regt.
Capt. the Hon. A. R. Hewitt, 1st E. Surrey Regt.
Major J. H. T. Cornish-Bowden; Capt. W. P. Buckley; Capt. C. B. Scott; Capt. C. B. Woodham, 1st D.C.L.I.
Capt. W. K. Evans, 2nd Manchester Regt.

The Military Cross

1st Devon Regt.

Capt. P. R. Worrall; Lieut. W. A. Fleming; Lieut. G. E. R. Prior.

1st E. Surrey Regt.

Capt. M. J. Minogue; Lieut. E. G. Clarke; Lieut. T. H. Darwell; Lieut. G. E. Hyson; Lieut. R. A. Montenaro.

1st D.C.L.I.

Capt. A. N. Acland; Capt. M. Crawley-Boevey; Capt. T. A. Kendall; Lieut. A. J. S. Hammans.

2nd Manchester Regt.

Capt. J. S. Harper; Capt. C. D. Irwin; Capt. A. J. Scully; Capt. G. W. Williamson.

A.S.C.

Lieut. M. Burke; Staff Sergt.-Major G. White.

R.A.M.C.

Lieut. W. McM. Chesney; Lieut. T. W. Clarke.

Distinguished Conduct Medal

1st Devon Regt.

Comp. Sergt.-Major E. Tabb; Sergt. H. Webb; Corpl. C. Jeffery; Lance-Corpl. W. Simmons; Lance-Corpl. W. Tremlett; Lance-Corpl. W. Webber; Pte. R. Ball; Pte. W. Dunster; Pte. J. Searle; Pte. W. Worsfold.

5th Signal Company, R.E.

Corpl. J. E. Adams; Pioneer F. Keevill.

1st E. Surrey Regt.

Sergt.-Major G. E. Hyson; Q.-M.-Sergt. W. Fisher; Comp. Sergt.-Major A. Reid; Sergt. A. Edwards; Sergt. P. Griggs, Sergt. M. Hill; Sergt. J. Packhard; Corpl. R. Williams;

Lance-Corpl. W. Harding; Pte. F. Grimwood; Pte. A. Hotz; Pte. F. Martin; Pte. J. Wilkins.

1st D.C.L.I.

Comp. Sergt.-Major W. Dingley; Sergt. H. Byard; Sergt. J. Roberts; Sergt. J. Wise; Corpl. G. Dagger; Lance-Corpl. J. Denton; Lance-Corpl. W. Stoneman; Pte. B. Barlow; Pte. H. Cox; Pte. J. Pennycock; Pte. A. Rex.

2nd Manchester Regt.

Comp. Sergt.-Major J. Lemon; Sergt-Major J. Parker; Sergt. A. Harrison; Sergt. H. Waters; Corpl. A. Bloor; Pte. A. Shalliker.

5th Cheshire Regt.

Pte. L. Pollitt.

R.A.M.C.

Sergt.-Major A. E. Spowage; Acting Corpl. J. Cartwright.

FOREIGN DECORATIONS

Légion d'Honneur

1st E. Surrey Regt.

Capt. E. M. Woulfe Flanagan.

1st D.C.L.I.

Lieut. A. J. S. Hammans.

Médaille Militaire

1st E. Surrey Regt.

Sergt. R. Hunt.

1st D.C.L.I.
Comp. Sergt.-Major J. Woolcott.

2nd Manchester Regt.
Comp. Q.-M.-Sergt. J. Morris.

A.S.C.
Staff Sergt.-Major M. Burke.

5th Signal Company, R.E.
Sergt. W. R. Carvell.

In the Northern Mists

Contents

A Mail-Bag and a Messenger	111
"Swakking"	114
Waiting for "The Day"	117
Sunday	120
A West-Country Ship	122
At Sea	125
"Guns"	128
Coaling	130
Concerning a Bucket	133
The Hand-Picked Life	135
"Stoker, First Class"	138
Destroying	141
Atmosphere	144
The Gun-Room	147
The Grand Fleet	150
Tropes, and Three Watchkeepers	153
My Servant	157
The Wedding Present	160
The Wedding	163
A War Widow	166
Elegant Leisure	168
Meals	171
Lower-Deck Love	174
The Patrol Trawler	178
"A Little Drop o' Leaf"	182

On the Sick List	185
Clothes Uniform and Otherwise	188
Sea-Soldiers	191
Guests	195
Religion and the War and the Navy	198
Hobbies	201
The Dug-Outs	204
Celebration	207
Mines and Mine-Sweepers	210
Equity	213
"Naval Miscarriages"	217
Romance	220
Promotions and Resolutions	223
Warrant Officers	226
Paper-Work	229
Hostility-Men	232
Wool and Water	235
"Wireless"—and a Cat	238
A Flap	241
The Beach	244
Sunrise and Sunset	247
The Acting Sub	250
Storm	253
Ranks and Ratings	256
Boy Giblets	258
Singing Sailormen	261
"Small Cords"	263
"Tonal'"	266
The Advantage-Party	269
An Indeterminate Equation	273
Aftermath	276

CHAPTER 1

A Mail-Bag and a Messenger

If at the time when I was first ordained and about to enter upon a quiet curacy some prophetic instinct had told me that after a considerable number of years I should find myself in my present position I should probably have quoted a few words concerning lying prophets: but then, as someone remarks, you never can tell!

I am "in the North Sea"; in a battleship in the North Sea; in an office in the battleship; in a mail-bag in the office. That is to say, the lower half of me is in a mail-bag, which, being made of stout canvas and drawn up close around the waist, forms a very comforting protection against the cold.

As to what I am doing in the office, the strictness of the censorship forbids me to say; but it is a certain job for which I have volunteered, as everyone must do his bit in these days. Certainly, the work does not come under the heading of pastoral duties, and according to the terms of the Hague Convention I am probably rendering myself liable to be shot by our friends the enemy if they catch me. Well, they are quite welcome to do it—if they can!

About four feet above my head, as I sit writing, is a steel deck; and upon this deck there are now being dumped down a large number of projectiles, weighing well over a thousand pounds each. As the process of dumping is not conducted with any undue delicacy, the resultant noise can well be imagined. Should one of these huge projectiles by any mischance explode, what death and havoc it would spread around! Of course, there is not the slightest possibility of such a thing happening; the precautions and safety arrangements make certain of that. But—let me spin a brief yarn with a moral. A man was once brought up before the captain for some misdemeanour, and, being a bit of a sea-lawyer, was fully persuaded that according to all the wording of the King's Regulations and Admiralty Instructions the captain could not punish him.—"'E can't do it, 'e can't do it," he kept repeating to himself; and so argued till the last moment "'E can't do it, 'e can't do it!—*But 'e 'ave!*"

There is one consolation. If I should prove mistaken in believing that the projectiles overhead cannot explode, I should have no time to exclaim, "But 'e 'ave"

Equanimity remains undisturbed. If I remember rightly, it was a part of the *Kultur* scheme that we in the Fleet were to be in-the-nerves-shaken and to-a-state-of-collapse-reduced by the fearful mental strain to which we should naturally be subjected, being harried and worried by perpetual alarms and fears. Another miscalculation! I am thinking of writing a book, in imitation of a reverend colleague in the Sister Service, and calling it *How to be Happy Though Harried*. For the men of the Fleet were never so cheerful and contented as now. Never have I known a ship's company so universally "happy" as that to which I have the honour now to belong. The sailor loves his growl, in normal circumstances. Today he has given up growling, and goes about his work with the smile that won't come off. And as for the dreadful strain, the only strain noticeable is that on the buttons of those many officers and men who, since the war started, have put on that flesh which argues a contented mind.

Outside the office a young bluejacket paces slowly up and down. He is my attendant satellite, and waits upon my bidding. As he occasionally strolls beyond easy ear-shot, the cry of "*Messenger!*" does not always bring him to me; and it has been a problem how to accentuate the word so as to give it the utmost carrying value. For a long time I tried "*Mess*-en-ger," and then "Mess-en-*ger*," with varying results; and finally discovered that the greatest penetration was obtained simply by calling out sharply the last syllable alone. Thus—"*Ger!*" Moreover, it is a great saving of breath. Possibly this was an unconscious memory of a scheme I once saw outlined by which the Eng vocab might be ren infin more simp by the very ordin meth of truncing ev unnecc syll.

I feed my messenger on peppermints. Kind ladies send me tins of these now and then, and, as there are not enough to go round amongst the whole of the ship's company, a choice has to be made.

I clothe him with mufflers. If he were peeled he would probably be found to be wearing six. There are plenty of these, thanks also to the kind ladies aforesaid. Mufflers are excellent for the upper works; but they cannot be adapted to the lower limbs; and that is where my mail-bag comes in—or, rather, where I come into the mail-bag.

The kind ladies' labours of love would be even more appreciated if they would now stop making mufflers for us, and knit us instead lots of stockings, long enough to come up well above the knee, and big enough to be worn outside the trouser-legs and inside the sea-boots. The coarsest and thickest wool would be the best, and they would be all the better for being made without turning the heel. Oh, how welcome they would be![1]

Part of the pleasure of living in a mail-bag is that when moving about the office I can revive ancient memories of long-past sack-races—in fact, I have to do so, unless I were willing to take the trouble of unhermitcrabbing, which I am not. Perhaps it is not a very dignified form of progression for a middle-aged clergyman of the Church of England—but then, think of the exercise!

Now I am going off duty for a while, and someone else takes my place. My messenger also gets relieved. I relinquish my comfortable mail-bag with a certain amount of regret. But I shall be in it again in a few hours' time.

---

1. As a result of these lines appearing, many ladies sent parcels of "woollies" to the ship; and the number of such gifts soon growing, the editor of the *Saturday Westminster* instituted a scheme for providing "Sea-boot Stockings for the Fleet," which proved of invaluable benefit. The Admiralty now issue all necessary gear of this sort.

Chapter 2

"Swakking"

All private correspondence sent from the ship is, very properly, censored before being placed in the sealed mail-bags, in order that no careless expression may chance to give away information of importance.

The sailor alludes to this process as "Censuring"—and indeed this is what it sometimes amounts to! Only this morning a chief petty officer approached me, more in sorrow than in anger, and displayed the remnants of a letter which he had sent to his father some days ago, and the latter had sent it back. No wonder! The first page was represented by a narrow ribbon of paper at the top and a similar one at the bottom; the remainder had been cut out bodily by the hardhearted censurer! Yet his was not an exceptional case; the policy of ruthlessness and frightfulness is pursued indiscriminately wherever it is thought necessary. The letters of the captain and all other officers are subject to the same treatment—and frequently get it!

There are two official censors—the fleet-paymaster and myself. But with a ship's company of over eight hundred letter-writers we are not enough to cope with all the work, so several other officers kindly share our labours. We settle down after dinner each night to a couple of hours' "Swakking."

This mystic word is derived from the fact that the sailor in love—and all sailors are always in love—makes a practice of writing on the tip of the envelope flap the letters S.W.A.K.

For a long time we puzzled our brains as to the meaning of these letters. Were they a secret code? If so, they ought to be "censured." The brightest brain among us guessed, just in time, that they stood for Sealed With a Kiss!

Alas for sentiment and romance! The actual kiss which seals the letters is given by an old red rubber sponge in a bowl of water. One sweep of the envelope across the sponge's moist surface, a blow of the fist, and all is over. The letter is swakked and ready to proceed on its journey.

Swakking is a little tedious at times. Nine letters out of ten inform Dear Beat (if the sailor's star is not named Beat she is a Flo, almost invariably) that the writer is in the pink, and the weather is very cold, but he doesn't mind it: he hopes to have a smack at the sausages soon, and is her ever-loving sweetheart.

But there are compensations, in the insight which swakking gives one into the minds and characters of the men of the Fleet, and in the closer touch with the "lower-deck" that results in many cases from having to read their letters.

One thing stands out with remarkable clearness—the deep religious feeling possessed by practically *all*. One does not suspect the sailor of being religious, as a rule; his ordinary language is not that of the saints, nor is his conduct always above reproach. Yet, if the quiet acknowledgment of God's power over all the world and the final triumph of righteousness; devout prayers for the blessing and protection of those whom he holds dearest; a complete trust in the Divine Wisdom to take care of him in life or death if these things mean religion, they are in nearly every sailor's letter.

"All the girls will be after Billy *when he has won this war*, but the only one he wants is Flo"; "I would rather have a kiss than a thousand drinks" (and this after many beerless weeks, too!), are sayings typical of him whom All the Nice Girls Love. One who signs himself "Yours for ever" is apparently a novice, for he says, "I asked you before what is the meaning '*Mizhap*' (!) at the end of your letter; please tell me."

The patriotic tone of the letters is simply splendid; they reveal just that some old fighting spirit which is half the battle. Not all express their patriotic feelings in the same manner. The style varies from the heroic to the comically devil-may-care. One man will bid his relatives take a pride in having so many of the family fighting for their country; while the next will pour out his hopes that the Germs may send out their high-canal fleet so that we may have a bump at them and see them off in rag-time.

There is a great deal of thorough-going righteous indignation against the enemy and all his works; but not the least among the many causes of resentment is the fact that by starting the war the blighters did us out of seven days' leave in July—yes, and our Christmas leave as well!

It is not only in their letters that the men express their longing for battle. There was a day when we quite expected to be going into action (it was months ago, and proved a false hope). Never should I have thought it possible for so much feeling to be put into one word as was heard in the word "Action!" passed delightedly from one man to another! As for our expectations as to the result of the action, I can do no better than quote the forethought of our marine officer, who took a spare clean handkerchief with him into his turret—"*in case my nose should bleed!*"

Chapter 3

Waiting for "The Day"

Barrili adduces the case of one of his friends who, although now of more than middle age, persists in wearing straps to his trousers in order to create the illusion that he is still but twenty years old. We retain, in the navy, a large number of trouser-straps for the fostering of ideas which belong to the post. As an instance, there is that custom of saluting the quarter-deck on coming aboard—the omission of which by a certain noble lord who honoured one of His Majesty's ships with a visit caused an old A.B. to remark to his shocked and offended topmate, "W'y, bless yer, Bill, wot do 'ee expect? 'E ain't niver bin to sea to larn manners!" The crucifix raised on the poop, which our forebears used to salute, no longer stands as warrant for the custom—though the Cross of St. George on the White Ensign fills its place; but the custom itself still holds.

But one of the chief illusions carefully tended by the navy is that we are only by accident sailors and fighting men, while really and essentially we are country gentlemen or, according to our degree, such gentlemen's retainers.

Drake and his compeers, it would seem, used to regard their estates and farms as their real life interests: now and then they were obliged, by force of circumstances, to leave their pleasant fields and take to the sea to wallop the Spaniard; it was rather a nuisance, and the best thing therefore was to do it thoroughly so as to get back again the quicker.

Much of our success as a naval nation is due, I believe, to our having carefully maintained this illusion that we are landsmen come to sea; our friends the enemy, on the other hand, fail because they take themselves too seriously as seamen—as, indeed, they appear to do in every capacity. I have seen something of the German Navy's discipline it is Kolossal!—Their whole naval system is based on carefully compiled text-books. But text-books never yet have provided for every contingency, and discipline overdone makes no allowance for the human element. The German is too much of the perfect sailor.

But with ourselves—even our naval titles sit awkwardly upon us. I served once with an admiral who had been at sea for forty years, yet his coxswain could never get out of the habit of alluding to him as Mister ———. The prints on our wardroom bulkheads are all of dogs and birds; our gunnery lieutenant and our navigator do not discuss the higher mathematics as applied to their own specialised arts like their German opposite numbers probably do, but debate instead the rival merits of the Tavy and the Walkham.

So now, while we are waiting for "The Day," our spare-time occupations are as un-naval as we can possibly make them. The commander can be seen any afternoon practising his swing upon a golf ball tied to a long cord. We have a hockey tournament now in progress; the players get into flannels before assembling for the game—on the quarter-decks! Our sailors, also, though they do turn up at the various lectures on the war given by different officers—attendance is quite optional—roll up in far greater numbers at the concerts and theatricals which are constantly being organised; and the favourite songs and "sketches" are those which have the least sea-flavour (the Admiralty, by the way, issues a very excellent collection of songs and chanties in the "Naval Song-book," but nobody ever sings them).

It is a long time since we in this particular ship have set eyes upon one of the Gentle Sex (so much for our "Skulking in Harbour!"); consequently, when one of our midshipmen appeared in the theatricals as a girl—and a very pretty girl he made, too—he was received with overwhelming favour; though to watch him recuperating after his efforts rather dispelled the girlish charm.

A wonderful good-humour prevails. One might imagine that the long period of waiting would be bound to tell upon the tempers of such a large number of men cooped up together; but this is not so. A fine example of our men's conduct to one another occurred only a few days ago: there was needed one man of a certain rating to be sent from the ship to a home port for a particular duty which would entail his living on shore for a long time in much greater comfort, of course, than can be found on board ship at present. Four men were equally eligible for the job, and in order to be quite fair they drew lots. Next morning the lucky winner came to his officer and asked that one of the others might be sent in his stead; he was a bachelor, whereas the other three were all married, and he would like one of those wives to see her husband.

But we are not entirely contented. It is not our fault if our record of this war must be, as one of Napoleon's generals, De Ségur, wrote of his part in the drama of 1812: "*Je fus là moins acteur que témoin*"; still, it is hard to reconcile ourselves to this. The fact that "Willy's Fleet" refuses to hearken to the old cry of "Dilly, Dilly, come and be killed" causes much grumbling against those cautious heroes: so much so that a little while ago some of our men fell in before the captain with the request that they might be *sent on active service!*

Chapter 4

Sunday

A profane rhyme, current among blue-jackets and of ancient date, parodies the fourth Commandment in the words, "*Six days shalt thou work and do all that thou art able, And on the seventh thou shalt holystone the deck and scrub the cable.*" This, of course, is an exaggeration, to say the least of it. Sunday is observed with us not only by custom, but by naval regulations, and indeed has always been so since the navy existed.

Certainly, our Sunday routine differs in some respects from that observed on shore. There is, I remember, an interesting paragraph to this effect at the beginning of one of the chapters of "The King's Own." I have searched the ship's library for a copy of the book in order to verify my reference, as every good parson should, but regret to find that it is no longer included in the catalogue; a pity, if this indicates that Marryat's splendid yarns of the navy as it was a century ago are no longer in demand! But, to draw on my memory, the passage explains that a due regard for Sunday is shown on board ship not so much by the formal religious observances practised as by the extra care taken in making the ship herself and everything about her neat and beautiful. The words are true of the navy as it is today, even in this time of war.

Myself, I hold that to observe Sunday by repeating the alphabet backwards and standing on one leg while doing so would be infinitely better than not observing the day at all. So, if the sailor has to dress in a better suit of clothes one day in seven as a sign that Christ is risen, this is a thing to be glad and thankful for.

But let it not be thought that in war-time we only mark our Sundays by a little extra bit of what the sailor tersely calls "spit and polish." On the contrary, on most occasions we keep to the same regular Sunday routine as in peace-time. Only there is a difference: there is a deeper interest and a greater fervour displayed in the Church services than ever before. It means more to us now when we pray that our gracious Sovereign Lord King George may vanquish and overcome all his enemies; and there is no one who can make request for peace in our time so feelingly as the man who has to fight for that peace.

Of course it will be readily understood that not all of our Sundays are of the calm order. The admiral possesses a power which out-Joshuas Joshua with respect to the passage of time, and "Next Saturday will be Sunday" is a signal which contains to a sailor's mind nothing humorous, but much satisfaction.

If this is out of the question, then we have, on a busy Sunday, "Stand-up Prayers," a term which explains itself. There is another name, not quite so self-evident in meaning, for the same thing; and I confess I had to reflect a while when first the commander said to me, "*padre*, I'm afraid we shall only be able to have Church by hand this morning." But in the New Navy, where everything, even to boat-hoisting, that used to be done by hand, is now done by machinery, and done much more efficiently, a make-shift substitute for the full Church Service performed decently and in order describes itself naturally to the modern sailor as "Church by hand."

For a certain period we had a temporary Roman Catholic chaplain attached to us. Some of our men were a little exercised in mind as to how the two rivals would get on together; and finally one came to me, very shyly, and asked me what I was going to do about it. At first I did not quite understand what he was driving at, but on his making his meaning clear I explained that on the following Sunday, instead of the usual service, we had arranged to have a ten-round contest, without gloves, to settle the conflicting claims of the Anglican and Roman Churches once and for all. My interviewer went away with a broad grin on his face; but I fancy that on the Sunday morning there was a more than usual interest taken in the arrangements for rigging Church.

Chapter 5

A West-Country Ship

Ours is a West-Country ship. Such is the unofficial designation given to a vessel belonging to and commissioned at the great Naval Depot of Devonport. This important naval centre has also an unofficial name by which it is known to all navy men: I regret to say it is the unromantic name of "Guzzle," but, seeing that the reference is to the good and plentiful fare of the West Country, it must be taken as a compliment. It is certainly a more expressive term than "Pompey," the naval nickname for Portsmouth; while Chatham, the third of the principal depots, is not distinguished by any pet name at all—except that crews from that vicinity are always spoken of as "Chatham rats."

There is something more than a geographical meaning in the term "A West-Country Ship"; a very distinctive character is also N implied. Foreigners—by which, of course, I mean people who do not belong to Devon or Cornwall—would explain it by saying, in naval phraseology, that we are "Chatty but Happy"—and "chatty" means lacking in those superficial qualities of cheap smartness and ostentatious cleanliness which to a Royal Yachtsman are the be-all and end-all of naval efficiency; or, in short, slovenly.

Of course, we are not slovenly, really. There may be a certain amount of slowness and deliberation about our methods, but, bless your heart, we get there all the same! It is no use trying to get a move on a West-Country crew beyond what they consider right and proper; but somehow the work gets done, and done in good time, too. What is more, it gets done in a happy, good-tempered way, if perhaps a little noisily. For "Westoes" cannot do anything without a power of talk. "What are you making all that noise about—quacking like a lot of old maids round a blessed baby!" roars an irate warrant officer with a fine broad Devonshire burr, incidentally making as much noise as the working-party he is addressing. But he might as well talk to the winds. The men grin back at him, and are quiet for a moment, but presently they are at it again as hard as ever, with the Warrant the most talkative of the whole crowd.

A stoker, clad in a piratical-looking suit of fearnought, passes my cabin door on the way to the engine-room; he does not walk, but progresses with a kind of roller-skating motion, and his heavy clogs, shuffling across the bare iron deck, resound half the length of the ship. And this noise, so agreeable to his ears if not to mine, he accompanies by an appropriate fragment of a rag-time ballad—

Glide, glide, keep on a-glidin'

sung at the top of his voice and in a particularly nasal tone. But they are singing all along the mess deck, too. They always are. So one more does not make any great difference. It shows that the ship is a happy one, and that is the great thing after all.

They poke a good deal of mild fun at us, those others. Pure jealousy, of course. They hint that we are all web-footed, and that we have become so by a process of natural selection induced by the West-Country climate. On Staddon Heights, overlooking Plymouth Sound, stands a long, high wall, built originally as part of a rifle range; but those who have the misfortune to be born elsewhere say that we built it to keep the seagulls out from the farmers' fields. Such remarks as these we treat with the contempt they deserve.

In this ship, as in all West-Country ships, there is a large contingent of Irishmen. Fine fighting men they are, and merry, good-humoured fellows in ordinary times of peace. Many of our naval surgeons, too, hail from Ireland. By a recognised naval convention they all come from "Shkibbereen," the birthplace of the famous *Skibbereen Eagle*, which really did warn Europe: "We have our eye upon the German emperor." One of these, a raw, newly-caught sawbones, seeing for the first time the menu of the wardroom mess, is commonly reported to have exclaimed: "Begobs, fwhat doiet! Mate three toimes a day!" And I, who write, had the happiness of being shipmates with an officer who asked, when the conversation turned upon the topic of collisions at sea: "Was ye iver in two ships to wance, an' they to meet?"

It is held against us who belong to the West-Country ships that we are inclined to be a little boastful. But is there not a cause? We have our share of heroes dead and gone, from Drake to Captain Scott. And if the records of this present war be examined it will be found, I think, that West-Country ships and West-Country sailors have not done so badly. And presently you shall see us back in our sweet old villages, when the gallant blue uniform shall flaunt it down the sunlit street, admired by all the village lassies; and on Sunday shall be seen conspicuous amongst those who come to render their service of praise and thanksgiving in the well-loved old church. And if, here and there, such a one be lacking, his very absence shall attest that he has kept up the honour of the West-Country ship.

Chapter 6
At Sea

It would interest and perhaps astonish the public if the intelligence were allowed to be made known of how many leagues of sea we have covered since the beginning of the war. Ours has always been a seagoing navy—as are not some other navies; and, far from letting a little thing like a war interfere with its usual habits, it has as a whole put in more sea-time within the last few months than in several years of peace.

A witty officer of my acquaintance described the war from the naval point of view as consisting of "long periods of extreme boredom punctuated by moments of intense fear." There is as much truth in this as can be expected in an epigram, remembering always that it takes a brave man to confess to feeling afraid. Even the boredom, however, has not been profitless; it has all tended to an increase of naval efficiency which is nothing less than extraordinary. Certainly the navy has always been considered fairly efficient, but even such a non-technical person as myself can see that there is simply no comparison between what it was seven months ago and what it is now. To watch the Fleet manoeuvring at sea was formerly a fine sight: it is now a revelation.

Scarcely less marvellous is the perfection of mechanical engineering displayed by the machinery of our ships, which instead of being slightly worn out by the amount of work got out of it is, on the contrary, in more perfect condition than ever like our ship's gramophone records, which require to be played a dozen times or so before they get into good condition.

I make a mental comparison between this state of affairs and that of the "High Sea" Fleet, with its officers and men getting no practice in seamanship, strategy, or tactics, and its untried engines concealing who knows what undiscovered defects; and I realise that if our Grand

Fleet were only half its size we might on this account still face a conflict with equanimity.

It means a good deal—this keeping the seas. It means, for example, a pitch-black night, with the temperature well below freezing; there is half a gale of wind blowing and a heavy sea running; a blinding snowstorm stings the faces of the look-outs, and makes it impossible to see more than a foot ahead. And through all this the Fleet is steaming at fast speed, *without lights*. The officer of the watch knows that there is a ship ahead of him and another astern, and he must keep his exact distance if he would avoid a calamity which might mean not alone the loss of hundreds of lives and of a two-million-pound ship, but the weakening of Britain's first line of defence. How is it done? How are any of a score of similar sea-marvels done?

The only answer is, by keeping on doing them. And not the least marvellous part about it all is that they who do these things do not realise that they are doing anything out of the way. I have often watched one who has just come down from the bridge at midnight or at four in the morning—a weird figure, looking as little like a sailor as I suppose our men in the trenches look like soldiers, clad in jacket and trousers of fearnought over three or four layers of ordinary clothes, and apparently at least a yard and a half wide, until he gradually peels off the layers and makes a pile on the deck of the snow-soaked, stiff coverings and the heavy sea-boots. But his one desire is for cocoa, hot cocoa, and lots of it; and his one complaint is that that lop-eared blighter Smith-Jones has relieved him ten minutes late!

The ship at sea, in the night-time, is a curious place. It is so different from what our friends from the shore used to see in those far-off days when they used to come aboard for tea-parties and dances! The long wardroom table has three officers "bedded-down" on it, and others in the same apartment have beds made up on chairs or on the settees. Almost at any hour of the night the smoking-room has a little group of officers chatting as in daytime; they have just come off watch, or are just going on, or they have sat up to hear the Poldhu wireless news, or they have come from their bunks to make an inspection of the particular department for which they are responsible. The guns' crews are at their posts, and when their watch is over clank noisily down the iron ladders to seek their greatly desired hammocks.

Down far below the stokers—whom for some unaccountable reason the newspapers will persist in calling by the distasteful name of the Black Squad—are working away with calm indifference to the fact that should the ship strike a mine or be torpedoed they are the ones who have the poorest chance of escape. Searchlights' crews, wireless operators, signalmen, and many others are all awake and busy. The ship never sleeps. Gradually the grey morning dawns, bleak and cold, and the huge forms of the other ships of the line begin to loom up—they are all in perfect station, ploughing along, "lost in the mists of the North Sea," and doing their appointed work. Which is *real* "Sea-Power"—this, or sitting close under a harbour's guns and strewing the seas with mines like poisonous tares scattered broadcast in a pleasant field?

CHAPTER 7

"Guns"

As touching the race of gunnery lieutenants, they are all exactly alike, only some are rather more so than others. I write this because our own particular representative of the type has just blown in through the wardroom door as though impelled by a charge of cordite, there to explode with rapid firing for the space of three minutes, then blowing out noisily through another door, leaving the wardroom and its occupants a shattered wreck amidst the fumes; and I, who have witnessed an identical performance on the part of many gunnery lieutenants through a long series of years, thought well to commit to paper at once some notes on the life and character of "Guns."

From his particular point of view the whole ship is nothing more than a gun-platform; the engines a convenient means of bringing his guns within range of an object; all the officers and men are considered by him according as they subserve in greater or less degree the great purposes of gunnery; and he mildly wonders that an inscrutable Providence permits the existence of some who are entirely unconnected with the great scheme; while as for his opinion of the torpedo lieutenant and all his works ... Even the weather gets drawn into it. Should you hazard the original remark that it is a fine day, he will agree with you up to a certain point: "Very nice, but not *quite* so much visibility as there was in the forenoon, do you think?" The heat haze has softened a little the sharp clearness of the morning light—and so a target cannot be seen at quite so distant a range now. An unexpected hot day, such as we sometimes get in early spring, is a little irritating to him, as it means that certain arrangements connected with gun-sights and graduated for definite temperatures must all be altered at once!

Do not, please, confuse the gunnery lieutenant with an ordinary common naval officer. This is an enthusiast, a dreamer! He lives for his guns; by, with, or from his guns, and, as the Latin Primer says, sometimes *in* his guns, or as far in as he can crawl, and certainly in the guns' turrets, where he is to be found half the day. Occasionally he descends from his Olympian heights to the lower world of the wardroom, clad in an overall suit of blue dungaree of the "boiler-creeping" type—such a rig as would have struck cold horror into the pure soul of any executive officer a dozen years ago!

Every type of gun is equally acceptable to him, from a tiny three-pounder to a huge fifteen-inch; they are the organ-pipes from which he conjures the music he loves; he has practised so long with ecstasy, and only awaits the hour when he may make them sound a grand Triumphal March!

And by virtue of his office he also takes a loving interest in any sort of machine that bears the remotest resemblance to that masterpiece of science and art, The Gun. Be it only a clay-pigeon throwing-trap, you will see him fingering it delicately and caressing it like a mother with her child. We had in this ship a toy, a game, sent by some kind friend to relieve our nervous tension, consisting of (1) a cardboard model of a roof; (2) *Horresco referens*, five cardboard pussies to place on the same; and (3) some catapults of wire and rubber with projectiles of leathern strips to shoot them with: a Hunnish conceit, in truth, and must surely have been made in Germany! But, would you believe it, "Guns" felt that this naturally came within *his* department, and at once took the whole affair out of our hands! In the most scientific way he "bracketed," spotted, and all the rest of it, getting the range in speedy time, and showing the greatest delight when the poor pussies were "put out of action"!

I suppose he has his counterpart amongst the German Navy. Possibly some *oberleutnant* is equally anxious to see the effect in action of his beloved *Kanone*: for what is the good of a war, anyway, asks "Guns," if we can't have a proper day-out with the big-boys? And if you suggest to him that there is just a possibility that the war may finish without a general fleet action he turns away in disgust, only staying to remark, "Then, for goodness' sake, let's have peace soon, so that we can get on with our battle-practice firing!"

CHAPTER 8

Coaling

The following soliloquy was overheard the other morning from one of the Royal Corps engaged in the daily task of zogging it off: "The greatest war the world 'as ever seen! And wot's a marine doin'? *Cleaning paintwork!*" Truly, it does seem at times that, if our destiny calls us to serve by standing and waiting, such service is, to say the least of it, a trifle dull! The crowded hour may yet come; but in the meantime we may perhaps be allowed the growl of those enforced to live the quiet life. Our commander remarked to me the other day that after the war there will be a great demand amongst naval officers for wooden-legged wives; the esoteric meaning of this dictum being that we have all become so accustomed to doing without amusements and excitements that those ladies will be the most sought after who will not want to drag us from our own fireside to partake of distractions whose allurements we have now outgrown.

One thing, however, which brings a little mild excitement at quite frequent intervals is Coaling Ship. In peace-time we used to look upon this as something of a severe strain, and grumbled if it occurred as often as once a month. But now! Why, the men look on it as a rather amusing form of athletics, a pleasant game to break the monotony, and if they were deprived of it for a whole month they would probably have a fearful moan!

Coaling ship in a man-of-war is a very different thing from what it is in a comfortable liner. There you lean over the rail and watch a mass of coal-laden lighters being slowly brought alongside by a puffing tug, while another barge brings a crowd of shouting and laughing men with glistening brown bodies, all ready to run up the sloping planks and disappear with their baskets of coal through the ship's side; and then you go ashore, to buy ostrich feathers, model catamarans, moonstones, or Teneriffe work, returning in the evening to the nice clean ship.

Here we begin by getting up several hundreds of coal bags from store-rooms down below. They are passed up through a round hole in the deck, covered usually with an iron plate, exactly like the supply to a coal-cellar on a London pavement. One such place is just outside my own cabin, as I am forcibly reminded every time we get the bags up. From another store come iron trolleys—hand-barrows for wheeling the filled bags. Then the collier comes alongside, and derricks and whips are quickly made ready. The men meanwhile have got into "coaling-rig"—for we are our own *coolies*, and do *not* have the assistance of "outside labour." The bluejacket loves nothing so much as to get into some costume different from his ordinary everyday one, and, as he is allowed to wear what he likes for coaling, you see something like an impromptu fancy dress party; one man has an old football jersey of stripes and colours, another sports a tattered khaki tunic, the gift of some soldier chum, while another is happy in the possession of a solar topee.

In each hold of the collier there is a party of men shovelling coal into the bags which are flung down to them in a constant stream. When eight or ten bags are filled a couple of men attach a strap to them, and signal to the motor-man; the engine buzzes round, and up go the bags into the air, and are swung over and lowered on the ship's deck. There another party of men are waiting; each seizes a bag, tilts it dexterously on to his trolley, and runs away with it along the deck to an appointed coal-shoot, where he tips the coal out so that it falls down into the bunker below, where stokers are waiting to trim it—that is, build it up cleverly, so that it occupies the smallest possible space. There is a great art in trimming. Officers as well as men take part in the coaling, and frequently those officers who do not happen to have any appointed share in the work will handle a trolley and work with the men. Very often the band "buck things up a bit" by playing popular airs from the top of a turret or some such spot where they are not in the way.

And what a rate they do work at! For 600 men at work 300 tons an hour is a record often attained. This means that every man must do the equivalent of handling completely half a ton, from the hold of the collier to its stacked-up resting-place in the bunker, in *one hour!* And after, perhaps, a day's work—or, it may be, a night's work—of this kind, the men must turn to and clean ship, and then do the ordinary work of the day in addition. But he is an extraordinary fellow, my friend the sailor! Give him a long coaling that lasts well into the night; let a drenching rain come down all the time and soak him to the skin; add a cold biting wind, and let the whole business, in short, be thoroughly miserable—and when things are at their worst it is ten to one that he and 500 of his mates will all at once be heard merrily singing at the top of their voices!

CHAPTER 9

Concerning a Bucket

Two mediaeval States once went to war about an old bucket. I wish I knew this story in all its details, as it ought to be a most exciting one; unfortunately I am ignorant of more than the bald fact. But I am able to give a fuller account of another quarrel originating from a similar casus belli which lately came under my notice.

The space outside this office is technically termed a "flat," and has nothing resembling the desirable suite of apartments which the word "flat" connotes on shore. It is more like the bottom of a well; Truth and myself residing there in congenial companionship. Occasionally this region is visited by a marine whose official designation is Flat-Sweeper, his duty being to scrub the place out each morning and keep it generally clean; and his were the lachrymose tones I overheard breathing out complaint to a sympathetic wardroom servant engaged in tidying his master's cabin in the same flat.

"First Lootenant, 'e blows along, and 'e says the flat ain't properly cleaned up; says it looks like the main 'old of a pig-boat, and asks me if I've never 'eard of the chemical properties of soap and water!"

"Well, why hadn't you scrubbed out?" asks the sympathetic one rather tactlessly.

"'Ow can I scrub out without a bucket? Tell me that! That's what I says to 'im, same as I says to you!"

"Well, where *is* your bloomin' bucket?"

"Someone's pinched it! I got that bucket from the Bos'n only last week, the old one being wore out and wouldn't hold water, and the Bos'n tells me to be particular careful of it, because there's only nine 'undred and ninety-nine of 'em or words to that effect, served out to this ship, and this was the last one he'd got until he drawed stores at the end of the quarter, so no one couldn't 'ave no more. And then some 'un must go and pinch it, an' me scrubber with it!"

"Didn't you have your mark on it?"

"Didn't I 'ave my mark on it? I spent the entire forenoon carvin' O.F. on it, standin' for Office Flat, with a knife I borrowed off the 'alf-deck messenger, 'avin' smacked his little 'ead because he didn't want to lend it; I put my own initials on it in a drop of the awfice red ink; an' I cut three notches on the rim as a private mark, signifyin' in me own mind the Three Days 10.A what I done for losin' the last one. I ask you, what could a man do more?"

"And can't you find out who's pinched it?" inquires the other voice, very compassionately.

"Might as well look for the badge I lost for tellin' the sergeant-major what I thought of him! Buckets might be made o' gold by the way they disappears in this ship! I've done my best—tried to pinch someone else's, but the people in this ship are that suspicious! A nice set of friends they must be used to, judgin' by the way they looks after all their belongings, as if it was the furnicher of a French *chatto* in the track of the clown prince! Disgustin' I calls it!"

"Well, and what are you going to do about it, if you can't find it?"

"I'm goin' to see the captain of marines about it. And if that don't do, I'm goin' on with it till till I gets to the 'Ouse of Lords. I'm goin' to 'ave someone's blood for it, and get justice done. I don't see why I should be treated with contumeely by the first lootenant, let alone sufferin' the risk of breakin' somethin' hi me inside by being redoosed to the necessity of not answerin' 'im back. I'm goin' to—*why, you've got my bucket! It's you what pinched it! You—you—!*"

It was true. The wardroom servant carelessly pulled back the curtain of the cabin just a little too far, and revealed the bucket in question, which he had converted to his own use in his zeal for keeping his master's cabin clean.

I wonder if the war between those two States in the Middle Ages began in some such way as this?

Chapter 10

The Hand-Picked Life

We were walking back together to the landing place, where the ship's boats lay waiting the return of the funeral party. One of our men, no youngster, but a man who had spent many years in the service, had died. For him, the Great War was over. A death in the hour of battle, with the sound of the guns and the cries of victory ringing in his ears at the last, was denied him: a common malady seized him, and he died quietly in his bed as though he had never seen the sea nor taken upon him to fight for his country. But we buried him with all the pomp and circumstance which attends the last rites of a man who lays down his life for the service of his king and in the defence of his native land, for such a man he was, and such was his end, at least in his goodwill. The volleys rang out by the lonely graveside and the buglers sounded the mournful Last Post, and there we left him.

Back through the bleak hills along the rough roadway the funeral-party retraced the miles along which the band had led them, setting the pace with slow funeral marches. Now they were marching at ease and smoking their pipes, and lively airs mingled with talking and laughter; for such is the way of the navy, and so it must rightly be where men are crowded together and have their own lives to live; they do not forget a comrade, but they cannot long continue openly mourning him. And even though the occasion be a funeral, it cannot be denied that a walk ashore is a pleasing thing to men who have long been cooped up on board, especially when the sun is shining and the fresh wind brings to the nostrils the unaccustomed smell of the good earth.

From the rude cottages, scattered rarely about the hillsides, and seeming an integral part of the boulders and the soil, wild-eyed children came shyly out to gaze wonderingly upon the strange sight; for them also the funeral made a holiday, to be the warp of discussions and conjectures woven by the shuttle of a child's lisping tongue across a speech to ourselves almost unintelligible, a dialect of a dialect.

The sounds from the band and the marching men came wafting faintly back to us, the officer-in-charge and myself, as we walked some half a mile in the rear of the funeral party. "We have been fortunate," my companion said, "in the small number of deaths amongst our ship's company." On further consideration we soon reached the conclusion that it was not unreasonable to hope for a low death-rate amongst a body of men all chosen by medical examination, all in the prime of life and leading a most healthy existence. "Yes," he said, "and I think it is not altogether good for us, *this hand-picked life* that we lead. We are sheltered from the sights of death and suffering and all the woes common to the generality of mankind; we see nothing of the troubles of little children; want and distress are kept from us. And men *ought* to know these things, it is good to have such experiences."

It was curious to listen to another usurping thus my own province of moralising; but there are few jobs that a sailor cannot turn his hand to on occasion, and even that of a parson cannot floor him. I am sure that he was in the right, but only from the selfish point of view of our own spiritual development, the value of which, in comparison with greater needs, may be assessed at, roughly, tuppence. It certainly is *not* good to breathe only the spirit of detachment far above the grosser air of the world's cares. What do we see of Belgium's sufferings except a subscription-list on the notice-board, of women and children murdered save in the pictures in the daily papers? Even those sorrows which are the common lot of all shore-going folk are removed from our ken as by the unseen hand of one who is anxious to shelter us from the knowledge of such things. Shall we forget, in the course of time, and assume the inhuman placidity of a Buddha or a Sphinx?

On the other hand, I am inclined to think that our living this hand-picked life is serving a larger interest than our own. It is for the good of the country that we should dwell in this detachment. No man can fight his best distracted by cares, nor concentrate upon the one supreme object a mind torn by sympathetic thoughts of outside woes. Let us live our hand-picked life for this present; by-and-by, please God, we shall see something of pain and care once more.

Meanwhile, we are not wholly free from our own particular griefs. There are some woes from which there is no escape by land or sea. Chief among these our younger men would probably number the pains of a crossed love, and I could find an instance in a sailor whose letter I recently swakked. It was addressed to a young lady in Ireland, and the love-lorn writer complained: "If you do not wish to have any communication with me, I think you might at least write and say so!"

Chapter 11

"Stoker, First Class"

The other day I read somewhere a very interesting article about the world's most popular tune, "Malbrouk," giving a list of the many different "words" to which that air has been set in various lands and ages.

I could have added one more to the list. Back in the long-ago days of Sunday-school picnics—St. Jude's was almost in the country then, and it was spring-time all the year round—the children used to return from their long day and tumble out from the packed and hot railway carriages into the arms of their mothers waiting on the platform, and there sing:

<u>God bless the Engine-Driver</u> (*ter*)

For driving us so well!"

It is a sentiment which I heartily echo in applying it to the Engine-Driver of the fleet. He is rated "Stoker, First-Class," to take the typical representative of his kind, and a first-class fellow indeed he is!

He has a deal of hard work, and precious little glory; although in this latter respect he is coming into his own at last. Popular opinion has vastly misjudged him, and, while ever ready to sing the praises of the glorious A.B., has rather looked down upon the Stoker as a grimy, underground sort of fellow only to be classed on sufferance with the lads in navy blue. How such an idea ever started, goodness only knows! Certainly it does not hold on board ship. *We* know that during this war-time the stokers have been the hardest-worked body of men in the ship, and that where a vessel has been in action the good steaming has had as much to do with the result as the straight shooting. Jealousies and odious comparisons between different branches are non-existent, I am thankful to say, and everyone recognises that it is not much good having gunnery at the pitch of perfection unless the ship can be pushed along to bring and keep the guns within range. And this is the stoker's part, a part he performs splendidly. "*You* heave the bricks at 'em—*we'll* shove the old 'bus along," I overheard a stoker saying to one of a turret's crew, and that illustrates pretty well the spirit that unites the upper-deck people with those down below.

Not that the stoker's work is always "down below," by any means. This is another of the things not by all understood, that a stoker goes through very much the same training as everybody else on board. He has his course of musketry training—and frequently proves himself the best shot at the range; he is taught how to pull—and not seldom in the races between different "parts of the ship" the stokers' cutter bears away the prize. On the same principle, an able seaman has to go through periodical stokehold training classes; for the work of a stoker is not a task that requires no learning, though many appear to think it is so. On the contrary, it is a skilled workman's, almost an expert's, task; and if anybody thinks it is simply a matter of shovelling coals on a fire, all I can say is, let him go below and try it! Also, a stoker is required to have a practical and theoretical knowledge of machinery of quite a high standard: altogether he is a thoroughly all-round competent man.

There are, of course, degrees in the stokers' hierarchy. The arch-priests are known as chief stokers, and wear a fore-and-aft rig, and very solid, staid, and sound members of society they are. I do not know why it should be so, but almost always the chief stoker has the breadth of two ordinary men; and to look at the little round hole that does duty for a hatchway on the deck of a destroyer, and then to go down it and discover a chief stoker actually there in bodily presence, reminds one of the narrow-necked bottles with models of full-rigged ships inside so dear to the old-time sailor.

I know of no more impressive sight in the world than three chief stokers walking abreast along the streets of a foreign port. Ponderous, slow, majestic, and inevitable is their progress; you watch them with awe, and you realise exactly how the British Empire has slowly swept its way across the world.

I heard a good story of a stoker lately. It happens to be absolutely true, but even if I did not know this for a fact, I should still believe it. One of our destroyers was in action, and in the course of the fight was struck by a shell which penetrated into one of her bunkers and there exploded. Fragments of the bulkhead and a litter of coal came flying out into the stokehold; and shot out with them in a cloud of black dust came also a stoker, who had at the time been trimming coal inside. He picked himself up slowly, gave himself a shake, and then, turning to the chief stoker, said: "I don't see that I'm doin' much good in there; the bloomin' coal's trimmin' itself!"

CHAPTER 12

Destroying

The Grand Fleet has, of course, the usual complement of destroyers, without which no battle fleet can be considered complete. They act as the eyes of the fleet, to use a common expression; which means either that they serve as a screen to ward off possible dangers or else that they fulfil the same office as the pilot fish does for the shark, searching out the prey for him to snap up—according to the way one looks at the matter.

In prehistoric times—that is, before the war—it was the ambition of every young lieutenant to obtain command of a destroyer. So it is still, but for a different reason. Then, the reason was that the promising young officer frequently had a promised young bride, and naval pay at the ordinary rates being insufficient for setting up housekeeping, the lady in question would fix the date for the wedding at the time "When Billy gets a destroyer." Because the command of one of those craft carries with it an extra allowance, officially termed Hard-lying money, just sufficient to translate the little flat at Southsea from the region of fairy dreams into reality. I should add that the expression Hard-lying money has really no connection with that occasional manipulation of paper-returns rendered so necessary by the exigencies of the service, especially in a destroyer where no assistant-paymaster is carried, but refers to the fact that in one of these vessels you lie hard in the sense of your life being not altogether a bed of roses.

But Billy's reason at the present time for moving heaven and earth to get a destroyer is that he thinks it would give him a better chance of seeing action, and perhaps of distinguishing himself; in which idea he is not very far wrong, for this war has proved to be, from the naval point of view, largely a destroyer's war. I was watching some of our destroyers the other day from the deck of my own ship. There was rather a heavy sea running. Each of these little craft was keeping her station splendidly; what strength in their build, and what power to drive them through the tumbling seas so steadily! The destroyer's side is no thicker than a piece of cardboard; but the engines, humming away to the tune of twenty thousand horse-power, drive that frail structure at the speed of an express train in the face of waves such as, breaking against a seawall, would rend the solid masonry into fragments! I watched, as one never tires of watching, other ships in company with one's own; down pinned each destroyer, bows under, into the grey seas, righting herself a moment later and rising heavily from beneath the weight of water which now streamed from each side of the focs'le in thick curtains of dazzling white; then, freed from its mass, while the last tattered ends of the waterfall were caught by the wind and tossed into the faces of the men on the bridge, she rose up and up, till her forefoot was quite clear of the water, and the keel could be seen for a third of its length.

Then she came down again with a thump into the next sea, and perhaps for a few seconds kept more or less on an even keel, cutting through the waters with the knife-edge of her bows. And so the process was repeated, hour after hour, knot after knot. (To be more correct, I should have said "mile after mile," for a "knot" is not really a seamile, but a unit to express the number of sea-miles travelled per hour.) Really, however, the destroyers as a rule do not make heavier weather of it than the big ships; and, granted that you once get used to their quick motion, they are not half so uncomfortable as they look. The worst thing is the amount of water that somehow finds its way inside when the sea is rough, and fills the mess-deck to a depth of a foot or more, making the "hard-lying money" not wholly undeserved.

They look so pretty and yacht-like, these destroyers, on a fine day; you long to take a little cruise in them. Some soldier officers had this feeling on an occasion I remember. The ship I was in had to go out for the day to run torpedoes, attended by a half-flotilla of destroyers. The soldiers were eager to be allowed to enjoy the sea-breeze and the sunshine from the decks of the dainty little craft, and out they came. Unfortunately, one of our torpedoes sank—a thing that happens, of course, with extreme rarity; and all destroyers had to spend the rest of a long, long day in that task whose very mention is enough to strike bitterness into the soul of the torpedo-man, "*looking for bubbles*" By the afternoon it began to breeze up, and in those shallow waters a swell soon arose, and the destroyers were rolling their twenty-five degrees, and all the soldiers were deadly sick. We in the big ship could not get back to the shore, either; and our only consolation rested in looking at the soldiers. Perhaps of all human pleasures, that of watching the misfortunes of others is the last of which we tire.

A destroyer story came to my ears the other day—a really true story. Two German officers had been rescued from the sea after one of the many minor actions of this war; they were taken down to the wardroom of the rescuing destroyer, and given dry clothing; next their preservers, now become their hosts, offered them whisky and soda and cigarettes, in all courtesy. The German officers were astonished at such treatment, and stammered out their lively thanks; it was not much they could do, they said, in such circumstances, to show how very much they appreciated the kindness of their captors, but if the latter could suggest anything, they would be only too happy to do it.

Then up spoke the irresponsible young sub. "Well, yes," said the bright youth, "there is one thing you might do; just get up and *sing us the Hymn of Hate!*"

CHAPTER 13

Atmosphere

The firmament that lieth above the waters has almost as much to do with the sailor's life as the waters themselves, and there is not a single branch of naval work which is not affected in some way by the atmosphere. The wireless operator's life is made a burden to him by what he vaguely terms "atmospherics"—are these, I wonder, identical with the little demons which an old retired paymaster of my acquaintance used to say were specially told off to annoy him on certain days when everything went wrong? The navigating officer is only prevented from returning two-thirds of his pay in the form of conscience money by the reflection that the atmosphere owes him a huge indemnity for the grey hairs it has caused him; and as for the gunnery branch, well, "when Willie's Canal Fleet comes out," it is the atmosphere alone that will decide whether the action is to be fought at close range or long. For the atmosphere can play strange tricks.

I have seen, for example, in Far Eastern waters, a perfectly good sunset with sun and rays and everything complete on the *eastern* horizon at the same time as the genuine show was taking place in the proper quarter. And on the African coast I have seen houses which were surrounded by miles of sand apparently standing in the middle of a lake: this, of course, was nothing out of the common, but what did surprise me was to notice that the houses were *reflected* in the non-existent water; the *Wonders-of-Science* books of childhood had never said anything about that!

Whether the physical atmosphere that hangs over the oceans has any connection with the spiritual one of naval life I cannot say, but there is no doubt that there does exist a definite naval atmosphere, quite different from everything else.

Let me say at once that it is *not* "breezy." If you want to make a naval officer thoroughly dislike you, call him a "breezy sailor." This popular conception is only to be found in comic operas of the "*Geisha*" sort, or amongst R.N.V.R. officers who have not yet been to sea: in real naval life he does not exist. As a class, that is; you do, of course, come across rare specimens of the type, just as you might find a breezy chartered accountant or a breezy veterinary surgeon, but these are, happily, few and far between, and as a rule they are much more appreciated when visiting other ships than they are in their own mess. For they are trying people to live with, these breezy people; it is all very well out of doors to stand up to the jolly buffets of the wind, but a breeze blowing all through the house upsets things and becomes a nuisance. No; if the naval officer can be said to run to type at all, it is of that kind expressed in his own words as "*mouldy*"; or, to get back to my theme, he lives in an atmosphere in which the elements of care and sadness form a large part. Certainly we have nothing to compare with a French naval lieutenant who came visiting on board one of our ships and, before he left, threw his gold watch overboard just to express his entire satisfaction with life in general and with the *Entente Cordiale* in particular.

Ours is an atmosphere, again, in which we breathe into our being a certain content with injustice, and learn that a measure of that unpleasant medicine is extremely salutary. Just like everyone on shore, so everyone in the navy, from boy to admiral, gets treated unjustly some time or other during his career, and possibly several times. But we come to recognise that it is a jolly good thing, and at the worst, take it philosophically, with the reflection that everyone has to stand his turn. There is no place, except perhaps at a public school, where this lesson can be learnt—though I cannot speak for the army; I daresay it is much the same there. The ordinary man on shore who finds himself treated with injustice is shocked that such an outrage can possibly happen to him; it is an unheard-of thing that such a deserving person should have been treated as though—well, imagine the remainder of his laments. "What am I going to do about it?" he asks himself plaintively, feeling that some steps ought to be taken to set matters right; a question to which the naval officer in like case replies in the wise and weighty words of Tiny Tim of the old *Vanity Fair, Hard Cases*—"*Do nothing.*"

On the whole, the atmosphere of naval life may be fairly accurately summed up in the words of the old *Gunnery Drill Book*, quoting from which the G.I. used to bid the men practising the routine for a funeral, "Assoom a *mournful but not too melan-cholly* a haspect, *subdood yet cheerful.*" And, by the way, in order to impress this and other facts upon their memories, he used then to pace slowly down between the lines, saying: "The party will now follow out the instructions as mentioned; *I will be the corpse!*"

Chapter 14

The Gun-Room

"*Si jeunesse savait*—if only the youngster had a grain of savvy," is the commander's lament as the midshipman of the picket-boat comes alongside and nearly succeeds in carrying away the ladder in doing so. But he probably did the same thing in his day, though, of course, he would strongly resent your telling him this, and would impress upon you that "when I was a gun-room officer, if I had ever shown myself such a hopeless ullage as all midshipmen appear to be nowadays," etc., etc., *ad lib*. The whole truth of the matter is that the commander has grown up; or, from the gun-room point of view, has already advanced far into the sere and yellow leaf stage with all the attributes of doddering old age crowding thick upon him.

For the gun-room is that part of the ship where Youth is at its flower; nearly all its occupants are in their teens, and the presiding member is a sub aged about twenty-one; the solitary specimen of hoary eld being the assistant-paymaster, who ploughs his long furrow in the gun-room till the age of twenty-six or so before becoming a "two stripe A.P." and entering upon the dignity of ward-room rank.

So here is young blood in varying degrees, from the squeaker just fresh from Dartmouth to the nearest thing we get in the navy corresponding to the complete nut. This latter type I can best illustrate by narrating how a friend of mine went to his outfitters for a suit of plain clothes, and explained that while he wanted something quite in the latest fashion, he did not wish for anything too dressy, too "I understand, sir," said the tailor; "*you don't want a sub-lieutenant's suit.*"

The midshipmen's berth in the days of Fielding, and even in those of Marryat, seems to have been a horrible dark hole far down below decks; the gun-room in those times was the mess of the senior officers, was a portion of the main deck partitioned off with three or four of the square gun-ports along its outboard side, the muzzle-loading guns mounted on their wooden carriages standing at the ports. Wardroom and gunroom were then synonymous terms; but at some date unknown to me the latter term was applied to the junior officers' quarters, and so remains at the present day, though there are no longer any guns within its precincts.

In respect of space, there is no very great improvement on the old midshipmen's berth. I wonder what the Health Authorities would say if it were proposed to accommodate five-and-twenty board-school children in a room about thirty feet by ten and seven feet high?

A great deal of this space is taken up by a long table, and there are seats built all around against the bulkheads, with lockers underneath. On the table is a litter of caps, sextants, dirks and belts, work-books, remnants of a watch meal, newspapers of the latest mail, gramophone records and a score of other things. One midshipman has cleared a space with a sweep of his arm, and is working out his sights with his *Inman's Tables* ready at his elbow; opposite him sits the engineer-sub, writing his home letters; the assistant-clerk, having struggled unsuccessfully with the ledger all the forenoon, vents his feelings by viciously kicking down a stack of hockey-sticks from the settee, murmuring sardonically the while, "Who wouldn't sell his farm and go to sea?" The two who were writing, annoyed by the clatter, and reinforced by a couple more who have just entered, rise from the table, crying, "Dogs of War on the Cheese-eye Pusser!" and there results at once a very fair imitation of a rugger scrum, with the unfortunate clerk representing the ball. In a few moments peace is restored, and all resume their normal occupations, and discuss amicably their chances of getting a game of golf later on.

The discipline of the gun-room is of the patriarchal nature, and is administered principally by the senior sub. Moral suasion is his ordinary method, and great are the qualities of wisdom and tact displayed in his rule; when such means fail the collective sense of justice of the gun-room supports him in having recourse to the old-fashioned remedy popularly known as "Six of the best."

Very much depends on the senior sub; the general tone of the gunroom rests entirely with him to make or mar. As a rule, he comes out not only well, but brilliantly, from such a really trying ordeal; learning, with some mistakes and with not a little opposition, to handle men in such a way that they may submit cheerfully to his ruling and may keep within restraints and yet not feel their pressure.

I was a guest once at the Coming-of-Age party of our one and only sub in a certain ship. The proceedings began with a ceremonious introduction to the hero of the hour, who was attired in royal robes and seated on a throne made of a couple of empty gin cases. Before him stood two statuesque dark-skinned attendants—the "native" pantry boy and third steward—each holding a six-inch-gun rammer as a staff of office; though what their precise office was no one exactly knew, being quite satisfied with the fact that they looked very nice and imposing. Soon it began to occur to the mind of the gun-room that the function of presentation, however dignified, was just a little tame; so they conceived the idea of a Private Entree for some of the smallest of their members; and, taking them quietly outside the room, shot them in headforemost through the pantry trap-hatch! This quaint conceit proved so pleasing that it was felt it called for repetition, and the "young gentlemen" were therefore presented some half a dozen tunes each, appearing like human bullets through the trap-hatch in what the gunnery lieutenant described as "rapid firing." I should not omit to say that the bullets enjoyed it as much as anyone.

Certainly the gun-room is the life of the ship. Its officers can always be relied upon for cricket matches, football, hockey, or any game under the sun, for the "funny party," for racy little verses in the ship's magazine, for sailing picnics, and for any fun and devilry that may suggest itself; the gun-room is on the top line for such affairs, always.

And not for such things alone. In keeping the enemy from our shores these bright young lads have borne their part, just as much in their own way as the admirals and captains. Without them the great machine could not run as it does.

How many of them, too, have given glorious proof that "*dulce et decorum*" is as great an inspiration to-day as ever! Willingly, heroically, they have gone to a sailor's grave, many of them going to sea for the first time as officers, only to be asked to give the supreme test of devotion at the very beginning of their career. It cannot be right to think of these splendid youngsters as "cut off in their prime"; rather do they seem as sons who, having an equal gift with others to offer to their mother, render it not in paltry inconsiderable driblets, thinning out their homage through the long years of a lifetime; but give splendidly, heaping all that they possess at her feet in one magnificent moment.

Chapter 15

The Grand Fleet

My most insistent grievance at present is the old one, that all the best things which can possibly be said about anything have already been said. I am not complaining now about Shakespeare, who, of course, in this respect is hopelessly incorrigible; my grievance is against Professor Seeley for having made a remark to the effect that the British Empire was acquired in a fit of absent-mindedness. Because I wanted to say that about the navy, and especially about the Grand Fleet. The German High Sea Fleet is the product of deliberate proposals; the officials of that country appear to have said at some definite moment, "*Happy thought*: good thing to have a navy: remember to get one from the stores when next ordering." But the navy of Britain came to us by exactly the reverse process, by pure absence of mind.

Of course, nothing that is worth having is ever acquired in any other way. No man by taking thought can add one cubit unto his stature; but by taking thought for quite other matters, such, for instance, as the defence of his country, drilling, and training in the open air, he finds to his surprise that he has added to his stature a very considerable fraction of a cubit, whereas the combined efforts of Müller and Sandow and a diet of vermicelli had previously failed utterly. The only way to keep the vision is to go away and feed the poor at the convent gate.

The Grand Fleet is a fortuitous agglomeration of units so entirely suited to its purpose that it affords a rare example of the beautiful and the fit, such as would have delighted the heart of St. Augustine in his Plotinian days. It is, in respect of this, comparable to the works of Creation, and has reached that result by being evolved on the same plan of chance that is not altogether chance. Nature never said: "Good idea: let's have a horse and an Englishman and a nice bit of grass"; but bungled along in a happy-go-lucky manner, evolving weird types of *protohipps*, *primequines*, *speluncahoms*, and *graminoid* bamboos, just like ourselves with our ironclads, turret-ships, fleet-rams, scouts, and coast defence vessels; until finally she arrived at the culminating perfection of the Grand National, and we at the Grand Fleet.

The term "Grand Fleet" was never used in recent times until the beginning of this present war. Yet it is an ancient expression, and the idea of reviving it was a most felicitous one. There is something very grand about the word "grand." And it is so essentially English. No other modern language, to my limited knowledge, contains a word exactly corresponding to it; just as no other navy quite answers to ours, and no foreign naval spirit is exactly the same as our own. For "Grand" seems to connote a dignity that needs not the trappings of magnificence, a consciousness of power that does not require to be kept awake by self-laudation, and boasts not itself against those of lesser strength.

Such, it appears to me, is the Grand Fleet. We have other fleets, working in various parts of the world, each of them forming a complete navy such as a more than minor power might well envy; but the Grand Fleet stands alone as the sure shield, under God, of the lives and liberties of the British nation and—Empire more, of the rights of the whole civilised world.

All that might be said concerning the composition of this great fleet, the various types of ships, and their numbers; its elaborate technical organisation; its skilful handling by those in both the higher and the lower posts of responsibility; its arrangements for the order of battle and its working methods during the period of waiting; all such matters must be left to the reflection of those who have a partial knowledge of them—for not even in the fleet itself are many who could claim to know fully—and to the imagination of such as place an implicit but uninformed trust in the navy.

The Grand Fleet is not absolutely undefeatable. No fleet is. Were ours ten times its present size, you could not make such a claim for it with any certainty. But it is undefeated, and, please God, will remain so. Entirely owing to this fact it happens that our fields can be ploughed and reaped peacefully, our womenfolk pursue their way without terror, our young men go a-soldiering with confidence as to the safety of their homes, and our factories work busily to supply the army's needs.

Until the Grand Fleet is defeated not a single German soldier can set foot on our shores. The enemy may exercise his childish malignity in sinking a merchant ship here and there, or may rain down indiscriminating murder from the risky security of the skies; but these are deeds of spite, not of war. Between him and the real object of his serious desires there lies a barrier which, by the help of God, he shall never break down—the Grand Fleet.

Chapter 16

Tropes, and Three Watchkeepers

Myself: There was a fellow in "Hudibras"
        Who ne'er his mouth did ope'
        But out there flew a trope.

First Watchkeeper: Well, of all the silly rotten things to say! Is it supposed to be funny? Do we laugh now? And what *is* a trope, anyway?

Second Watchkeeper: It comes from the Eyetalian *troppo*, meaning *Too much of your back answers!* You ought to know that if you've been up the Straits. Dry up and give the *padre* a chance.

Third Watchkeeper: No, it comes from the Greek *tropos*—hence the term Tropics. The idea is that whenever the chap opened his lips you heard some pretty hot stuff!

Myself: A trope is a word turned out of its original meaning in order to add emphasis or wit to a remark. It also means a metaphor, or—or, well, almost any old thing of that sort.

First Watchkeeper: Like saying that So-and-So has "had a one-gun salute"[1]; is that the idea?

Myself: Something like that. My aim is to make a collection of such naval tropes. So I want you to help me.

Second Watchkeeper: *Padre*, that's all very well, but don't forget that the majority of naval sayings have been handed down from days when polite conversation was not quite so restrained as it is at present; so, unless your collection is to be a private one—

Myself: It may need Bowdlerising? Perhaps that can be done.

First Watchkeeper: How will this do for you? One of my turret's

---

1. Meaning that he has been court-martialled. The ship in which a C.-M. is held fires one gun at 8 a.m. on the day of the Court.

crew is going to be married, and, being very ignorant and nervous about the Marriage Service, he came and asked me whether it would be possible to get the chaplain to give him a *dummy run!*[2] .

Second Watchkeeper: Poor effort! This is rather neater: I asked the waiter at dinner last night if the chicken was fit to eat, and he whispered confidentially in my ear, "Well, sir, I think 'was an old hen just coming up for her third badge!"[3].

Third Watchkeeper: Ever meet old Jones, a Siwash Gunner?[4] . One of the Hungry Hundred[5] he was; I remember him training a racing cutter's crew, mostly Selborne's Light Horse[6], and shouting at the stroke oar: "Call that pulling? You couldn't pull your best girl from the arms of a soldier!"

Second Watchkeeper: I was shipmates with Jones once. He was a proper Messman's Horror[7], always stowing his hold[8]—used to ship a face like a sea-boot[9] if there was only Fanny Adams[10] for lunch. I hear he's in one of the mine-bumpers now.

Myself: One of what?

Second Watchkeeper: One of the Third Fleet ships. And I hope he's living on Navy[11] now; it would serve him right!

First Watchkeeper: If I wasn't two ends and the bight[12] of a fool I

---

2. At certain firing practices the ship steams along a buoyed course, aiming the guns at the target but not actually firing, as a rehearsal or dummy run.
3. A man comes up before the captain to apply for his third good-conduct badge after sixteen years' service, "man and boy."
4. A lieutenant who earns a shilling a day for carrying out gunnery duties in the absence of a more fully trained gunnery officer, more commonly known as a Bob-a-day Gunner. A Siwash (N. American Indian) duck is a disappointing bird which looks like a wild duck but isn't one.
5. A name given to the first lot of supplementary lieutenants entered straight from the Merchant Service.
6. Men entered for a period of five years only, under a scheme originated when Lord Selborne was First Lord.
7. So fond of his meals that he ate up the messman's profits.
8. The Scots say: "Filling his kyte."
9. A common naval expression, both verbal and facial.
10. Hash. Fanny Adams was a woman who was murdered some years ago, and her body was found a considerable time afterwards chopped in small pieces and packed in a box.
11. To live on Navy is to have Service rations with no private additions.
12. The bight of a rope is the loop lying slack between its ends, so the expression means the complete rope—or fool.

should be in one of those ships myself, bung up and bilge free[13], and getting a drop of leaf now and then by the aid of the Married-man's-friend.

Myself:———?

First Watchkeeper: Pet name given to a German submarine which, so the yarn goes, kept one of the bug-traps[14] bailed up in a narrow harbour for a week by waiting off the entrance ready to squirt a mouldy at her directly she showed her nose outside.

Myself: Ready to?

First Watchkeeper: To fire a torpedo at her, of course! All the bundle-men [15] wanted to subscribe and send out medical comforts [16] to the submarine's crew to induce them to stay. But their Number One, who was single and Salt-Horse [17], went about with a face like a scrubbed 'ammick [18]; he used to say that married men were as much use to the Service as sweethearts to a nun.

Third Watchkeeper: Look here, we're not getting on with these what-names for the *padre*. There's any amount of naval expressions which are rather well chosen when you come to look into them: "Angel's whisper" for the defaulters' bugle-call; "body-snatchers" for the ship's corporals; a "holiday" for a scamped bit of paintwork; "spun-yarn tricks" for underhand dealings.

Myself: What's the origin of that last?

Third Watchkeeper: Much the same as "having everything on a split yarn"—that is to say, ready to start at once. *Padre*, anyone would think you had only been a dog-watch in the service [19], not to understand plain English! At evolutions—"out-nets"—for instance, the practice *has* been known of getting everything ready the night before

---

13. A method of stowing casks on board—snug and comfortable.
14. Gunboats.
15. A bundle (of good things) allegorically denotes a wife.
16. Among which a Sick Bay Port: a term of endearment amongst sailors for wine of all kinds.
17. A non-specialist lieutenant. Salt-horse (beef in brine) was the plain, ordinary fare of old-time sailors. Salt-horse officers are frequently more of the briny old sea-dog than their scientific confrères.
18. Another naval expression similar to the sea-boot face. A freshly scrubbed hammock looks about as un-joyous as anything in the world.
19. The dog-watches are the shortest, only two hours each. People who "have only been a dog-watch in the navy" are not encouraged to express their opinions about service matters.

and the proper fastenings replaced with pieces of spun yarn which can be cut through with a sailor's knife as soon as the signal is made. Of course, it isn't playing the game: that's a "spunyarn trick."

Second Watchkeeper: A dry business, all this quacking! I say, *padre*, this is a pretty long ship, isn't it?

Myself: About five-fifty to six hundred feet in length, I believe; but why do you ask?

Second Watchkeeper: In order to be your honoured guest. Don't you know that "a long ship" means one where it is a long time between drinks?

Myself: You've earned one. Press the bell, will you?

Second Watchkeeper (after a brief pause): Well, here's luck! Precious little clear-lower-deck [20] about this soda!

First And Third Watchkeepers: But what about us?

Myself: Certainly. Call the waiter again. Well worth it, as the sailor said when he got seven days' cells for kissing the admiral's daughter.

---

20. At the order "clear lower deck" men come tumbling up from below to the upper deck, like the bubbles in good soda-water.

Chapter 17

My Servant

One great advantage enjoyed by a chaplain over his brother officers is that he is the only individual in the ship able to talk to all sorts and conditions of naval men on equal terms. I have frequently spent a pleasant half-hour with one whose free spirit could not brook restraint, and his vile body consequently had to; have sat by his side on the plank bed of his cell and picked a small portion of his oakum; and then have gone almost immediately to pick a small portion of the admiral's grouse "in the hupper suckles of the cuddy," as the wardroom puts it. In each case it was my privilege to be able to talk as man to man—or, as I once heard a devout young warrant officer say in a Gospel address, using a common name for a sailor with astonishing inappropriateness, "to speak as fellow-flatfoot to fellow-flatfoot."

The ordinary naval officer cannot do this; even if his training has not dulled his perception of the fact that an admiral or captain stripped of official paramountcy is but a human being of his own social class, yet his sense of discipline prevents him from putting that knowledge into practice. Similarly, a well-defined barrier exists between officers and men. This is as it should be, and does not forbid a splendid spirit of comradeship such as cannot be found in any other navy in the world; but it does forbid any excessive familiarity. A chaplain, however, is not only privileged to be in closer personal touch with the men, but is expected to be so to a certain extent. Therefore it happens that the officer who shares a servant with me refrains for service reasons from talking much with him beyond giving him necessary orders, whereas I can indulge in the full enjoyment of his conversational and other talents.

Let me first describe these other talents. He looks after my clothes and cleans up my cabin, washes my clothes, and in short "does for me," to use a technical expression, as a kind of combination butler, valet, tweeny-maid, and boots; and he performs these diaconal functions—serving tables and the rest—remarkably well and for a ridiculously few shillings a month.

Then, as a private in the Royal Marines, he has to acquit himself well in various other directions. "Soldier and sailor too," he sometimes vanishes from my ken for the greater part of a day to take part in coaling ship; when I see him again he is once more spruce and clean save for that which is most difficult to get rid of, a rim of coal-dust on the eyelids, showing up well against the healthy fresh skin and giving him a handsome pair of "Irish eyes." At other times he dons overcoat and mufflers to keep a night watch on deck as sentry; we have met occasionally at 4 a.m., when he has had the middle and I the morning. He lands for route-marches, well turned out; he can pull an oar with any seaman, and is as smart a soldier as any in the king's army.

He is an artist, too, of no mean order. Much of his spare time he spends in his mess or, by special permission, in the cabin, making an enlarged copy of some picture postcard that has taken his fancy, and doing it very well indeed; he takes a brotherly interest in my own attempts at water-colour sketching, and has given me many useful hints on the subject.

Have I mentioned that he is a good-looking young fellow? At any rate, there is a girl in Bristol who has no doubts on this question, and to give this young pair a little wedding present will be more of a pleasure to me than is the case with many other such offerings. The occasion will arise, I hope, at no distant date: I have already published his banns on board.

Early in the war, by the way, it was possible for a service man to get a special licence from any bishop at an hour's notice for a couple of guineas, without any preliminary banns or notice. This was a very great convenience, and I cannot understand why it is now "a washout." There are, every day, men coming back to their homes unexpectedly who would seize the opportunity to get married, but are prevented from doing so because the legal twenty-one days stand in their way. A recent criminal trial has proved that our marriage regulations do not preclude the possibility of fraud, and in my poor opinion their only effect is to render marriage difficult for the sailor and the soldier—which is asking for trouble. The two-guinea special was a good tip. and I am sorry it no longer holds good.

To return to my servant and his varied energies—it is as a conversationist that he chiefly shines. Mine is mostly a listening part, and very little encouragement is needed to get him to air his views.

Let it not be imagined that his speech and expressions are those of the comic marine found in a certain type of naval stories and sketches. He talks grammatically and without accent, having been fairly well educated and coming from a very respectable and "superior" social class. I wish that people on shore would understand that a large proportion of our men are like him in this respect, and that the rollicking, roystering, semi-savage of their ideas is as dead as Nelson himself.

My servant's views on things in general may not be very original, but they are very sound; and they would make a socialist orator gnash his teeth with rage. One of his pet phrases is "It is ridiculous." For example, it is ridiculous to think that we can do without rich people; it is ridiculous to imagine that they enjoy greater freedom than the working man, or have less burdens to bear. Their lives are different from ours, but not easier, and without them the State would quickly go to pieces. It is ridiculous to make any sharp distinction between the upper classes and all others and to rail against the former; everybody knows that there are innumerable grades amongst the working classes themselves, and if people find themselves in a lower grade it is generally their own fault. No one spoils the game for the working man so much as the working man who is content to live like a beast and behaves like one. "Some of the people in my mess," he says, "won't understand these things; you can argue with them as much as you like, but they can't take it in—they don't seem to have the intellect!"

On the subject of Germany he is mildly contemptuous, yet pitying withal. The whole trouble with the people of that country is" that they want to get everything without earning it, and they must be shown that the world isn't run on those lines. Their bombastic claims strike him as purely silly; such childishness comes from living in a ring fence and never having any ideas of what is going on outside. I am afraid that on the subject of the *Kaiser* he is even more contemptuous, but still without a trace of bitterness; he sums up the All-Highest's attitude in his favourite expression—"It is ridiculous!"

Chapter 18

The Wedding Present

We had a right-down regular genuine old-fashioned ward-room cag about it. One of our number was to be married shortly, and as is customary on such occasions the mess wished to combine and give him a present.

We in the ward-room do not let such an opportunity for argument and debate evade us easily. In peace time we might perhaps settle the business in a day, and the amount of words expended over it would not be more than enough to fill a couple of volumes of Hansard; but not so during the war, when fresh topics of conversation are hard to come by and the standing debate between optimists and pessimists is apt to pall.

Be it noted here that the common form taken by ward-room discussions is liable to be misunderstood by the uninitiated. A group of Maltese boatmen talking over their private concerns in a friendly manner appear to be engaged in such a violent and deadly quarrel that you instinctively turn to look for the nearest policeman to separate them; and in like manner our discussions, though most unparliamentarily both in method of procedure and in the choice of expressions, do not really give rise to bodily assaults or life-long hatreds, as you might imagine they would. The main object is for each man to express his own opinion and not to listen to the ideas of others. When a chance does occur of an unaccompanied duet a bullock-driver would as soon expect to get a move on without the aid of a little profanity as a naval officer without a few nicely worded personal affronts.

A preliminary question as to whether the gun-room should be invited to stand in with us was disposed of with disappointingly calm celerity; the proposer put forward his suggestion with a hesitating lack of confidence in his own ideas and found no backers, and after some withering remarks on gun-room officers in general and our own in particular the question was allowed to drop quietly.

Next came the consideration of what amount should be contributed by each officer. Everyone was willing and even eager to give to an extent, within reasonable limits, but that was not going to be allowed to interfere with our enjoyment.

"Let everybody give one day's pay," was the first suggestion. "Too much! We don't want to give him a solid gold bedstead with diamond knobs on the end!"

"Well, we want to do the thing decently, don't we? I suppose *you'd* like to give him an ormolu clock and a case of pipes suitably inscribed, and the remainder of the hevening was spent in 'armony! This isn't a dockyard matey's wedding, it's a naval officer's!"

"How about a half-day's pay?"

"Too hard on the juniors. Why make a hard-and-fast rule? There's no need to do everything according to the drill-book; you'd like to regulate how many eggs we can eat for breakfast, two hard-boileds for three-stripers, and one split scrambled amongst the junior watchkeepers!"

"And what about allowances? Some of you people are getting princely allowances while the real hard workers have to live on their bare pay; I vote that the idle rich pay the super-tax if we're going on these lines!"

"Oh, why not let everyone give exactly what he jolly well pleases? Here, give us a piece of paper, I'll write down the amounts. Come on, how much will *you* give?"

"What has it got to do with you how much I give? I don't see that you've got any qualifications for running this show beyond a nose like a Yiddisher money-lender and a talent for faking your quarterly returns!"

"No, I'll tell you the best way to do it. If any officer is too modest or too mean to say openly how much he is willing to subscribe, I don't mind sitting at the receipt of custom in my cabin and you can all come and give your money to me privately."

"Ho! You want to pay off Gieves, do you? Put it down in the mess-bills, whatever else we do."

We finally settled this part of the discussion to the contentment of at least a working majority.

Having reached this point, we then proceeded to try to settle what form the present should take. This act of the drama was divided into several scenes, such as the Quarter-Deck, An Officer's Cabin, The Ante-Room, etc., with groups of from two to six people taking speaking parts in each, the last scene comprising nearly the whole of the caste.

Somebody suggested "Knives." A few were already becoming wearied with the contest immediately agreed to the proposal; but a more virile number heaped scorn upon it. "*Knives!*" he echoed sarcastically, "why not give *blankets!* A nice romantic, dainty present, *knives*, I must say!"

That killed knives.

"A standard lamp," said one; "a silver tea-tray," said another; a third, "a spirit-kettle"; a fourth was for spending the money on not one but several useful presents. "No," said an objector, "this mess-present is going to be something that they will take a pride in, something different to all the other presents. What is wanted is a gadget that the bride can show off in years to come as the present that came from her husband's ship."

"Well then, why not ask them to choose for themselves?"

"No, I'm dead against that," struck in a confirmed bachelor who will probably be one of the first to fall a victim when peace brings him again into the society of the gentle irresistibles. "I'm dashed if I'd allow her to have any voice in it. This is our present to him, not to her. These women have got to be kept in their places. Let him choose if you like; but she must understand that she has darned well got to take what's given her."

A married man: "My poor fellow, you may say what you please, and think what you like, but this present is going to be the bride's property—and quite right, too! Moreover, if there's any idea of letting them choose for themselves, don't you make any mistake, *she* will do the choosing, and *he* will only *think* he has had a hand in it!"

"Suppose we elect a committee, and give them a free hand?"

This suggestion met with opposition, but not much, and was adopted.

So the theatre of operations was narrowed; but it still left room for a combination of two against one. The allies wanted each of the three committeemen to make a separate choice, so that everybody's ideas might be more or less acted upon; three alternatives being submitted to the interested couple, from which they might make a final choice.

The opposing member was at last brought into line, and a list of three articles was prepared.

And, of course, it was the bride who made the choice. Equally, of course, she chose something that was not in the list so carefully drawn up by the committee.

Chapter 19

The Wedding

I have officiated at a good many naval weddings in one part of the world or another, but this one was different altogether. The rest were all in the piping times of peace, while this one had an added air of romance and certainly an air of mystery from the fact of its being our one war wedding.

As for the mystery, that all arose from the strictness of the censorship and the necessity of allowing nothing to leak out concerning the movements of the ship. Poor bridegroom-elect! He had fidgeted until he got me to read his banns, twice over, and even to start them for a third time; for months he used to count the stones in the greengage jam at seven-bell tea and mutter despondingly, "This year, next year, some time, never" he used to cheat now and then, and put back some of the jam into the jar, preferring plain bread and butter to the unkindness of the *sortes* (what is the Latin for *jammy?*). He could not go away from the ship to get married, nor could he arrange with the lady to come to meet him at any place for the same purpose, because he did not know where the ship would be, and if he knew he might not tell! The bride in her distant home must have been in an equal if not a worse perplexity; but one has the feeling that she bore it with greater patience and placidity, being of the anabolic and not the catabolic sex, which is the scientific way of saying that women have more common sense than men.

All these difficulties were, however, suddenly and unexpectedly overcome—it is not permissible for me to say how—and, as the society papers say, "A wedding was arranged between —— and ——."

I use the word "arranged" of set purpose, because the bridegroom himself had but little to do with it. He would have been content with the barest legal and ecclesiastical essentials; but we, his messmates of the ward-room, had different views. The bride, too, was quite prepared for a registry-office wedding, or at best a Dickensian one, with a snuffy sexton and a rusty pew-opener for witnesses.

We felt, though, that it was our show, not theirs, and so we arranged it all for our own satisfaction.

One of our lieutenants, who is a handsome fellow and has a way with him, said that we really must have some bridesmaids; so he proceeded to call upon the ladies of the district and persuaded them to lend three of their pretty daughters for this purpose; and very charming bridesmaids they made, too.

The gunnery lieutenant provided an excellent substitute for the conventional red carpet out of a bolt of "Canvas, Scene Painting, Red," commonly used for targets. For my own part, I fell in the Funny Party, and drilled them well in two hymns and the Marriage Psalm; Barnby's "Venite," day twenty-one, is a chant that goes to any words, and all sailors know it.

We also raised a couple of motors, and instructed the driver of the one which was reserved as the bridal chariot that he was not to "turn on the juice" on leaving the church, but leave matters to the bridegroom's division, who were standing by with concealed drag ropes.

The boatswain, as was his customary job, constructed an enormous garland, such as is always hung from the stay on these occasions; it is made of evergreens, and is really a kind of globe formed of three garlands joined together, with long streamers attached.

A bouquet was raised from somewhere, and wedding presents were not lacking, though, of course, the majority of these had been sent to the bride's home.

One of the kind ladies mentioned above was given the temporary acting rate of Mother-of-the-Bride, and was ready with hospitality and warm welcome to take her fair charge to her kindly arms, and see her safely to the very altar.

So we had a gay wedding after all! I ought, I know, to describe the bride's dress, but all I can say is that it was some white stuff, and I think it was serge. At any rate, I am sure it was a travelling dress. And she had a hat.

I rather pride myself on being a specialist in the Marriage Service, and will guarantee to take a pair of people utterly and completely ignorant of the drill and to put them through it in such a way that it seems the most natural and easy thing in their lives. These two backed me up in my boast, anyhow.

And the harmonium rose to the occasion, playing the Wedding March when it was all over as if it really felt itself to be for the time a great cathedral organ! While it was playing all the officers had quietly made their way out of the church and had formed up outside, in such a way that when the bride came out with her husband—why, she had heard of the custom before, and seen it pictured in the papers, but this was *her* wedding, hers and his; truly it was for their own two selves that the swords were flashing in the air, and she was walking by her gallant man's side beneath an arch of steel raised by his gallant comrades!

That is just the one part of the festal ceremonies which, as the officiant, I have never seen; I am still in the vestry, taking off my surplice and putting away the books. If I hurry to come out while yet in my black cassock, the church is empty and the glad party are already on their way. For a few minutes I enjoy the artificial pleasures of melancholy, and pretend to feel that I am left out of it. They have made use of me, and I am not wanted any more. This is all make-believe, remember; I do not really feel like that at all. But how can a body understand or sympathise with the great crisis of life—of other people's lives, I mean—except by acting a part in a little toy theatre of one's own making and using the cardboard figures to try to construct the real scenes?

Chapter 20

A War Widow

It was at a Church Service on board ship that I saw her; the exact locality I will not mention. She does not know me, and will not recognise herself from these notes; the less chance of that happening because her sad little story is hardly distinguishable from several thousand other sad little stories dated any time these last twelve months.

She was the prettiest and dearest girl in all the countryside, and had lovers more than you could count from now to Michaelmas. Amongst these came many a smart young officer of the king's navy—yes, and many besides, who, though no longer young, were still smart of bearing, and could throw their rank into the scales, with gold in plenty to bring up the weight.

Amorous middle-aged captains and love-sick boys of midshipmen, she dismissed them all, with others of every intervening rank and every other branch. At last, however, the inevitable happened—the right lad came along, and the lass was his.

It was a love-match. He was a handsome young lieutenant with a laughing face and merry eyes, and besides these recommendations very little beyond his bare pay. All the rejected lovers came and danced at the wedding, which took place scarcely more than a year ago.

Little more than a year ago—and now he lies cold beneath the waves of the North Sea.

What touched me most when I saw her in church was that, although clad in the deep black that becomes a new-made widow, her clothes and headgear were by no means the conventional widow's weeds: she wore the hat and dress of a young girl, the style most suited to her age, for she was not more than twenty; and these clothes, of so young a fashion and so deadly sombre a hue, seemed to me more pathetic than any widow's garb I have ever seen.

With the others of her party she sat amongst the sailors, surrounded by officers and men; and as the simple service proceeded there were many times when I saw her childish eyes fill with tears. No doubt she had recollections of going to church on board the ship she had learned to call proudly "my ship"; recollections, possibly, of enduring little prickings of her tender conscience for wishing the service to be over, so that she might again join her handsome lieutenant, who sat apart from her, looking so debonair in his frock-coat with the bright gold stripes on the sleeves, then sit by his side at a merry lunch party in the after-cabin, and go ashore with him in the whaler and watch how splendidly he sailed it!

Seeing her, I felt as one does at the sight of a seagull with a broken wing; the beautiful bird, so perfectly adapted for happiness that one demands nothing from it except to be perfectly happy, has been broken and *spoiled*; and the first natural ejaculation that springs to one's lips is not so much "What a pity!" as "What a shame!"

Well, the seagull's wing may mend—if it be not too badly broken. There was a time when a love story was ruined for me if the heroine could debase herself by becoming affianced to the wrong man, through the misunderstandings of the middle chapters, before clearing matters up with the hero on the final page; while as for a second marriage, that showed, in those days, that the author had no conception of what true love really was.

It is possible, I hope, to keep the romantic ideas of earlier days and yet to temper them with a little common sense. It might be a very splendid and loyal action on the part of this girl-widow to live out the rest of her life in bereaved loneliness, true to the memory of the husband of her youth; but I cannot help seeing that it would be better if she could bring herself, a little later on, to—well, putting it coarsely and bluntly—to make the best of a bad job, and take another husband. He will not be able to give her back the happiness she has lost, but it may be he will help to make the loss less bitter.

Poor little war-widow! How monstrous she would think these sentiments if she were to read this! God's pity on her; she has a long way and a hard way to go before she realises that there may be something in them, after all.

Chapter 21

Elegant Leisure

There was a day when the loud trump of war dwindled to a thin, piping note, and the temporary lull imitated peace so closely that it was possible to go ashore for the whole day, forgetting the ship and spending the blissful hours in elegant leisure.

My plans were made for me; the P.M.O., who is an ardent fisherman, had long been persuading me to follow the craft. Weakly enough, I had allowed him to give me a lesson in "casting" on the quarter-deck a few days before. That settled it. I now found a rod prepared for me, all complete, with a made-up cast and with certain feathered things concealing unforeseen contingencies, which the P.M.O. called flies. There was no getting out of it. The steamboat was called away early in the morning, and, together with three of our lieutenants, known as Uncle, Mud, and the Bulgar, w made for the distant shore. We walked awhile and came to a lake. The P.M.O. and I got into a boat and pulled about a mile to a likely spot. (For myself, in future, it will be a not-likely spot.) Then it rained. Hard. Then t came on to blow. Hard, also. Yet for three solid hours I really honestly tried to break the back of any unseen and unsuspecting fish by smiting it hard with my whip-lash. I didn't succeed in hitting one. Well, no more did the P.M.O., which was one consolation. I also hoped the other blighters weren't getting any, and said so; but the P.M.O. told me that was a very unsportsmanlike remark; still, I meant it!

The rain cleared, and after we had flogged the lake for weeks and weeks, we came ashore and had lunch in a roofless, stone boathouse. Here we unpicked the entomological specimens from the ends of our strings and tied on six other weird atrocities. A second venture on the lake proved no more successful than the first, so once more we pulled to the beach, and the P.M.O. suggested that we should fish from the bank, he going on about a hundred yards ahead of me.

Casting from the bank is quite a different science from casting when sitting in a boat. Did you know that? I am not really an expert angler, but I am a very good entangler: this I discovered quite soon, and therefore, having made quite sure that my mentor was well beyond shouting distance, I stealthily made my way back to the roofless boathouse, and there sat me down upon the grass. I felt it was a cruel thing to take life, and that if it were really necessary to do so—if we actually *needed* fish—a big net or a stick of dynamite would prove much more efficient than the method we had been pursuing. This might be debated, but I felt quite positive that I was not really a born fisherman.

The lintel of the boathouse door was one huge stone, and I wondered why these modern lacustrine peasants had spent so much effort for such a humble purpose, gathering from their scattered huts to close round the mighty monolith and raise it on their sweating shoulders; and whether they were unknowingly following the custom handed down by their forebears of a million years ago.

Around me, as I lay upon the ground, were a score of pretty weeds, of whose names and habits I was ignorant; I might have been taught them at school in the time I spent learning the method (which I have now forgotten) of making bad Greek verse; but the penalty for being uneducated has now to be paid by missing large delights which are at hand everywhere. A cow looks upon the wild plants with more discernment than I do: she at least knows that some are good to eat and others are not. It seems strange to go through life and amass little more knowledge than does a three-year-old child who has grasped the fact that these are "pitty f'owers."

We all have our own peculiar ideas as to how to make the most of our leisure time ashore. I remember a bluejacket at Gibraltar who had exhausted the pleasures of the land, and, having some money still left in his pocket, determined to spend his last half-hour of liberty in the grand style; so he hired all the shore boats he could find—there were ten of them, in fact—and made them all join up in one long line, towing the last boat, in which he sat in lordly state in the stern-sheets, and in this manner he came alongside his ship, feeling that his money had been well spent.

I have been told of another who went ashore at Pernambuco and came back on board with a live sheep, for which he had given five pounds; he said that he could not see anything else to buy!

You rarely see sailors going for a walk beyond the limits of a town. The pleasures of a country stroll have no attraction for them. They do not mind hiring bicycles, and often pay large sums for a carriage and pair, in which they will make excursions into the country, passing on the way their officers, who are content to trudge it along the dusty roads; this disinclination of sailors for walking has always seemed to me quite inexplicable. Certainly they are ready enough to tramp about the streets of a town, and are always keen on sight-seeing, though the sights that attract them are not always such as you would imagine. "Haven't you been to Bethlehem?" said a young sailor, whose ship had just come from the Levant cruise; "Oh, you ought to go there and see *the electric light works!*"

Our leisure when we are "on the beach" is generally spent in an irreproachable fashion; I have seldom been at a foreign port where the local papers have not devoted a special article to the exemplary conduct of the British sailors. If there are sometimes exceptions to this rule, let it be put down to the fact that "there be landsharks." Sometimes our shore-going friends themselves lead us astray, as the following true tale will make clear.

An officer friend of mine has an uncle, a man well past middle age, and of the most intensely respectable outward appearance; he looks like a bank director, and his benign and dignified air would inspire confidence in the most suspicious; even his clothes alone would almost do this. Unfortunately, he has never grown up. My friend was once taking a railway journey in his company, and as the train was slowly steaming out of the station the uncle beckoned courteously to a gentleman, a perfect stranger, who was standing on the platform. The stranger came forward briskly to the carriage window—anyone would have done the same for such an eminently grave and reverend *seigneur*. Then said the uncle, as the train gathered way, "You will excuse me, sir, I trust, but I really *must* pull your nose!" And he did so.

Chapter 22

Meals

Meals in war-time assume an importance far greater than they possessed in the peace period. Then they were the mere punctuation marks of the day; but now they have become the principal paragraphs, with large blank spaces between them. *"Let us eat and drink, for tomorrow we die,"* has quite a new meaning now, for if the British Army marches on its stomach, the British Navy steams on the same portion of its anatomy, and it is only common sense to pervert the scriptural phrase into sound advice for fighting men, avoiding the original meaning thereof, which I take to be homoousian with that of the words I once read on a Melbourne restaurant menu, *"Have a good time while you're living, for you'll be a long time dead."*

Caesar's *legionaries* refused with scorn their rations of mutton and beef—soft stuff, they said, not fit for men's eating—and demanded good honest corn which they could feel between their teeth. (I present this argument from the classics to all vegetarian propagandists, and am surprised that they have not discovered it before.) *Quantum mutati* are we sailors now! For our official rations, as served out to us by our maternal Admiralty, provide us with the sole alternative of mutton and beef or beef and mutton. Sometimes, indeed, we call the mutton lamb, but it is only the aspersion of mint sauce and the giving of a name that make the difference.

The men of the lower-deck, however, would not suffer any change; and they only follow Caesar's warriors to the extent of growling at any interference with what they regard as their proper diet like all good fighting men in every age; I have known them to chuck overboard a large consignment of grouse sent to them as a special treat, and, on another occasion, several hundred fresh salmon; Gallio-like, they cared for none of these things, and fell in at the paymaster's office, complainingly demanding their beef-and-mutton rights. We in the ward-room rely for the joint upon the same staple articles, and though we do introduce a little variety on our own account, even in this variety we are still bound to the wheel; full rightly may those grand old words be applied to us: "*Nee coenum nec animal mutant qui trans mare currunt*"—that is to say, we still stick to the same old cold supper o' Sunday nights, with the same old Palaeolithic chicken.

The greatest of all Sacraments was created out of a meal partly for the reason, I think, that we might learn to make every meal into a sacrament; and certainly in the navy do we at our meals find the inward and spiritual grace of knowing ourselves to be one communion and fellowship. We have no "places" at table, but the greatest sits down with the least, and the last-comer, be he three-striper or one-ringed man, has to take what vacant chair he can find. There is a general interchange of conversation and everyone is at his brightest. I am referring to dinner-time principally. A ward-room dinner in peace-time has always seemed to me a very picturesque sight; down the long table gleam the gold lace and white linen against the dark blue of the naval uniforms, brightened at one or two places by the flaming scarlet of the marine officers' mess-jackets, while the necessary artistic touch of sombreness is added by the befrogged coat and black silk waistcoat of the chaplain—for it is one of his very few naval privileges that he is permitted of an evening to disguise himself as an Ecclesiastical Dignitary!

The marine waiters in white jackets with blue facings and silver buttons give the scene a further touch of brightness, and altogether it looks as people say of a specially brilliant sunset—exactly like a picture. During this present distress, however, the brilliancy is gone; we do not "dress" for dinner now—it would be impossible, seeing that officers have to hurry off to turrets, or get to some other warlike work immediately afterwards. But this does not prevent the good-fellowship of the meal; it still remains the great medium for drawing us all very closely together and cementing friendships. Understand, it is only of dinner that this may be said; lunch is a hurried, go-as-you-please affair, and as for breakfast—well, there are very few people who are at their best at breakfast-time.

Once, long ago, I bade a cheery, a *very* cheery "Good-morning" to a shipmate, and proceeded to follow up my kindly greeting with various bright remarks and inquiries after his general well-being. "*Padre,*" returned he, more in anger than in sorrow, "have you never read what it says in the book of *Proverbs* about people like you?" I confessed my ignorance. "Then," said he, "listen well to this: '*He that blesseth his friend with a loud voice, rising early in the morning, it shall be counted a curse to him.*'" I didn't believe that these words were in *Proverbs* at all. But they are!

We still keep up the custom of having a Guest Night once a week, and sometimes have the opportunity of asking officers from other ships to come on board. Even when this is impossible, as, for instance, when we are at sea, the messman holds to his contract of giving us one or two extra courses on this weekly occasion; for which reason Guest Night is frequently known in the navy as Camel Night, the underlying idea being that one then needs the same interior arrangement of space as is devised in the Ship of the Desert, which, I understand, is blessed with three central compartments, divided by transverse bulkheads, instead of having only one, like us poor humans.

As for the sailors, they eat five meals a day, and how they can manage it is more than I can tell; but they are always equal to any odd snacks they can get between meals besides.

At the other end of the scale come the meals at the admiral's table. There is a good game that can be played at admirals' dinner-parties; it is called Pineapple Loo. You play it by surreptitiously wrenching off the top of the best pineapple and counting the leaves, with a small wager as to the result. You would hardly believe that there are so many leaves; perhaps you might hazard a guess at twenty-four or so, but as a matter of fact you would be safer if you were to say a hundred and fifty. It is a very interesting game, but it is not good for the pineapple.

It was at an admiral's dinner-table that I once heard a German Consul disprove the theory that all Teutons are quick at acquiring the niceties of foreign languages. The fish had been served, and the butler came insinuatingly behind the consul's shoulder and murmured, "'Ock, sir?" The foreign guest showed by his puzzled face that he did not understand. Again came the butler's invitation, "'Ock, sir?" and again the uncomprehending blankness. For the third time the patient entreaty was uttered, and at last the light broke upon the German's mind and illumined his features as he exclaimed, "*Ach, Ox-tail!* Yess!"

Enjoyment of food is, like all other human interests, an affair of mixed motives and complex foundations; delight in the unaccustomed forms, I suppose, one of the principal factors. This may explain the inner mind of the sailor who told me recently that he hoped the war would be ended soon so that he might go home and have a nice piece of fried fish! Alas! it may account for the peculiar leaning of many naval officers towards kippers at afternoon tea.

Chapter 23

Lower-Deck Love

There is a passage in the *Antigone* beginning with:

> Ἔρως ἀνίκατε μάχαν,
> Ἔρως ὃς ἐν κτήμασι πίπτεις—

which the classical master at my school, having a taste for rhyme-making, insisted on translating:

Love, unconquered in the battle,
Love, that lightest on the cattle—

a version which certainly brings out the interesting fact that the ancient Greeks were in the habit of speaking of cattle as "The Things", just as we do down in the West Country (*vide* Eden Phillpotts, *passim*)—proof positive that we are the inheritors of the true Greek spirit. But, to return to Sophocles, I would hazard the opinion that his verses may be more correctly rendered:

Love, what an undefeated sport you be,
You pounce on every blessed thing you see!

For what but Love is it makes gallants turn collectors sometimes even "purveyors"—of gauds, toys, *gew-gaws*, apricocks and dewberries, articles of bigotry and virtue, gold and silver, ivory, apes and peacocks, from Eastern bazaars, foreign ports, looted towns and rifled palaces— what but Love, aching to lay its tribute at a mistress's feet?

And do the goddesses really value the gifts heaped lavishly upon their shrines? Why, no, bless your heart, not a bit, except for the giver's sake!

We have amongst us here a misogynist who always speaks of **Τὸ θῆλυ γένος** as "those selfseekers"; and if he had sufficient acquaintance with Biblical language—which he hasn't—to know the phrase "*Daughters of the horse-leech,*" he would hug it to his bosom; he is in outer darkness, and has yet to learn that if bright eyes become brighter at the gift of a milky coconut or a diamond tiara, it is only because such homage proves Lysander or Bill still fond and true. And the real pleasure that the incomparable She derives from the tribute is the pleasure of knowing that her man is pleased in believing himself to be giving her pleasure. Our misogynist does not know this—yet: but I expect he will find it out, some day.

Nothing pleases Jack so much as to send a present home; he never wants to keep anything for himself, but delights in making up a parcel for Flo or Beat. Those pretty little brass boxes, graciously presented to us last Christmas by Princess Mary, were originally intended to hold tobacco: but I would wager that nine out of ten of those sent to the navy now contain—*hairpins!*

Love-tokens take varied and curious forms when Jack has the run of the shops, especially in a foreign port; but, now that his opportunities are so restricted, he is obliged to make the best of what he can find near to hand.

Cap-ribbons, too, are much in request as tokens of affection; and when you see a girl with the same ship's name upon her sailor-hat month after month until the gilt letters gradually become faded and tarnished, it is a sure sign that her undimmed love is glowing in the inverse ratio of brightness; but out upon the fickle jade who collects ships' ribbons like trophy scalps, heartlessly and without care for the original owners, to make a cushion cover or deck a banjo!

It is not by gifts alone that the bluejacket shows the sterling qualities of his affection. As husband or as sweetheart he takes a lot of beating—and takes it with wonderful patience, as a rule!

Mr. Punch's twelve-year-old candidate for a Naval Cadetship, who, on being asked his reason for wishing to join the navy, replied, "Because a sailor has a wife in every port," was the victim of a delusion founded upon a gross libel, and should have been made to commence his naval studies with the Sea-Songs of Dibdin, where he would have read:

That girl who fain would choose a mate
Should ne'er in fondness fail her,
May thank her lucky stars if fate
Should splice her to a sailor:

and I am proud to testify that Dibdin's words are as true today as in his own time. Having opportunities of knowing the sailor-man's most intimate and undisguised feelings, the more I get to know him the more am I struck with admiration at the wonderful love he bears towards the girl of his heart. In fact, there are instances, sometimes, when circumstances point to his being a long sight too good for her, and I should like to give the hussy a real good shaking!

Love on the lower deck is not seldom a matter of arrangement, just as it is so I am informed in the highest circles of our nobility. Tom Trunnion (A.B., 30 Mess) writes to his sweetheart that he has a chum, Ben Backstay, in the same mess, who has no young lady at present, and would like someone to go with when on leaf, so does she know of anybody? And Will Clinker (Leading Stoker, 17 Mess) talks of his young sister Polly to an unattached friend on board, and refers the matter to his mother, who agrees that if the friend is a respectable young fellow it may be a very good thing for Polly when she is a little older.

Sometimes the unblessed bachelor has no friend to work for him, and is forced to take matters into his own hands; and in such a case, hiding his shyness behind the walls of the post office, he will write to "Dear Miss"—a damsel he has seen when on his walks abroad—and say that although he has not the pleasure of her acquaintance he would very much like to write to her and to get a letter and her photo in return, and trusts that she will not consider this a liberty. Signing himself "Your ever-loving Sweetheart, Jack, x x x" More power to him! We parsons know that there is such a thing as taking Heaven by storm; while, as for his signature, it is well known that the girl who marries a sailor always has a sweetheart for a husband!

Gallant enough in his intentions, but not equally so in his method of expressing them, was the man who came up before the captain to ask for forty-eight hours' leave. "What do you want the leave for?" was naturally the first question. "Trouble ashore, Sir," said the man. "I'm sorry to hear that," exclaimed the sympathetic captain "what sort of trouble?" "Want to get married, Sir," replied the devout lover. (Leave approved.)

Without doubt, those girls who "join the navy" have many hardships to bear, not the least among which is that long and heart-breaking loneliness when the husband is away on a foreign station, and the scanty pay will not permit of going out to him; especially if there is a little one to keep.

Unhappier still the wife who is one amongst that frantic crowd outside the dockyard gates, where captain's lady weeps upon the neck of weeping Poll, her sister in sorrow when the Casualty List is posted up!

But, hard as the lot of the sailor's wife must always be, she has her compensation in knowing that she is the Pole to which her True Love's Compass-Needle always points; and she smiles amidst her tears at the new version of "I could not love thee, Dear, so much," when she reads, "Of course I wants to come back to you, but we've got to put the Strafers in their place first."

CHAPTER 24

The Patrol Trawler

Who is the Happy Sailor? Who is he that every young N.O. would wish to be? Well, I can tell you quite definitely who he *isn't*: the officer selected to go away in the patrol trawler.

Upon the happy circle in the wardroom bursts one who wears a brass hat and an expression of gloom: he bears in his hand a signal-chit, and scans it, muttering softly.

"Tell us the news, commander," cries one of the watchkeepers; "let us know the worst at once! Is it another regatta?"

"Worse than that," replies the second-in-command, who sometimes describes himself bitterly as a "perishing maid-of-all-work"; "we're told off for the patrol trawler, and I've got to send away one of you and a snottie; just when guns comes moaning that I've taken away all his turret officers and the skipper says there *must* be a lieutenant in charge of the boys' sailing cutter! Nobody loves me!"

With a fine disregard for anybody's troubles but his own, the watchkeeper, who had eagerly asked the news, now makes a swift calculation with the help of his fingers and realises that he himself is the one on whom the choice must fall. Summing up the situation in a few well-chosen words, he concludes with: "And I shall be as sick as a dog, I know! I always am! Well, I may as well have something to be sick on." So he orders ham-sandwiches, hard-boiled eggs, beer in bottles, sardines, apples, and chocolate, calling loudly the while for his oilskin, his binoculars, and his largest pipe.

Picture him some few hours later. The night is dark and very cold, and a heavy sea is running. Every few minutes a chilly rain-squall comes lashing down. The trawler is fairly dry—by which I mean that she takes in few seas; for the wetting of the rain counts for nothing. Like all these North Sea craft, trawlers, drifters, and the rest, she is built with bows nearly twice as high out of the water as the after-part in order to ride the big waves easily; and by just keeping her shoulder to the heaviest seas it is possible to keep her dry and snug in a howling gale. Yet tonight a green sea sweeps the decks from time to time: it is because the weather is such that if the trawler were engaged in peaceful fishing she would run for shelter or else lie hove-to until the gale moderated; but now she is on patrol duty, and must stick it out.

The lieutenant pulls up the collar of his oilskin and takes shelter under the lee of the wheel-house. He is not concerned about the navigation of the vessel; he has his own duties to perform—and has a very poor opinion as to their importance. "Here am I," he reflects, spitting contemptuously into the sea, "doing absolutely nothing at all! Living in the lap of luxury" (a green sea slops over the side and surges up to his waist) "while those beggars in the trenches are getting all the work! If we don't get a fleet-action sooner or later our name will be mud with the people ashore!"

He fails to see that what he is doing is just as useful as firing twelve-inch salvoes at the enemy's ships—and far more trying work. There is no excitement about it, and no glory; but it demands nerve and endurance to the highest degree. Almost anyone could screw himself up to the pitch of exaltation in a fleet-action, I fancy; but I do not envy the enemy that gets up against a ship manned with people who have done the Trawler Patrol!

Up in the tiny glass-sheltered wheel-house the skipper peers out into the darkness, and keeps a light hand on the ever-shifting spokes. He is a Tynesider, or else a Grimsby man, or maybe a Scotty or a Shetlander, and all his crew hail from the same place as himself; probably half their number are part-owners with him in the vessel, and all are equally qualified to take on the duties of skipper or mate or cook just as convenience may direct. There are no shore-lights to guide him in his navigation, but he has to keep to his appointed beat, in spite of the fact that the tide is setting strongly and the vessel must be making leeway with all this wind. How does he manage it? Partly by an occasional sight of the loom of the land, but mostly by that intuition, earned only by many years of flogging the seas, which he would describe as "smelling his way."

Towards morning the midshipman comes on deck to stand his watch and relieve his senior. But the lieutenant, who has been up all night, has an idea that there is just a chance of his being required, or, as he puts it, "Shouldn't be surprised if there was something doing when the dawn comes," and decides under the circumstances not to turn in at all.

Down below in the tiny saloon there is an atmosphere that makes the one hanging oil-lamp burn with a struggling blue flame and a temperature like midday in the tropics. Trawler-men like a good froust, and, as they get plenty of fresh air and cold when on deck, they like a change when they go below! There is a round stove in one corner, nearly red-hot; every scuttle is screwed up tightly, and the cabin door is carefully closed, to exclude all possible "draughts"!

On either side of the long table are four bunks, ranged in two tiers, and at any time of the day or night some of the crew will be found sleeping here, for they work watch-and-watch in the trawlers, and the sleepers take every precaution against chills by drawing the heavy bunk curtains when they turn in!

It is in this cabin, in the spare bunks, that the patrol officers have to sleep. One of our lieutenants, detailed for this duty, did not mind any of the other hardships and discomforts, but rather shirked sleeping in the cabin. He was a lover of fresh air, the very personification of cleanliness, with an extremely sensitive skin and a deep abhorrence of dirt—and all that dirt breeds. So before turning in he approached the skipper of the trawler, and with a certain amount of hesitation, not wishing to hurt his feelings, inquired: "I suppose you haven't any—any, well, *live-stock* on board, have you?" "Oh, no, sir," the skipper reassured him; "no, sir, not one! Nothing of that sort! *But she's infested with fleas!*"

Another of our officers, philosophical enough with regard to this particular form of discomfort, was yet a little troubled about the preparation of his food on board the trawler, being somewhat fastidious in culinary matters. "I couldn't stick plain hard-boiled eggs," he related on his return; "some people's souls never seem to rise above hard-boiled eggs, but mine does! So I made an omelet. I'm rather a good hand at an omelet!"

"How did it turn out?" I inquired.

"Well, do you know," he said, "it was a *very* good omelet; there was just that light touch of the expert about it, that *je ne sais quoi*—in fact, well to tell the truth"—here he paused, and the expression on his face gave me to think that pride in his achievements was mingled with some unexplained regret.

"Well, what was wrong about it?" I asked.

"It was the beastly, beastly frying-pan! They had been using it for herrings—and there were very strong reminiscences of onions about the darn thing besides! My omelet was wasted!"

"Couldn't you eat it?"

"Oh, yes, I *ate* the beastly thing! But it was wasted all the same—*afterwards!*"

Different people have different ideas as to what is best to take away with them in a trawler. One of our people came back the other day and told us that he had been relieved by a sub-lieutenant whose provision for nourishment and amusement during his turn of duty consisted of a melon, a bottle of champagne, and *a set of bagpipes!*

Chapter 25

"A Little Drop o' Leaf"

In the very explicit words of the *King's Regulations and Admiralty Instructions*, which always aim at putting you in your place, and none of your nonsense about it, "Leave of absence to officers and men is to be granted or withheld, as the circumstances of the Service may render expedient," the same idea being expressed by the familiar sentence, "*Leave is a Privilege, not a Right.*"

I am happy to be able to chronicle the fact that the circumstances of the Service have rendered it expedient to grant this privilege to certain of our number. My own feeling about the matter is that we should have had no cause to grumble even if we had been kept on board our ships from the start of the war to the finish, but we certainly did appreciate being let loose! I myself had been home once only during the previous eighteen months, and then for no more than three days, and there were others of those who went with me in like case; so it can readily be imagined that we looked forward to our leave with considerable eagerness.

This time it was not to be a mere "Dickie Flurrie"—that is, a brief, wild, glorious spree of a few hours on shore—but an affair of days, in which we might once more pick up the threads of civilised life, hear the opinions of ordinary normal people, see shops and trams and trains, and the "movies," and, above all, everything connoted by the picturesque naval term "Skirt."

The anticipation alone made a wonderful difference to us; no longer did the ante-room after lunch present the usual *tableau* only semi-*vivant* of gassed naval officers sitting like their grandsires cut in marble. We began to be quite animated, and formed ourselves into a committee of ways and means to discuss how the few days might most profitably be spent.

Perhaps it was natural that the ideal programme as outlined by the majority should include the maximum possible number of theatres and music-halls. The play is much to my taste though I prefer to pay my half-crown for something thoroughly unintellectual: Backchat comedians delight my soul; and it will be a sad day for me if ever the stage relinquishes the fine old English tradition of letting fall and breaking a pile of plates. But on this occasion all my craving was for plain, unadulterated Leader and Yeend King: to the great contempt of the young surgeon, who witheringly remarked, "*The country!* Oh, well, I don't object to the country—you must have something to put round London!"

A bluejacket from our company landed with a chum, and, as he told me, "As soon as we got into the main street we saw a woman wheeling a pram; my chum seemed to go suddenly mad, for he clutched my arm and dragged me forward, shouting, 'Come on, I say, Bill; here's a woman and a real live child!' The woman looked, naturally, rather surprised, but my chum apologised and said, 'I beg pardon, ma'am, but it's twelve months since I've seen one!'" I think we all felt much the same, even if we were not quite so demonstrative about it.

Comparing notes with others afterwards, I found that we had all been alike in taking at least a couple of days to get our land legs, thereby upsetting the calculations of our sisters and our cousins and our aunts, who were for dragging us off to various amusements with such terrifying energy that we began to understand why excursions and alarms are always bracketed together.

We were all of us curious to see to what extent old habits and routines had become changed, and to find out whether any one great prevailing idea had come to birth during the war; we had been long enough away from shore life, we thought, to get the right perspective. But it was by no means easy to obtain just the impression we wanted; the fact of there being plenty that was new to see and to hear proved to be no more help in forming an idea than a cartload of artists' materials would be a help in painting a faithful picture of an elusive sunset. The mind is a wayward child; you may seek to divert it with a host of magnificent and expensive toys, and it will turn away and concentrate all its attention upon an old broken clock or a handful of common shells.

It was so in my own case. I kept on saying to myself, "Look here, surely you can make something out of all this." Here's the tramping of armies, the marching of men; schools turned into hospitals, and the children working hard in a hundred little war-ways; wounded soldiers attended by girls who only a year ago never thought of doing a hand's turn of work; high prices and smiling faces—yet not so very high, the prices, and the smiles often those of courage rather than of gaiety; gossiping tea-parties transmuted into sewing-guild meetings, and the Army of a Dream really come true. Does all this convey *nothing* to you?

But my mind refused all these proffered aids, and would not fix itself upon anything more phenomenal than a bill-hoarding to be seen from my window. On it were three posters: the first inviting the public to come without paying and see a religious picture of the war, painted by a great artist; the second calling for men to come and work at making munitions in the new factories; and the third advertising the performance of the world-renowned Somebodies at a music-hall. And side by side these posters, so diverse, made their mute appeal to the passers-by.

Which thing was to me an allegory. Religion, art, work, and play, we have always had them with us, but never before standing side lay side as now. They are old elements combined to make an entirely new compound. England has found out that to sweat at lathe or forge can be true religion, and it is not wrong to laugh or even to make others laugh, and the conscientious workman is a true artist; and the complete man—something so very different from the Complete Mensch of Teutonic philosophy—must have a little of all these elements; and, in short, that all things work together for good to them that love God and their Country. It is a new type of national character that will come out of "*The Melting-Pot*"—a phrase of recent coinage which has a happy augury in its relation to the old Biblical promises of a nation being purified in the refiner's fire.

But I did not spend all my leave in peripatetic philosophising. I meant to have a real good time—and I had it. So did the others. And we came back quite ready to spend another winter at the same old game—or another ten, if necessary!

CHAPTER 26

On the Sick List

A little while ago I was on the sick list, and in bed, or perhaps I should say in bunk, for a fortnight; an inglorious business and most unsatisfactory, since from an artistic point of view a carefully placed shrapnel wound might have been much more effective and less painful. But the P.M.O. did not find it unsatisfactory, by any means! Trade has been so slack with him that he just gloats when someone falls into his clutches. This is such a thoroughly healthy life that when the next Blue-book on the *Health of the Navy* is issued it will be found that our absence from the microbe-haunted land justifies Horace Walpole's expression of thankfulness that "England is safely at war again." But to the P.M.O., chock-full of science and keenness, it is nothing short of dreadful that there should be so few brows wrung with pain and anguish for his angelic ministrations. He therefore made up for lost time by starting three different treatments on me all at once.

And, after he had had a rub at me, the young surgeon blew along. This medical luminary said "Hum!" at me twice; and then, seeing that I was not impressed, proceeded to try to vindicate his professional qualifications by telling me that a worm has eight hearts. Fancy a worm, of all people, having eight hearts! That burning problem, *Can a man love two women?* so dear to modern novelists, must I suppose be extended in the vermicular world to *Can a worm love sixteen she-worms?* Quite possibly the Junior Man of Blood deliberately intended to distract my mind by turning it into such psychological channels; at any rate, I am sure he would take the credit for it if the idea occurred to him; they are wily fellows, these doctors!

Sometimes, of course, a little wiliness is necessary; one of the rare cases of malingering in the navy was that of a man I once heard of who was continually coming up to the sick bay and complaining of pains which were undoubtedly imaginary; all that he really suffered from was a constitutional dislike for work of any kind. However, it was impossible to prove this, and the man still kept coming up. At last the fleet surgeon, who was an irascible Irishman, grew tired of this, and, having made the man strip to the waist, said soothingly, "Me poor man, I see what 'tis ye're wanting"—and then added in a blood curdling voice, "*Shteward, bring me a big knoife!*" The patient gathered up his clothes and fled.

As a general rule, though, the men are of a very different type; they do not trouble the doctor unless it is absolutely necessary, and when once they get under his care they are exemplary patients. I knew one man who suffered an injury to his knee overnight, and said nothing about it till the morning, when he was quite unable to walk. "But didn't you feel any pain in it during the night?" asked the doctor, as he examined a knee about the size of a football. "Well, sir, it did seem a bit stiff like," was the extent of the patient's willingness to own up.

All the encomiums I have read lately about our Tommies as hospital patients, their cheerfulness, and their pluck, I can echo about sailors when they are "on the list"; a long illness or a serious operation they will endure smilingly; and when it is only a case of a minor ailment that lays them by for a few days their one growl is that they cannot get out of bed and go back to work again. Often has a man in the sick bay said to me: "I used to think I should like to get Guard and Steerage" (*i.e.*, an extra hour's lie-in) "every morning, but now anybody that likes can have my place."

The patients, both in the naval hospitals and on board ship, are looked after by the sick-berth staff, a most superior class of men, for whom I have the highest admiration. There are exceptions, of course, but taking them "big and large" they are marvellously tender and careful nurses, and possess a professional knowledge of no mean order. Their training is very thorough, and covers a wide ground, and their examinations are of a very high standard.

I was once told a curious piece of information with respect to the training of probationary Sick-Berth Attendants at Haslar; it was said that these youngsters on their first introduction to the operating theatre were lined up in a row against a wall, With a rope stretched taut close in front of them just below the waist level; so that if anyone of them should faint at the unaccustomed sights he would fall forward, the rope preventing him from coming to the ground, and being thus suspended by the middle he would automatically recover by the rush of blood to the head. It was further said that on a good day a dozen of them might be seen bobbing up and down in rapid time, fainting and recovering and fainting again, looking like so many *kow-towing* Mandarins, and nobody taking the slightest notice of them.

I regret to say that this story is entirely untrue in every particular.

How is it, I wonder, that when you are on the sick list you read books that you would never dream of reading when you are well? I went solidly through one of the silliest stories that were ever written, by one of the best storytellers that ever lived—Nathaniel Hawthorne's *Transformation*;[1] yet the basic idea—a man being descended from an ancestral Faun—had great possibilities; the story failed chiefly through the faun-man being respectable to the point of frightfulness; for the rest, it seems a good rambling guide-book to the Rome of 1860. For all that, I read it to the last page, and enjoyed it after a fashion. And another officer, whose natural bent is all for mechanics and inventions, "went sick" for a few days and feasted his mind on Carlyle's *French Revolution!*

Making use of this curious fact of the reading taste being changed by sickness, I give the patients in the sick bay a great deal of literature of a sort they would not ordinarily care to read. The plan worked very well, in most cases.

But not always. There was a time when a celebrated murder trial was in progress, and the interest in it spread even to the bluejackets' sickbed. Many a time then did I visit our patients, to be met by the request given in the weakest of voices—"Can you tell me any news, sir, *about Crippen?*"

---

1. This story a.k.a *The Marble Faun* can be found in *The Supernatural and Weird Fiction of Nathaniel Hawthorne* Volume 2 of a 4 volume set published by Leonaur.

Chapter 27

Clothes Uniform and Otherwise

The war has done one thing for naval officers—it has taught them how to wear their uniform on shore without looking and feeling awkward and ashamed. Formerly, uniform was never worn ashore except when on duty, or occasionally in foreign ports; and the wearer never quite escaped the feeling of being rigged out for private theatricals; but now that its use is compulsory—at least, in the big naval ports—the strangeness of it has vanished. In fact, I heard of two naval officers who went to a theatre in London, and decided beforehand that they would go in plain clothes as the more comfortable and accustomed rig; but when they got there they found all parts of the house filled with people in khaki, and felt so uncomfortable that they were constrained to return to their hotel and change into uniform!

But it is not only the wearers who are unused to naval uniform on shore. One of the two officers who were at the theatre belonged to the medical branch, and consequently displayed between the gold stripes on his sleeve a backing of scarlet (typifying, in the words of Shakespeare, that "*this is a bloody business*"). "A naval officer, I think, my dear," said a lady seated in the row behind to her daughter. "Surely not," whispered back the girl, who by pleasant experience had lately become learned in the many *minutiae* of military uniform; "he must be a staff officer—notice the red upon his sleeve!" A third fair speaker, unseen, and, like the others, believing herself unheard, broke in at this point and corrected both the others with, "Neither of your guesses happens to be right—he is a Belgian!"

This same absence of general acquaintance with naval uniform on the part of the public brings with it occasionally certain disadvantages. There was, for example, a certain fleet paymaster who had to make a long railway journey in that particular variety officially described as "Frock-coats without swords"; he arrived at his destination in an extremely angry condition, due to the fact that at various stations *en route* he had been consistently mistaken for every single grade of railway official, from stationmaster to porter, and treated accordingly; it is rumoured that at one place a dear old lady pressed two pennies into his hand and requested that he would get her a bun and keep the odd penny for himself; but as I am very particular about telling the truth I will not vouch for the accuracy of this part of the story.

But there are also disadvantages in not wearing uniform, as one of my own branch discovered some time ago. He was on a foreign station, where chaplains frequently wear white suits of semi-uniform cut, with pearl buttons instead of brass ones. Going ashore one day in this rig, he was met by the picket and promptly stopped by the petty officer, who charged him with being an officer's steward ashore without leave.

"You are making a great mistake," said the cleric; "I am the chaplain of the *Nonesuch*."

"I've heard that yarn before," said the P.O.; "you come along o' me to the picket-house." And he had to! It was hours before he succeeded in establishing his identity.

One of the most delightful of naval phrases is connected with clothes it is the order for the men, before any work that might soil their ordinary garments, to "*clean into a dirty rig*"; another one, "*a make-and-mend*," has become synonymous with a "half-holiday," since the time originally given for overhauling and replenishing the wardrobe is almost universally spent in having a little shut-eye, with the messtables and benches for couches and ditty-boxes for pillows.

The order to wear uniform on all occasions has been somewhat liberally interpreted. Surely some of the old-time rigid sticklers for propriety in dress would faint to see officers going ashore for golf or a walk in a monkey-jacket and grey flannel trousers! All the "glad rags" of yester-year, the "dog-robbers," "poodle-faking suitings," and cherished ancient Bantry tweeds, are stowed away in drawers or sent ashore for safe keeping now, and changing into plain clothes to go ashore is a thing of the past.

There was a captain once who was always most particular about having fitting honours paid to his dignity; and, being ashore in plain clothes, he was on one occasion met by a young seaman of his ship who omitted to salute him. The captain, very irate, sent the man on board, with orders to put himself in the report. The case was brought up before the captain in due course, and the man was asked what excuse he had. "I didn't recognise you, sir, in your plain clothes," was the answer. "Then you must learn to recognise your captain in whatever costume he may choose to wear! You will come and look at me at intervals of two hours, night and day, for the next three days!" And so the unfortunate man had to go and study the appearance of the captain in every rig or lack of rig, in uniform, plain clothes, in bed, in pyjamas, and in the bath!

It is an inexhaustible subject, but I will close it now with one more apt expression: any article which can be bought in the shops to serve a purpose similar to that of the corresponding government article is termed a "plain-clothes" thing. You can have, for instance, a "plain-clothes rifle"—and I suppose an ordinary shore-going parish priest would be a "plain-clothes parson."

Chapter 28

Sea-Soldiers

Many regiments carry on their colours a long list of battle-honours; the Royal Marines have but one.

The reason is that if all the battle-honours to which the marines are entitled were to be set down the job would be one for a publisher, who would have to bring out a small edition of the *Gazetteer of the World*.

Always, when a difficult military nut has had to be cracked, the word has been passed, "Send for the marines," and the marines have come along, smiling and efficient, have cracked the nut, and have been rewarded with—the nutshells. There you have a brief summary of the history of the corps. For fuller details read the history of the principal British campaigns for the last three or four hundred years. And see the splendid part which the marines have played and are still playing in this present war, in which about sixty of their officers have now been killed and more than that number wounded, and the rank-and-file in proportion—for when it comes to following an officer's lead, be it to the gates of death or beyond them, a man of the Royal Marines has no intention of being left far behind. What St. Vincent said of the marines in Nelson's days remains as true now as then:

> There was never any appeal made to them for Honour, Courage, or Loyalty, that they did not more than realise my expectations. If ever the hour of real danger should come to England the marines will be found the country's sheet-anchor.

Afloat, the marine finds himself in a curious position, to which he has adapted himself with the same ready facility displayed by him in all other circumstances. He becomes subject to the Admiralty, and is no longer under War Office control; the men become seamen to all practical intents, though they still wear their own distinctive uniform, and their messes are termed the "barracks." As for the marine officer, his position on board has undergone great changes of recent years; there used to be an old joke against them—and against my own branch, too—relating how one sailor put to another the conundrum, "Which of the orf'cers has the least work to do aboard this ship?"

"I dunno! Well, the chaplain, I s'pose?"

"No; 'tis the cap'n of marines."

"How d'ye make that out, Bill?"

"Well, you see," said Bill, "the chaplain, he's got nothin' to do all day long; but the cap'n of marines, he's got nothin' to do neither, but he's got a subawltern to help him!"

Nothing but modesty forbids my denying the soft impeachment with regard to the chaplain, but in the case of the marine officers the point of the jest has certainly become blunted. I well remember the great excitement caused when they were first required to keep watch in harbour; the upper decks of the whole fleet were alive with men swarming up to watch with great delight the strange spectacle of the "young soldier" pacing the quarter-deck with a telescope under his arm. It does not look at all funny now, when he performs a score of assorted jobs which in former days were done by the naval officer alone.

In a big ship there may be as many as a hundred and fifty marines, consisting almost equally of "gunners," or "blue marines"—the R.M.A., and of "red marines"—R.M.L.I., sometimes known as "the Royal Light Fut," and both are frequently classed together by the affectionate term of "*Bashi-Bazouks*," though I do not know why!

Every sailor will readily agree that the marines are the smartest and best-disciplined men of all on board; it is their training when in barracks on shore that makes them so, a training which has the effect of fostering in the men a feeling towards their barracks composed in equal parts of reverential loyalty to a sacred institution and profound affection for a home.

Since the beginning of the war the major has naturally become Our Military Expert. We go to him for the meaning of bridgeheads and saps and fougasses, and other such fearful wildfowl; he explains to us how a salient may sometimes be a tophole thing to have, and sometimes simply rotten; the minor details of tactics and the deeper mysteries of strategy he has alike at his fingers' ends; he tells us just why the military correspondents of all the papers are all wrong, and he sticks the little flags in our war-maps with a precision that makes us regard him with silent awe, as knowing more than it is good for a mere human being to know.

Like all other marine officers I have ever met, he is an enthusiast on the subject of field-training. Put him ashore for a day with a half-company of marines, and he will dig trenches enough to spoil the best landscape going, and point to his horrid work with pride. No matter if the terrain (notice his influence upon my vocabulary) be solid rock or quivering bog-land, he will have it all entrenched before the day is out, and in all probability he will have marched his men fifteen miles in an hour and a half into the bargain, practising scouting by the way.

For the last half-hour of his time on shore he will most likely slate his men thoroughly and comprehensively for being a useless, rabbit-backed, idle, loose-kneed set of eviscerated nursemaids, who may thank their stars they were not in the corps ten years ago, when a day's work really was a day's work; and he will then stand them beer at the local pub. For, you must understand, they are his children, every one of them. Nobody else must say a word against them, but he may say what he pleases; thinking all the while in his own heart what a thundering set of fine fellows they are, and how he would like to lead them against three times their number of Germans, Austrians, Turks—or, if it comes to that, Hivites, Hittites, Perizzites or Jebusites, anybody in the world, so long as they could put up a good scrap.

I suppose this love for field-training springs from the same source as the sailor's ambition to run a farm when he retires, that longing for the shore which possesses all sea-going folk.

There comes to my mind a marine on shore—out in South Africa. He was up a tree—doing something scientific in the field-training line, of course. When I sighted him he was about thirty feet above the ground, but the next moment he was at the level of my boots, and a loud crash signified that his descent was both rapid and involuntary.

"Hurt?" I inquired, prepared to render first aid.

"Broke, sir, I believe," said he.

"What arm or leg?"

"Why, the branch, sir; I've spoiled the look of that tree!" returned the marine, amazed that I should imagine a mere thirty-foot fall could even dent a marine!

And this is another true story, which I cull from the *Globe and Laurel*, the marines' magazine, a story of the North Sea action against the German battle cruisers:

Our small bugler—15 years 5 months old, and 4 ft. 11½ inches high—did powder-monkey in regular Trafalgar Day style; he told himself off to fill up the tubs for the rammers at the 6-in. guns, and because he was not big enough to carry a mess-kettle full of water he towed it along the battery, fore and aft, at the end of a piece of string!

Yes, the man in *The Flag Lieutenant* was quite right when he characterised the Royal Marines as "*the finest corps in the world!*"

Chapter 29

Guests

"Monarchs I have met" would form an article that might be written by most naval officers, for there are few who have not frequently "hobnobbed with royalty"—to use their own light-hearted expression—though the royalty has been in varying degrees, down to coal-black, semi-nude West Coast chiefs, and including dusky *sultans* and dignified *emirs*, minor European serene transparencies, and great kings and emperors. For almost every potentate in the world has been a guest on board one of His Majesty's ships at some time or other.

The very last occasion of all was of almost historical import—when the German emperor came as an honoured guest on board H.M.S. *King George V.*, just four weeks before the outbreak of war, and there flew his flag as Admiral of the Fleet in the British Navy—an honour which he no longer holds.

Another renowned occasion of a different character is connected with a certain officer in command of a small gunboat on the West Coast, who arrived at Simonstown hoping to have a few weeks' rest and cool weather after having sweltered for months threading steamy tropical rivers or rolling rail-under off the coast. But to his great disgust he was ordered to go back immediately, and prepare some of the local kings for a visit which the admiral would very shortly pay to that part of the station. He *did* prepare them! He took back with him in his gunboat three top-hats and a quantity of gold paper. And a little later on, when the flagship dropped anchor off the coast, the royal guests came on board, one by one.

When the first was piped aboard, the junior king of the three, great was the astonishment of all to see a solemn black nigger wearing an immaculate silk hat garnished with commander's stripes in gold, and above them, also in gold, the word "*Dirt*"! The admiral and the captain laughed convulsively, though the commander did not seem very pleased. Then the next king was ushered on board, and he too had a similar hat; but there were four stripes on it, and the legend was "*More Dirt*"; the captain pulled a rueful face this time, which tickled the admiral still more! When, however, the third king arrived, there was trouble, for his silk hat had an *admiral's* stripes, and "*Still more Dirt*" was gleaming above them!

One more story of a rRoyal guest, and this is of our own most gracious king at the time when he was Prince of Wales. It was an occasion when he honoured the Royal Naval College at Greenwich by coming there as a guest at dinner, and afterwards went into the billiard-room for a game. The marker was much perturbed at the honour thus suddenly thrust upon him, and somewhat at a loss as to how to comport himself. Seeking aid in his difficulties, he approached one of the officers present, and asked in an undertone, "Beg pardon, sir, but would you mind tellin' me what I ought to call 'im—'Your Royal 'Ighness,' or '*Spot White*'?"

The war has taken from us our opportunities of walking with kings, not losing the common touch. We have opened a new brand of guests now, for the most part captains of colliers and store-ships, fine hardy seamen who sit awkwardly on the edge of our wardroom chairs and wish us "Best respex" over the top of their glasses. Or else they are of the opposite extreme, garrulous and reminiscent, quite easy to entertain, and not exacting towards their listeners. We had one such on board not very long ago; he talked for weeks and weeks, but all I can remember of his conversation is that his wife was the most beautiful woman in England.

But we are glad enough to see these splendid fellows, who risk so much in their perilous seafaring, and risk it gladly, in the thought that they are "doing their bit" and a brave fine bit it is too! We like to hear their tales of what is happening in the ports from which they hail, their wondrous information from the highest authority, their mysterious hints as to further knowledge which they must not reveal.

Guests from other ships are, of course, somewhat rare nowadays, but we do see them occasionally, and very pleasant it is when they do come. Our own language neglects to give the solemn warning conveyed by so many other tongues in which the same word does duty for "host" and "guest," thus teaching that if you are a host tonight you will probably find yourself a guest next week and it is such a bother to get out of your own ship! This is the only drawback to having a guest to dine with you.

Much could I write of guests in distant parts of the world—English guests, I mean, people who build the Empire that we go to protect—as, for example, how I met in East London my best and oldest pal, after many years, and found a schoolfellow serving behind a counter in Bombay.

Or of foreign officer guests, of various nations, some now allies and some enemies; but all alike in this respect, that they prefer their champagne sweet. So that the invariable order is given to the wine-steward when such guests are expected: "Bring up a case of the Foreign-Officers' Champagne."

Chapter 30

Religion and the War and the Navy

I filled some pages of my note-book with remarks on the above-named subject—and then I tore them up.

They contained a number of sayings which seemed to myself distinctly smart and amusing, and I was not ill-pleased with them on the whole.

But I tore them up, because, although I was really only smiling, other people might have thought I was grinning. Now, Religion is a very lovely thing, and you may smile at it—or some people may—but you must not grin at it. And, alas, even a smile is forbidden to me, for that is a privilege reserved to God's saints, who may jest about their sweet beliefs because they love them so; but, at the same time, I certainly do not want it to be thought that I could grin on such a subject.

So I am writing my notes all over again, and the ship is asleep as I write—as much asleep as the ship ever is; nearly a thousand men are within a stone's-throw, sleeping in their hammocks or hidden away at their work, yet by the silence and the solitude I might be alone in the world; so am I far from their hidden thoughts, though I hear their voices daily. What the war means to them, how can I or anyone tell? Have they traced the finger of God in this terrible upheaval of the nations, or has their faith suffered such a shock that they have been led to deny God's existence? Or have they thought about the matter at all?

Surely upon the majority there must have been made some impression—by which I mean some religious impression; for although we have no personal experience of tragedies and heroic deeds, of imminent death and marvellous escapes, yet into all our lives has come something of the deep solemnity of the war. Many have lost their dearest friends, and without them life can never be quite the same thing again. Not a few have brothers now in the trenches, and others—*had* them. We, too, have not been without our risks, and the casualties by sea have plainly taught that in war one must be prepared to give all, willingly and without hesitation.

But whether any impression made by such reflections may be a deep one or simply momentary and fleeting, that, again, lies hidden. And, it may fairly be questioned, is a momentary impression necessarily fleeting? That was no more than a momentary impression which broke off the marble arms of Milo's Venus, yet the effect has not yet vanished; and men of science say that nothing is ever forgotten; only, some things are tucked away in a little back cell of the brain, pigeon-holed and docketed for future use if necessary, to be brought out again when occasion calls for them,—at the hour of death, maybe.

Once more I think of all these hundreds of men so near me, deep in that counterfeit of death which becomes so much more realistic when you remember that a sailor's hammock also forms his shroud when his body is solemnly committed to the deep. For every one of them the smoke of many censers has risen this evening, from the incense of the prayers of good women, whose breath of love has fanned the glowing flame. Can it be that there is no effect—I do not say from the prayers themselves, for that is unquestionable, but from the knowledge that such prayers are being made?

Even without the steadying influence of the war, as an added impulse, most sailors are religious men—in their own way. Many are openly and avowedly so; others more secretly, as is the Englishman's way. And even those of the swearing, drinking, loose-living sort—am I convicted of condoning sin if I call these but wild, unbroken colts, with no real vice, but with certain tricks of which they have to be cured before they are yoked to the Chariot of the Lord?

Faith and unfaith are both of a very simple kind in the navy, and philosophic doubt is a growth which flourishes very badly aboard ship. That, I think, is because there is always plenty of work to be done, and the people who get troubled with intricate religious doubts are mostly those who have nothing to occupy their time. So the sailor as a rule accepts the puzzling affairs of this world with a childlike faith that all "works for some good," even though "by us not understood."

One of our men had sent him a card of prayers for special use during the war: he was not pleased, and his comment was, "I don't want any card to tell me how and what to pray—I should think that any man who believes in prayer at all cannot help praying at such a time as this!" He could make no allowances for the good intentions of the sender, nor for the condition of any men who might be taught to make their prayers more real: either you didn't pray at all, or else you prayed properly, was his point of view, which I imagine is a typical view amongst naval people.

But let it not be thought that I would limit the term "naval people" simply to those who man our ships and establishments. A friend of mine in a shore billet was once going out to dine, and reminded his housemaid that he would require his white mess waistcoat laid out for him. "Sir," the maid answered indignantly, "do you think I don't know that, after *being in the navy* all these years? "

Yes, they are "in the navy," heart and soul, tens of thousands of wives and mothers, sisters, sweethearts, and faithful servants; and no attempt at writing on naval religion during the war would be complete without mentioning them. Dreadful as the war is, it has at least given a new colour to this side of naval religion, rousing to wonderful fresh activities of practical religion those who are so closely bound up with ourselves. Have not many of them found out that the most Christlike service is that of "going about doing good," or doing good even without going about, but in any case *doing* good, and not only *being* good?

The gifts which have been showered upon us, and the sincere kind letters accompanying them, are ample proof that thoughtfulness for others has taken deep root; and much self-denial has not seldom sprung up with it, for there are many who have given out of their poverty from the burning desire to be of service, and in sending gifts to the navy have really cast upon the waters the very bread so hardly earned by them.

CHAPTER 31

Hobbies

There is an old saying which begins, "*Set a sailor on horseback*," and then proceeds to describe tersely the manner and the destination of his riding. The saying is equally true when the steed is a hobby-horse. Few there are of us who fail to keep, and keeping, fail to ride furiously, our own particular hobby; and a very good thing, too, under the present circumstances, when the individual whose only favourite pastime is fighting German ships finds himself at a singularly loose end.

War-hobbies are quite different from peace-hobbies. They have to be. For example, motorcycling is a thing of the past; it has been superseded by the hobby of taking motorcycles to pieces. Almost any make-and-mend afternoon nowadays you may see one of our erstwhile scorchers busied up in the superstructure with the disintegrated anatomy of his beloved stink-wheel, the deck all around him strewn with nuts, bolts, pins, wheels, and many other of those unseen influences which have made England what she is—from the pedestrian's point of view—while the owner himself, one mass of oil, proceeds to justify the national indictment that we take our pleasures sadly by spending most of his time in trying to collect elusive ball-bearings, a pastime which makes the road to Berlin a mere infant's amusement by comparison.

The great universal naval war-hobby is, of course, sleep. What prodigious quantities of sleep we do take, to be sure! And at what odd times! When you see an officer folding his tent like an Arab, and silently stealing away immediately after lunch, with the remark that he is about to have a little of the stuff that knits up the ravelled sleeve of care, you think that nothing at all unusual; but when you see one stretched out at full length on a settee and fast asleep at ten o'clock in the forenoon, or just before dinner, or just after dinner, you begin to realise that tired nature's sweet restorer has really become a war-time hobby. I know one officer who invariably makes a practice of getting into pyjamas and turning into his bunk on Sunday afternoons. Much of this is due to the fact that the distinction between day and night has largely lost its meaning for us; it is hard to make people realise that the modern sailor's life has very little of the Blow-ye-winds-Yeo-Ho, Salt Spray and Dazzling Sun business about it, but resembles more the life of a booking-clerk in a tube railway station so far as a big ship is concerned. Once grasp this, and you can realise the point of view taken by one of our decoding officers, who does not at all mind being called upon to decipher messages in the early evening—that is, up to 3 or 4 a.m.—but objects strongly to being turned out in the middle of the night, by which he means somewhere about 7.30 a.m.

A hobby much affected by the young gentlemen of our gun-room is one which I think has been invented by themselves. At any rate I have not heard of its being indulged in by any other ship of the Fleet—though it may be, for all I know. It is called Photograph Pool. Those who take part in it put, each of them, a shilling in the kitty; then they write a polite letter to various pretty actresses in the town of London, and, according to the answers received, so the money in the pool is distributed. I am given to understand that a signed photograph counts five points and a letter two; but a letter containing an invitation to tea on the next occasion the young gentleman is in town counts three; if, however, the lady's invitation is to take tea with herself *and her mother*, that counts only one!

This is not one of my hobbies.

The mention of photographs reminds me of another hobby which has suffered a sea-change through the war. Formerly there was much more certainty of finding a camera in the possession of every naval officer than of finding any of that varied selection of articles, such as a copy of the King's Regulations, of which he alleges his ownership once a year by signing "Yes" against a list of them; as to which it may be remarked that if a woman's No sometimes means Yes, a naval officer's Yes frequently means No; but all this camerawork has now gone the way of motorcycling, and has turned into a pursuit known as enlarging. All the old negatives of Lang Syne have been dug out and pilloried before a lamp that by some clever manipulation picks out the tit-bits and serves them up in an enlarged and entirely new form, much as our wardroom cook picks out the presentable portions of last month's chicken and artistically arranges a totally new landscape labelled "Indian Pilau."

Engaged in this pursuit, officers disappear into their cabins for hours at a time, and you are not allowed to go in and play with them. Or, if you are, you find that the electric lights have been painted over with a lurid red, and every air-hole has been pasted up with newspapers; you are shown a cruel snapshot of one of your messmates, or possibly of yourself, being slowly magnified till each trifling defect becomes a glaring misdemeanour and the spot of light at the tip of your nose shines like a good deed in a naughty world. And the worst of it is that when you would fain stagger out, breathless and half-fainting, you are not allowed to, for fear you might spoil the plate or something!

The study of foreign languages is another very persistent hobby of these days. There are several of our number who indulge in this. One in particular may frequently be seen in the wardroom, at such a time as a dozen others are all talking or playing some game, or having a friendly scrap; but he in his corner is quite blind and deaf to it all, and is quietly reading a French novel carefully selected for him, laying down the book every now and again to look up the hard words in a dictionary.

Then there is the gramophone, which ought to be allowed to coin a new proverb, to the effect that an officer is known by the records he plays. There is one of us who always looks after the interests of Russia; and he invariably celebrates a Russian victory by switching on a particularly lugubrious bit of "*Parsifal*"!

Many other curious hobbies there be; but perhaps none of them all equals that of a certain post-captain, who smokes Wild Woodbines all day long!

CHAPTER 32

The Dug-Outs

"When I retire from the navy I shall walk straight inland carrying an oar over my shoulder, and never stop till I come to a place where someone asks me 'What's that thing you're carrying?'" How often have I heard this classical remark quoted! And I have watched many old shipmates one by one dropping out of the Active List and putting this resolve into practice with the most conscientious adherence to the spirit if not to the letter of the quotation. They settled down on shore, enthusiastic supporters of Back-to-the-Land principles, and, to use a phrase minted recently amongst much other similar war-coinage, they regularly "*dug themselves in.*"

But now they have become the Dug-Outs, a term which, I suppose, will stick to them, though it is a very unjust name, seeing that all the digging-out has been done by themselves. They have come back, answering the first sound of the call of the drum, some of them, like the silly sailors who found that they could not live without their sea, only too pleased at returning to a life which they had abandoned with the honest conviction of disliking it intensely; and others, not recanting their comminatory creed, yet responding to the imperative summons which, unanswered, would make a hell of the heaven wherein they basked at ease.

One such I knew well—as fine an all-round sportsman as ever I met, and a brilliant young officer, having no taste for a sailor's life—he was always seasick at the beginning of every cruise—and, seeing before him the hopeless prospect of long years without chance of promotion, he left the service as a two-stripe lieutenant. An Indian fortune-teller who came off to the ship one day told him, "Master not really liking fighting: master only pretending he liking it"—a soft impeachment, which he laughingly admitted to be quite true. A man without nerve?

Hardly that. At King Edward's Coronation, being on the roof of a tall building to watch the procession, he shinned up a chimney-stack, and must needs stand on the very top of a chimney-pot, where there was but barely room for his feet and absolutely no support of any kind, with a sheer drop of an appalling distance to the flagstones below.

I asked him why he did it, and he said, "Oh, well, my brother was doing the same thing on another chimney-pot, so of course I had to!" On leaving the navy he took to himself a charming wife and settled down tea-planting in Assam. But he is back again now and in harness, and, I doubt not, doing excellent work somewhere, a Dug-Out who can no longer be classed as "a loss to the service."

A Dug-Out of a different type was one whom I met not long ago, a lieutenant-commander who retired from the service full five-and-twenty years ago! Yet he still kept young and fit, and was keen to get back to a job where he knew he might be useful. He was given a ship; and when he turned out in time to keep the morning watch without being roused there was some surprise that he should have kept the trick of this after a quarter of a century on shore. "Not at all," he explained, "I have never dropped the habit; I have been sailing a boat of my own all these years." Here at least was one Dug-Out, then, who belied the proverbial opinions of the retired sailor-man!

Another old messmate of mine was a major of marines, of an activity in inverse ratio to his girth. We camped out together in a certain sub-tropical land, and I remember that his ideas of commissariat were that we should require "A little eggs and beef and whisky." The last I heard of him was that he was at Gallipoli, camping out under similar skies but very dissimilar conditions. Yet another old messmate, amongst the Dug-Outs, one of the most efficient officers we had in the ship, and the one who you could be certain would always be picked for a difficult job that required a steady and competent officer. Once, in the Persian Gulf, our whaler got blown away and lost to sight in one of the violent sandstorms so prevalent there; this was the officer picked without hesitation to man the cutter and go in search of her.

It seems strange now that the service should have allowed such a number of highly trained and most useful officers to retire, while at the same time entering a crowd of raw lads; but so it was. And in course of time these same freshly entered youngsters would have grown to the stage at which they were really useful, and then would have retired likewise, many of them. But war has altered all that.

My own accounts of Dug-Outs could easily be enlarged, and

could, no doubt, be matched by the experiences of everyone else in the service. There must be some very curious instances, and some very noble ones. Amongst the latter I would give a place to those retired officers of high rank who have volunteered to come back and work in any lower grade, and are actually serving, and serving splendidly, in ranks from which they were deservedly promoted twenty years ago.

Chapter 33

Celebration

Sunday morning dawns. Not heralded by any coming of the pleasant daylight, for this my cabin never sees. While I am yet sleeping my servant enters quietly and turns on the electric light, then takes from a cupboard my folding altar and sets it up, with frontal and fair linen cloth. Before he has finished I am awake, and do not need his quiet rousing me to tell me that "Church is rigged." I dress myself and make ready. Little by little that becomes a chapel which has been till now a bedroom. The door-curtain drawn well back lets in a plentiful breeze to make the cabin sweet and clean. I lift the altar bodily into its right position, and arrange the candles on it, taking care that the match-box is ready to hand and filled. The sweet reasonableness of this proceeding would, I think, be allowed even by those who object on principle to the use of altar lights, for without them we should often be left darkling in the midst of the service; the circuit by which my cabin is supplied is often switched off about this time in the morning, and for a minute or so I have to read the prayers by candlelight.

Next, I take from their cumbrous oaken case the chalice and the paten which are supplied by the Admiralty, leaving in its compartment the enormous flagon which forms part of the outfit, and is of solid silver like the rest. Our thoroughly conservative navy still issues this massive Georgian flagon, which I suppose is never used by a single chaplain, so unsuitable it is. Indeed, the whole set of "communion vessels"—which, by a curious and typically naval arrangement, are in *the carpenter's* charge—might with advantage be replaced by a smaller-sized but more complete set costing about half the money.

The oaken case, however, comes in useful, for I place it on its side upon my writing-table, and cover it with a white linen cloth. This forms a credence, and upon this I place glass cruets of wine and water and a box of altar-breads. And now, in transition from bedroom to chapel, the cabin becomes a vestry; the narrow wardrobe from which the folding altar was taken contains also my surplice and stole—in addition to a host of unecclesiastical gear. I robe myself, and wait to begin the celebration.

The worshippers come in. Sometimes in numbers sufficient to fill all the available space in the cabin, and sometimes only one or two. But if there be one only, yet I consider myself dispensed by the circumstances of ship life from the rubric which requires more, and the celebration proceeds as usual. And when there are more the service becomes indeed a communion, in a sense that has no parallel in anything else that takes place on board, not even in the Parade Service, in which all are supposed to join; for here captain and officers kneel down side by side with the ship's boys; midshipmen, petty officers, members of the admiral's staff, and second-class stokers shuffle along on their knees and make room for one another before ever they can begin to join in that higher union and fellowship wherein the Sacrament lifts them all up to the same level.

It is a strange setting for a celebration. To the right of the altar hangs a large print of Hacker's beautiful *Annunciation*, and *The Light of the World* is over the writing-table; there is also a photograph of the chancel of the cathedral in which I was ordained; and these are all that can be considered even faintly reminiscent of a church. For the rest, the bulkheads are adorned with cherished water-colours, with paintings of former ships, and photographs of family and friends. The top of the chest of drawers is filled with books, which overflow into many other odd corners. A big armchair forms a *prie-dieu* for two or three of the clustered congregation; and behind it hang my dressing-gown, oilskin, and overcoats. The wash-hand stand closes with a mahogany lid, and this also makes an occasional prayer-desk. A tobacco jar and a pile of official papers, the big church Bible, and some boxes of lantern-slides, a few ornaments, and odd litter of various sorts, combine to fill all the remaining spaces with such tidiness as can be managed. Outside the cabin the tramping of feet and all the many voices of a ship are incessant.

How different from the beauty and the stillness of a large church at an early celebration! That subtle loveliness, so utterly different from anything else that either nature or art can offer, brings with it a delight about which I can never make up my mind whether it is purely sensuous or truly ethereal; the large spirit in which all the adornments are planned, the uncarnal beauty of stonework and woodwork, the very height of the building where sight wanders and is lost, and that even temperature maintained both when the blazing sun beats against the outside walls and when the biting wind drives the snow across the perch, all work together to produce something which seems as nearly like the courts of heaven as anything on this earth can be.

And since in such an atmosphere earthly cares drop off and earthly passions seem shameful, and the pettiness of this world is really seen to be petty, and a heavenly frame of mind replaces all else, though it be only for a little time—I care not whether the influence that can do all this is sensuous or not; or if, as in my heart of hearts I am inclined to suspect, a verdict on the question of fact would be given to the cold Puritan, yet I cannot side with that theological school which treats religious feelings as of no account.

All these external aids are missing, however, on board ship. Perhaps, though, more is gained on the whole than is lost in our simple service. The worshippers are of very diverse schools as regards Churchmanship: some cross themselves devoutly when they receive the sacred elements, others are earnest "Evangelicals"; but these barriers are broken down, like many other barriers also, when men meet at a morning celebration in a ship's cabin

Chapter 34

Mines and Mine-Sweepers

I have noticed in some of the more depressing comic papers many attempts to formulate a joke by playing upon the double meaning of the word "*mine*." Now, a mine is not a thing to be joked with—at least, it demands an exceedingly delicate touch; handled heavily, it is apt to recoil upon the joker with considerable force. That is why our mine-sweepers treat their particular work with becoming seriousness. Indeed, the only way in which a mine can really be regarded as a joke is when it is viewed as the *ridiculus mus* brought forth by Germany's mountainous boast, "*The Trident must be in Our Fist.*"

Though, of course, this is by no means the only bit of quiet humour for which we have to thank Germany; the other day, for instance, I surprised an officer shaking with silent laughter in his chair, and on my inquiring the cause of his hilarity he replied—it seemed to be a quotation—"*Will the English Fleet never come out?*"

But to return to mines. There are some kinds that have horns—like a dilemma; and any logician will tell you that a dilemma is a very dangerous thing for the inexperienced to handle. It is better not to break the horns of the ungodly in this case, for when the horns are broken the mine explodes. Some are arranged to come up to the surface long after they were hidden in the depths, and at unexpected times, like regrettable incidents from a hectic past. Others are constructed with fiendish ingenuity to wait after touching a ship until they have felt out its most vulnerable spot before exploding. Some are made to float about at random, as a malevolent wit flings abroad his spiteful jests, caring not whom he wounds. And others, more dangerous still, drift when they were meant to remain anchored: and these, when they are cast up on the German coasts, our enemy is ever ready to describe as *English* mines—never German, mark you. But it is a rascally people, that cares nothing for the difference between *meum* and *tuum*.

The task of sweeping for all these different brands of tinned doom is almost as great as that of the old lady in the nursery rhyme whose job it was to sweep the cobwebs out of the sky. The labour of Sisyphus was child's play compared to it. For this labour must go on incessantly, over a vast area, and often with a doubt whether the desired results have been fully or only partly accomplished. Added to this, somewhat on the principle of making a big hole for the cat and a little one for the kitten, there are frequently found, near the surface above the big mines laid deep to catch large vessels, smaller ones designed with special forethought to entrap the mine-sweepers engaged in clearing the field.

What the country owes to the men employed in mine-sweeping can hardly be estimated. They are the men who keep destruction away from our fighting ships, great and small, and preserve the navy in a condition to uphold its tremendous responsibility; they sweep the mines from our path, and from the path of the thousand merchantmen that come daily to supply the needs of those who live at home.

Many are the craft that have been enlisted in this service; some designed long ago for this very purpose, and others that first took the water with very different ideas about their career, dreaming of the crowds of happy holiday-makers they would carry, or stolidly resolving to settle down to a life of humble industry. Now, like many a gilded youth and many a hard-working apprentice, they have changed their ideas and their way of life, to their own very great surprise, and to their much-increased usefulness.

One of these vessels came alongside us some time ago. She was told off to be our chummy-ship, to take a few days' rest after her battering by the mighty seas, and to have a brief respite from her perils.

Fine fellows they were who formed her crew; laughing, polite, rampageous daredevils with an allotment made out to the wife at home and a tendency to sit at a sewing-machine in their spare time; they might have walked straight out of one of Dumas' romances—supposing him to have ever written about the sea—and yet were as unconscious of it as though they were living in Sandford and Merton.

The big mother-ship found many things she could do for her temporary foster-child: carpenters and electricians and armourers and others lavished their attentions like so many suddenly converted Scrooges, and our limited possibilities in the social line were offered and accepted with much mutual pleasure.

A Sunday coming within the period gave me the opportunity of holding a lantern-service on board in the evening. The offer of it was hailed with much delight; and, if you think that this is rather an exaggerated expression, please remember that if you had been walloping about the North Sea for weeks and weeks you might be glad enough to go to a lantern-service too, or a dog-fight, or anything!

So much was this the case that I had a little difficulty in making clear without saying so the fact that this was not a "show." Many willing hands rigged the screen for me, and unshipped the tables down in the confined mess-deck, which was the men's home, and all were prepared for any mood that might invite them. But Guido Reni's Head of Christ, switched suddenly on the screen and allowed to remain there for a few moments without comment, accomplished its object, as I was confident it would. Pipes and cigarettes were dowsed, unasked; and when a Sankey's hymn followed on the screen the whole ship's company in that little hot and crowded space were soon singing the words with, I hope, as much inward feeling as outward sound. Followed the story of the Prodigal Son; but there was one phase of his downward career upon which I felt it inappropriate to dwell, and the slide that represented it I passed over very rapidly. Perhaps you have seen the set of slides to which I refer? The artist has thrown so much feeling into his picture of the Prodigal indulging in riotous living and wantonness, and has allowed his imagination such free play, that the resulting impression, upon men forced to live a life of more than monastic severity, without even so much riotousness as would fit out a Sunday-school treat, might well be the opposite of that repellent effect intended to be produced.

The mine-sweeping captain really deserves a note all to himself. He is often a young lieutenant, and this is his first command; so he is charmingly proud of it. He walks his little quarter-deck, which is half filled with mine-sweeping gear, as though it were the deck of the *Queen Elizabeth*. And it is a fine thing to see him speaking as a brother captain to some dignified and courtly grey-beard in command of a mighty battleship. All very right and proper, too; and even a finer sight to see the veteran *preux chevalier* accepting the young blood on an equal footing, with the great spirit that is his; not feeling himself lowered thereby, but raising the other to his own high level.

Officers and men and ships, all are of a fine type. None but the best could be chosen for such drudgery. From which I could point a moral, to cry *sursum corda* to all others who toil with little recognition in those dull tasks which are the most important in the world.

Chapter 35

Equity

It is not enough that the law, as administered to nations and individuals, should be perfect of its kind: a further requirement is that it should be readily accepted, and its perfection acknowledged. Otherwise there is trouble.

Look at Ireland. And look at Stoker Daniel Whiddon.

Look at his case, I mean; for his personal appearance is not sufficiently attractive to invite inspection even now, though it is much better than when he stood amongst the defaulters a few days ago, waiting his turn to be brought before the captain. For at that time one eye was totally obscured by a puffy swelling of lurid and vivid hues, while the other did duty for both by gleaming a double share of rancour and resentment.

The rest of his face was veiled from the public gaze by a thick layer of coal-dust, and a like indication of his profession had toned to a neutral tint the whole surface of his canvas working-rig. On his right hand stood an able-bodied seaman from the picket-boat, in his number one suit, spruce and immaculate as though he had just stepped out of a naval recruiting poster; and on his left a cook's mate in kitchen cap and apron. Others of his companions in misfortune were a boy, very frightened at appearing for the first time in the defaulter's list; a leading-stoker in blue working-rig; a sick-bay attendant, with the Geneva cross upon the sleeve of his fore-and-aft jacket; and three or four others, making up a small company that might have been pictured as types of the British Navy, or the supers and scene-shifters in a nautical play.

The case immediately before his own having been settled to the satisfaction of everybody—including the culprit, who had reckoned on getting seven days' cells, and was agreeably surprised at being let off with three days No. 10—Stoker Daniel Whiddon heard his name called by the Master-at-Arms, and, stepping forward to face the Captain across a green-covered card-table, he was ordered to "off-cap."

Next came the formal Reading the Charge, which in this instance was:

> Did on the 10th of the month bite the swimming-collar of Leading-Stoker Peter Davy.

The captain's face lighted with a momentary flicker of mild surprise; he was accustomed to all sorts of unusual "crimes," but this one was rather more than usually unusual. Biting swimming-collars is certainly wrong, and if persisted in may degenerate into a bad habit, but it is not a sufficiently common offence to be provided for in the Articles of War or the King's Regulations, though these between them cover the ground from pitch-and-toss to manslaughter; nor is it easy to say how to make the punishment fit the crime, though there is a range from "*Death, or such other punishment as is hereinafter mentioned*," down to *One day's pay and grog stopped*. For all this, there was no doubt that the pastime of biting swimming-collars had to be discouraged.

"Have you anything to say for yourself? "asked the captain.

"Yas, zur," answered Stoker Daniel Whiddon, turning his phrases in the accent of his native Widdicombe under the stress of his emotion, "'e 'it me. L'adin'-Stoker Peter Davy, 'e 'it me. 'E did'n 'ave naw right to 'it me. I cud'n''it un back, cos tid'n allowed, so I bit 'is swimmin' collar, w'ich was 'angin' round 'is neck like, jest fur to shaw un as I wad'n gwaine fur to be putt upon by the likes o' 'e!"

"Is Leading-Stoker Davy in the report?" asked the captain, suspecting that there would probably be a counter-charge; "if so, I'll investigate the two cases together."

"Leading-Stoker Davy," called the Master-at-Arms, and then added, "Defaulters, shun! Right turn! March to the other side of the deck," a procedure which is followed when a leading hand or petty officer is being tried, in order to save his honour from the curious ears of underlings.

"Did on the 10th of the month strike Stoker Daniel Whiddon," announced the Master-at-Arms.

"Any witnesses?"

"Yes, sir; Stokers William Brewer, John Stewer, Peter Gurney, Henry Hawk, and Chief Stoker Thomas Cobbley."

Here was the promise of an intricate case. Remember that for minor offences the Briton's Birthright of trial by his peers has no existence in the navy. The commander and the captain sit in judgment like the *kadi* of an Arabian Nights' story, and the verdicts which they give are usually unquestioned. This is because they fashion their rulings after the principles of equity, which overrides the Common Law, and arrive at their decisions with the speed and accuracy of a Solomon. It is quite certain that if *Jarndyce and Jarndyce* could have been brought before a naval captain sitting at "Defaulters" the case would have been polished off in less than five minutes. If necessary, the evidence is occasionally treated with the disregard that evidence frequently merits, and a decision is reached simply by common sense; and I have known cases where a man's punishment might be described as perfectly unjust but thoroughly well deserved!

Leading-Stoker Davy, being questioned on the charge of hitting Daniel, admitted the fact. He said that Daniel had refused to stop talking when admonished, and so he had "just given him a little tap, like." Had Daniel been talking? Daniel acknowledged that he had. "I was only spakin' to 'Arrry 'Awk, zur, and tellin' of un not to swear an' blaspheme so dreadful! W'y, I niver did 'ear sich talk, an' 'im brought up strict an' a member of the chapel down to Widdicombe, same as me!"

"What did he say?" the captain asked.

"Aw, I cud'n repayt it, zur! 'Twas tew bad!"

"But, my man, I'm afraid you must! I can quite understand your dislike to repeating bad language, but I wish to hear all that took place."

"Naw, zur, I cud'n do it, I tell 'ee. I wud'n sully my lips wi' sich words as they."

"But I insist upon your doing so. The case must be investigated thoroughly. You, apparently, were the only man to hear the language which you took upon yourself to reprove, and it is necessary that you should repeat it."

"I've told 'ee before, zur, an' I tell 'ee again, I wud'n sully my lips wi' it!"

"But I order you to do so. Once more, I give you the chance. And I warn you, if you do not tell me, you will be punished for contumaciousness. Now then, what did Hawk say?"

"I wud'n sully my lips wi' it!"

"Oh, take him away," cried the captain, thoroughly annoyed at the man's stubbornness, "and let him do seven days' number 10!"

"*Hooh!*" snorted Stoker Daniel Whiddon, "an' this 'ere's naval justice! *Naval Justice!* I thank 'ee!—Blank an' dash 'ee, you adjectival ole to-ad!"

From which it may be agreed that although the offence of biting swimming-collars is not provided for by the regulations, yet Daniel was not altogether unjustly punished. Also, that the law, though perfect of its kind, is *not* always appreciated by those whom it affects.

Chapter 36

"Naval Miscarriages"

From the limbo of the past there comes to mind an incident at a meeting of the college Debating Society. What the subject of debate was I have entirely forgotten; but the discussion drifted into a quite irrelevant side-issue as not infrequently happens at college debates—dealing with horses and horsemanship. One "honourable member" sarcastically ventured to question whether his opponent had ever been on a horse in his life; whereupon the latter, a military man of much over the average undergraduate age, retorted that he had not only been *on* a horse, but had also been *off* a considerable number of horses, and in every conceivable way that it was possible for a man to fall or to be thrown from a horse. After this the first speaker had no further remark to make.

History shows that the British Navy has in the past experienced many a fall from its high horse; it has suffered defeats of every possible kind, in fleet actions and in single-ship actions, with inferior numbers and with superior numbers, glorious defeats and defeats most egregiously inglorious. It was not in spite of these falls, but because of them, that the navy finally learnt to ride triumphant.

We can talk and write quite dispassionately now of such "regrettable incidents"; we can even feel a certain pride in them, like Beau Brummell's valet when he came from his master's boudoir laden with a trayful of crumpled but unsoiled cravats, and explained with a lively satisfaction, "*These are our failures!*" Even when we cannot actually feel proud of our naval failures, we at least do not mind openly admitting them.

A navy which has no past history and has played not the smallest part in the making of its nation cannot bear the reproach of ineffectualness, and writhes when it meets with undeniable defeats. In this respect it resembles a *parvenu* who lives in constant horror of committing those solecisms of speech and manners which in a well-bred man are not only permissible, but even acquire a certain grace; being sure of oneself, it is no great matter to have to admit some few defects in actions connected with deportment—or some few defeats in actions with the enemy at sea.

So little unusual were such defeats during the Napoleonic wars that we actually coined a term to describe them: we called them "Naval Miscarriages," and the occasions on which the term had to be applied to our enterprises were far from infrequent.

When at Mauritius I heard of a curious example of the naval miscarriages of that period. Our ships were patrolling the Indian Ocean, and Mauritius, at that time a French possession, was cut off from supplies and reinforcements. But the brave islanders, nothing daunted, set to work to cut down trees and build ships of war for themselves. Having completed these vessels and fitted them out with guns I suppose from the shore batteries they put to sea, met the British squadron, and defeated it! This incident is too unimportant to find mention in general histories, but it is so interesting that I should like very much to possess a fuller account of it.

Nations with a long and honourable record at sea, such as the French and ourselves, know perfectly well that in naval warfare, just as in land warfare, a cause is not necessarily ruined nor even greatly endangered by misfortunes and follies, and that the side which eventually wins is the one which does not make quite so many mistakes as the other.

This morning we were pitching heavily in a seaway; a loud crash in the wardroom pantry advertised the fact that a lesser naval miscarriage had occurred in connection with our glass and crockery. But, seeing that a kindly Admiralty makes an allowance for breakages and freely replaces 15 *per cent*, of our stock each year if required, we may be pardoned for not regarding such a contretemps in the light of the disaster it would seem in a small household.

And a still worse misfortune has befallen our ship—according to many-tongued rumour; we have been sunk—indeed, several times. A German cartoon I have seen shows a woebegone John Bull writing off his losses, holding a long list of sunken ships, in which this ship occupies a very prominent place. It was quite thrilling to sit before the wardroom fire in a sunken ship and look at this dramatic cartoon! But, even supposing the picture had registered the truth, would there have been much for our friends the enemy to crow about? If the fortunes of the sea or the fortunes of war take toll of our glass and crockery or of our steel sea-fortresses, we can say to them, "We have plenty left for our needs—but what does *your* bill for damages amount to?"

Naval miscarriages are very frequent in the career of the average midshipman in his junior time. When he is first put in charge of a whaler he generally succeeds in carrying away the mast and losing half the boat's gear; later, when promoted to a picket-boat, it is a marvel if he does not begin by staving in its bows by ramming the ship's side, thus making himself thoroughly unpopular with everybody from the commander to the carpenter; and he is very liable to incur further dislike by breaking up the gangway when going alongside the flagship. There are all sorts of wrong things he can do when on board his ship, and he generally manages to do most of them.

As midshipman-of-the-watch, signal midshipman, tanky, or commander's doggie, he finds ample opportunities for many and varied naval miscarriages; but somehow or other he lives through them all, gathering useful experience from every mishap, till he develops into a thoroughly capable officer. And when he achieves the dignity of two stripes as a full-blown lieutenant he will recount with pride the many unfortunate incidents of his youthful career—how for this lubberly trick he got a dozen of the best, and thoroughly deserved them, or how his leave was stopped for a month on account of his thinking when he didn't oughter think, or *vice versa;* and he will end up sententiously by remarking that it would be a lot better for the navy if the midshipmen of the present day were treated as *he* was, etc.

And to this degree he is right: that the value of a seaman, like the value of a navy, is to be reckoned in direct proportion to the number of naval miscarriages in the years or the centuries that are gone.

Chapter 37

Romance

We were coaling ship, and it was a miserably cold day; the wardroom fire could not be lighted, because the skylights were closed down and the fans switched off; there was a dreadful fug, and everything was beastly. Those of us who on this occasion belonged to the more leisured classes took up a position on the settee in front of the empty stove, and pretended there was a cheerful fire blazing.

An outlet for pent-up wrath was provided by a reference to certain things that have appeared in print about the navy. The practical-minded man seized upon this opportunity. It is a pity that the word "Pshaw!" is no longer in fashion, because I am certain he would have found it very useful to start in with. As it was, he began like this:

"Sloppy, I call it! Just pure sloppiness! Sentimental tosh! It gives me the dry heaves! What do people want to write like that for, making out that we're a set of Little 'Eroes living in a world of romance? Boo-ah!" (This last word cannot be written phonetically with any degree of precision.)

"But, surely, you will admit that there *is* a certain amount of romance attached to the show?"

"Romance? Grrrr! Well, there may be some in the case of the submarine fellows, and those people who have been kicky enough to get a scrap; but, as for the Grand Fleet, there's just about as much romance about us as there is about a chucker-out at a theatre! He's big and strong, and so are we, and that's all there is to it! '*Watching and Waiting in the Northern Mists!*' Boo-ah!"

"Well, that's just what we *are* doing, isn't it? Possibly it doesn't seem very romantic or dramatic to ourselves, but that is just because we are in it, and have to take too close a view; but consider the Grand Fleet as seen from the perspective of people at home, or from the historian's point of view, say, fifty years hence?"

"Bosh! The soldiers, now—!But here we have all the comforts of a well-appointed club—don't talk to me about our romantic life!"

Well, perhaps he was right. Who shall decide? It depends largely upon what is meant by Romance. Love and adventure and death, and so many other things, come under the heading, and some of these elements we undoubtedly lack.

But not all of them, I think.

That very same day one of us received orders, at only a few hours' notice, to leave the ship and take up another appointment. He had been expecting this for some little time, but it was only when the orders came that he really found out how sorry he was to go; and we how sorry we were to lose him. For, in a "happy ship" such as this, the war has unquestionably had the effect of making us, like Nelson's captains, "a band of brothers."

We decided at once to "dine" him that same evening, of course. That is the utmost we can do to speed the parting guest—make him a guest indeed at his last dinner on board, and then go up on deck to "see him over the side," with the band to play "Auld Lang Syne" as the picket-boat bears him away.

During the afternoon our guest had been packing his gear, a most prosaic occupation. We saw him at intervals, and told him that he was very lucky to be getting a change, and we wished we had his chances. Precious little room for any sentimental feeling about getting away from this mouldy existence! But I noticed that each time he talked of going away his eyes filled with tears.

As Guest of the Evening he comported himself with that delightful ease of manner which is so peculiarly his own. And the dinner went merrily on, though not without those frequent interruptions which always occur—a midshipman coming in to ask the commander for certain instructions, or a signalman bringing a message which may have to be attended to at once. For instance, on this very occasion a man came bearing an order to the torpedo-lieutenant that searchlights were to be burnt forthwith, and this for a little while broke up the party to a small extent.

After "The King" the president passed the wine for the second time, and when all glasses were filled he rose to make a little speech, short and not flowery, but very much to the point. And when, after a short pause, our guest rose to return thanks, we felt that he meant every word of his expressed regrets at the coming parting.

These serious speeches being disposed of, we considered that some "comic relief" was needed, and so called upon our chief wit for a few words. But, instead of being funny, he surprised us all by making a splendid little speech, which—I cannot put it otherwise—touched all hearts, and won him a round of genuine applause.

The boat which was to take our guest away had to leave very soon after this, and we all escorted our guest to the upper deck to see him leave. It was bitterly cold, and a keen wind was blowing; the picket-boat surged heavily against the foot of the gangway, and the seamen in their oilskins were kept hard at work to fend her off with their boat-hooks.

The searchlights were still burning, and made a pretty and romantic sight. Where the beams fell upon the surface of the sea from the ships all around the water took on a hue of vivid green, as the greyest water will when under a searchlight's ray; and against the green the tops of the breaking waves showed dazzlingly white. The display brightened up the parting, and seemed almost as though made specially to honour the occasion.

A last grip of the hand all round, a cheery word of farewell, and our messmate through all these long months of war hurried down the gangway and was gone.

Then we learnt the real reason of the searchlights; they were lighted up for another farewell—a longer one. A man had fallen overboard from one of the other ships, and an effort was being made to discover him. But in that rough sea, and weighted with heavy oilskins and sea-boots, the man never had a chance. The search was hopeless from the first. The searchlights burnt for half an hour longer, and then all was darkness.

CHAPTER 38

Promotions and Resolutions

Just at the close of the year comes a day when a certain number of lucky naval officers awake to find themselves entitled to wear another ring upon their sleeves. Which is very likely the origin of the expression, "*Ring out the Old, ring in the New.*"

The list of promotions is awaited with the keenest interest, especially by such as consider themselves within the zone, so to speak. It is generally promulgated late at night, by wireless, and begins with the words, "The following promotions are announced by the Admiralty"— and *then* you have to hold your breath and scan rapidly down a list of names to see whether yours is amongst them—or not!

Only one branch, the executive branch, is affected by this half-yearly promotion-list, In all other branches—Accountant, Engineering, and Medical—promotion to a higher rank comes automatically with a certain stated seniority, and therefore is not nearly so exciting a matter; moreover, in these branches promotion does not mean an increase of pay—sometimes it means actually a decrease, as in the case of an engineer-commander with whom I was once shipmate, who lost sixpence a day by being promoted to engineer-captain.

As for my own branch, the only promotion that (possibly) lies in store for us is of the nature foreshadowed some little time ago in the daily list of Admiralty Appointments, which announced "Chaplain the Rev. —— ——, to *Glory.*"

Promotion to the ranks of commander and captain is made not by seniority but by selection; at the same time, seniority does enter somewhat into the decision, since the selection is made as a general rule from amongst those officers who have served a certain number of years in the preceding rank; a lieutenant-commander enters the promotion-belt at about his third year, and—if he is unfortunate—

leaves it at, roughly, his sixth; the zone for "commanders to captains" stretches similarly from the fifth year to the eighth. War promotions, and those made for specially meritorious service, are, of course, exceptions.

In either case the selection is made entirely according to merit. No favouritism enters into it—in spite of the *dictum* of one of our greatest admirals, that "*Favouritism is the backbone of efficiency!*"

But how do aspirants for higher rank "acquire merit"? There are various ways; and perhaps they can best be differentiated by quoting the saying of another distinguished naval officer: "Some run in ordinary shoes, some in tennis-shoes, *and some in spiked shoes!*"

It is handed down by tradition that in the good old days many a promotion was earned by the lavish expenditure of paint and gold-leaf; but those were the days of spit-and-polish, when for Admiral's Inspections not the least thing aimed at was to make the ship "look tiddly." Many an interesting tale could be unfolded with respect to moneys advanced to impecunious first-lieutenants for this purpose, if the bumboatmen of Malta and the China Station would reveal the secrets of their account-books!

All that is past now; greatly to the relief, I should imagine, of the many who enter what is proverbially "the poor-man's profession "for a livelihood as well as for a career. Gold-leaf has gone the way of masts-and-yards; and as for paint, the official allowance of the business-like but unbeautiful "Admiralty grey" is sufficient for even the most confirmed ship's-husband.

Promotion comes now to the man who does his job well, and the plodding and practical "Salt-horse" man has as good a chance as the specialist.

Everybody in the navy looks forward to the publication of the list; if a man is not directly and personally interested in it he is sure to have friends whom he hopes to see promoted. Certain hot favourites are studied with as much nice judgment as goes to the weighing of the chances of Derby entries, and a Promotion Sweep is a most popular form of amusement at this time of year.

Every man within the promotion zone is an Ishmael to the others. And even when the victor has won the semi-crown of oak-leaves which adorn a commander's cap-peak the struggle is not altogether finished. As I will now proceed to illustrate by an improving story.

A young commander of exactly six months' seniority was looking at the new list of officers promoted to commander's rank. "A splendid list of promotions," he observed to his wife, "simply *splendid!*"

"What, are they all friends of yours, dear?" she asked sympathetically.

"Friends of mine? *Friends*, did you say?" exclaimed the horror-struck husband. "No, Heaven be praised, I don't know one of 'em! The last thing I want to see is any of my friends promoted!" They were all old "passed-overs," who would not be likely to interfere with him later on.

Few things, I take it, are more chilling than to look for your name amongst a list of successful candidates and not find it. There will be some unlucky men, you may be sure, who will have this chilly feeling for some few days after the promotion-list comes out, and after all their hoping and striving will pessimistically agree that

"*There's a divinity that shapes our ends—rough!*
Hew them how we will!"

But they will soon cheer up again, and look forward to being promoted next June—as I hope indeed they will be! And, be sure, their New Year's Resolution will take the form of a determination to get that "brass-hat" in another six months, if human endeavour can accomplish it.

I think that we all of us cling, half-ashamed, to the old-fashioned practice of making New Year Resolutions, though it is supposed to have gone out of use—laughed out of existence!

I cannot say that I see any subtle humour about the fact that such resolutions are commonly soon broken.

Even if they last for one whole day, that is better than nothing.

Practice before precept? Certainly—here goes! "*Resolved*, That next year I will read more of the Writer than I have done this year." During the past twelve months I have only read *David Copperfield, Little Dorrit*, and part of *Martin Chuzzlewit*—take shame to myself!

There is another New Year's Resolution, not of my own invention, which seems so admirable that I may as well put it in the form of an exhortation for general use. It is this:

If you come down to breakfast and find yourself cross, do nothing:

But if you come down to breakfast and find *everybody else cross*—
Then take some medicine.

CHAPTER 39

Warrant Officers

Warrant officers are the backbone of the navy, as any naval man will tell you.

Their exact position is a little difficult to define; in moments of bitterness they will complain that they are "neither officer nor man," while in strict theory they rank inferior to a sub-lieutenant but superior to a midshipman who is inferior to a dog but superior to a weevil; so there you have it. They get plenty of hard work and responsibility, and very little honour and glory; but they wear the cocked hat and sword, and are the only officers—you should be very careful about this—who must *always* be addressed as "Mister"; I do not know what would happen if anyone, even the First Lord of the Admiralty, were to omit the "Mister" when speaking to a warrant officer! We of the wardroom may sometimes speak of them in their absence with freedom and familiarity as "old Smith" or "that fellow Brown"—much as schoolboys talk airily of their form-masters; but we should not dare to withhold the rightful dues of the "handle "to the name when speaking face to face with them, whether on service or on those social occasions when they are our guests in the wardroom.

They are always allotted cabins on board, and well, I have been trying hard to reckon up what other special privileges are theirs, but all I can think of is that they are the only officers who are allowed to take up the daily ration of rum.

Warrant officers all come originally from the "Lower Deck," but in our democratic service they figure in the list of officers without distinction of persons. And how very democratic the Navy List is may be seen by opening it at the letter R, where you will find set down:

Russias, *His Imperial Majesty*

Nicholas II., Emperor of all
the, K.G.—Hon. A. F.

(*i.e.,* Admiral of the Fleet); and immediately following:

Ruston, Arthur.—Gr.

which is short for gunner. So that this latter gentleman may rightly claim to be "*with but after*" our august Ally.

Many a young midshipman joining his first ship has cause to be grateful to some warrant officer who becomes a regular "Sea-Daddy" to him, getting him out of scrapes, teaching him much of his work, and regaling him with wisdom in the form of yarns drawn from his vast experience. The *locus classicus* is, of course, to be found in "Mr. Midshipman Easy," where the hero's debt to his warrant officer friend is probably an affectionate remembrance of the author's own early days at sea.

Marryat, in fact, delighted in bringing warrant officers into his stories—which, alas! are so little read by this generation of sailors—and drew them very skilfully and accurately, if one may judge by their antitypes; for his "Mr. Dispart, the Gunner," "Mr. Chucks, the Boatswain," and the rest, can be matched in every squadron of our present Fleet—almost in every ship.

Practically all the non-consumable stores on board a man-of-war are under the care of warrant officers, who are the regular store-keeping officials afloat. How vast a responsibility this is may be gathered from remarking the wide range of such stores, from the ship's anchors, which are under the boatswain's charge, down to magic-lantern slides, which are under that of the carpenter.

All such stores have to be mustered at stated periods of a month or so—a fact which has given rise to a proverbial naval expression; for, although very willing to lend any of his cherished "stores," a warrant officer usually accompanies the loan with an injunction to "remember the day of the month," with an eye to the date of the next muster; so that when you lend anything and do not wish your action to be construed as a deed of gift, it becomes convenient to quote the saying, "*Remember the day of the month*," thus conveying your meaning by a delicate hint.

There is another saying, proverbially ascribed to the gunner and used by him instead of a watch for the purpose of timing a ten-second salute; *mutatis mutandis*, it runs as follows:

Twenty years a gunner, and then to be called the son of a dog! Well—I'm—blessed!—Number one gun,—fire!

A shorter sentence, used for a five-second salute, is:

If I wasn't a gunner I shouldn't be here! Number one gun, fire!

The attitude of the warrant officer towards his subordinates is usually of a nature that may best be described as "unbending"; and a good "Warrant" will get more work out of the men than a whole covey of commanders. Their rigid authority seems to be a tradition passed on from one generation to another; for our own boatswain, himself a stern disciplinarian, tells me that when he was a boy he ventured on one occasion to "argue the point" with the gunner who was giving him instruction. "Boy," said the gunner, "please to remember this—that when I am right, I am right; and *when I am wrong, I am right!*" There was no more to be said.

The boatswain has been known from very ancient days as "Tommy Pipes"—a name derived, of course, from the silver whistle or "pipe" which he wears slung round his neck for the purpose of sounding various orders. He is, so far as I can remember, the only warrant officer to whom Shakespeare has allotted a "speaking part."

The gunner's nickname of "Bluelight" is not so obvious; but "Chippie" for the carpenter, and "Shovel-Engineer" for the artificer-engineer are more self-explanatory.

These four ranks held undisputed sway for many years; but latterly their numbers have been added to largely. Warrant electricians, armourers, stewards, telegraphists, writers, and cooks now occupy a place in the Navy List; and it is pleasing to see such recognition given to men who have thoroughly earned the right to wear the uniform of a king's officer. For in the warrant officer, you must understand, you see the survivor of the fittest; they are good men and true, one and all, and deserve all that they get, and a good deal more besides.

Give all the praise you like to famous men, admirals, captains, and commodores and their kind; but remember, when all's said and done, that it is the warrant officer who has made the navy what it is!

Chapter 40

Paper-Work

It has to be done, so let us get it over quickly. There is a confession to make. Now—stand by—*We are no better than the Germans in the matter of ante-bellum miscalculations!* Granted that they excel us in the mere number of their unintelligent adumbrations—

One moment, please. This splendid word "adumbrations" is a gift from the literary gentleman who composes the Poldhu messages: it came in last night's Press News, and I discovered the P.O. Tel, strafing the wireless operator who took in the message for having muddled up the whole thing by mixing several words together. *Adumbrations!* Clearly, the operator must have missed some syllables, and nobody could tell now whether it meant the Argonne, Dr. Dumba, Brazil, or Ratisbon! I explained that "adumbration" was a Sunday word for "forecast," and so succeeded in restoring peace.

But, to go back to the high road again: in the mere matter of number, the Germans excelled us with regard to unintelligent adumbrations: Ireland was going to be plunged in civil war—(I tried once to explain to a German officer that the so-called Sedition of Ireland is on exactly the same footing as the Golf of Scotland, a national pastime to be laid aside when more serious business arises; but he couldn't see it, poor fellow!)—India was going to revolt, the Dominions were going to break away, and so on.

What are all these lesser miscalculations, however, to the one hideous example which may be laid to our charge!

I speak for the navy alone, be it understood. We said that if ever there should be a war *all paperwork would be a wash-out!*

And, what is more, we believed it!

All reports, returns, requisitions, reference-sheets, were to be done away; memos. and letters were to be heard of no more; digests, notifications, and schedules were to be reduced to a negligible quantity; and, in brief, all papers were to be swept into the rubbish-bin by the cleansing besom of war.

So we said—in our haste.

But the sad truth is that in the matter of paperwork the little finger of war has proved considerably thicker than the loins of peace. The naval officer's pen may not be mightier than his sword, but it is much more often in his hand. We all spend quite a good portion of each day writing something or other in the official line, and if we are not all of us turned into literary experts by the end of the war it will not be the fault of our betters.

Speaking for myself alone, I am not troubled with very much paper-work in ordinary peacetimes, and have very little more to do in this direction than to fill in the school report of the ship. There is, however, another report which I am always careful to fill up myself: it is the report on "Chaplain's Duties," required at every Inspection, and contains seven questions relating to the assiduity and efficiency of the chaplain. It will be readily understood that by attending to this matter personally I invariably do my bit towards getting a good Inspection Report for the ship.

There are some classic tales concerning paperwork current in the navy. The gem of them all, of course, is the incomparable story of The Shovewood. And there is also the story of Whale Island and the Poker, which any gunnery-lieutenant will tell you.

Several of such tales relate to ways and means of getting rid of inconvenient papers or of avoiding filling in returns under awkward circumstances, the time-honoured excuses of "Eaten by rats," or "Destroyed by damp," having long ago worn thin, and a suspicion having arisen at headquarters that the latter of these two excuses was no more than a playful euphemism for "Thrown overboard," as indeed was often the case.

A more original expedient was that of a certain officer in command of a West Coast gunboat. He had several times been politely requested by the Admiralty to send his ship's books and papers home for inspection, and as on each occasion he failed to make any reply, much less send the papers, the request gradually lost more and more of its politeness, until at last it became a peremptory demand. But, unfortunately, all the desired reports were so hopelessly in arrear that it was beyond human ingenuity to compile them with any appearance of verisimilitude.

But the lieutenant, being abundantly dowered with that unfailing resourcefulness which has so often in our naval history turned a defeat into a victory, soon hit upon a way out of the difficulty. Having procured a tin-lined case, he bored several tiny holes in it, and placed therein the blank books and papers. Lastly he placed inside a couple of dozen healthy West African cockroaches.

And when the box arrived at Whitehall there were some small fragments of leather, a mass of infinitesimal scraps of paper, twenty-three plethoric cockroaches the size of frogs, and one who had been cut off in his prime by devouring a binding dyed with arsenical green.

The lieutenant, of course, was entirely exonerated from all blame.

Chapter 41

Hostility-Men

A strange tide has flowed from the land to the sea, a stream of fiery voluntaries, with ladies' faces and fierce dragons' spleens—or sometimes *vice versa*—who have come from desk and consulting-room, office, farm and pit, to make a hazard of new fortunes here during the period of hostilities.

Navy Jack calls them, for short, "Hostility-men." Some of them are R.N.V.R. men of many years' standing, brimful of zeal and equally chock-full of knowledge, able to take a part in the more scientific work of the ship, and to take it very well, too. Their training has been very thorough, and they brought with them to their apprenticeship an immense enthusiasm which helped them quickly over all its difficulties. Often have I heard them say, "If ever a war comes, we want to be sent to sea; we don't care in what sort of jobs; we should be quite content to do the dirty work, the unskilled work, of a ship, and to release better men for better work." A fine spirit! Though, of course, there is very little unskilled work on board a ship. Well, they have got their way, and have been sent to sea, and the knowledge they acquired ashore has made them far more useful than ever they dreamed of becoming.

But these are not the *real* Hostility-men; the title properly belongs only to such as never gave a thought before to the service of the sea, yet at the outbreak of a war which appeared naturally destined to be a war of sea-fights heard within them the call of the ocean, rose from their places, and came down to the great ships.

It is, to my mind, astonishing what a great number there has been of volunteers for the navy. I can understand men joining up with the army, for, after all, the land is the land, whether it be in Leicestershire or Flanders, and to hunt all day or trudge behind a plough is not so essentially different from riding in a cavalry charge or marching with a regiment. But what brought these, these studious clerks and quiet scientific men, these grimy inland toilers and raw upland youths, to adventure themselves upon a world of waters as little known to them as the encircling *flumen oceanum* to Herodotus?

Perhaps it was that little drop of sea-water that is said to be in the veins of every Briton.

From the point of view of the commander of a ship, Hostility-men are an agglomeration of tearful surprises. Until they have been licked into shape, of course. For you must understand that commanders as a class are base material souls who don't care a hang about patriotism or enthusiasm or any rot of that sort. "*Point de zèle*" might well be taken as the motto of their Order. What they look to is, How much *work* can be got out of any given individual? So it may easily be understood that the arrival on board of a small batch of Hostility-men is not always the subject of loud thanksgivings on the part of the second-in-command.

Imagine the despairing sighs of this sorely tried officer when he interviews a handful of such new arrivals to see what use can be made of them. "What were you doing before you joined?" he asks.

"If you please, sir, I was a groom."

Heavens! Does the man think we keep a racing-stable down in the hold? Or perhaps he wants to join up with the Horse Marines!

"And what were *you*?"

"Market-gardener, sir."

The commander thinks for a moment, and then ingeniously hitting upon a task that seems to be in the man's own line bids the master-at-arms to "send him forrard to weigh the potatoes"!

A more suitable job was found the other day for a newly joined Hostility-man who came to one of the ships of our Fleet. The usual question was put to him, "What were you before you joined?"

"I was a painter," said the man, and the commander at once heaved a sigh of relief.

"Thank Heaven, at last I've found a man who can make himself of some use," he said; "let him join up at once with the mess-deck painting-party."

A couple of hours later the commander strolled along to see how the work was progressing. He discovered the self-styled painter in the midst of a most unholy mess—paint on the decks, on the mess-crockery, on himself, everywhere, in fact, but on the bulkhead where it should have been, and that showed nothing but a few feeble dashes of various colours trickling down and blending one into another like a post-impressionist sunset!

"What the deuce do you mean by this?" cried the irate commander. "Call yourself a painter! Why, you don't know the first thing about it! It's quite evident you've never done anything of this sort before in your life! Why, bless your pretty eyes, I could paint a bulkhead better than that blindfold! What did you tell me you were a painter for?"

"I'm not used to this sort of work, sir," apologised the man.

"Then why did you tell me you *were?* Didn't you say you had been a painter?"

"Well, so I did," explained the other. "You see, I didn't think of putting it any other way. Most of my work I *exhibit at the Royal Academy!*"

For the most part they soon settle down very comfortably to the ship's routine, whether they find themselves on the mess-deck or amongst the "after-guard." There are some who have lived the extremely sheltered life ashore, and must feel themselves in a rough, wild world at first; but what a lot of good it does 'em! Others are more nautical than any of their new comrades who have spent their life at sea—I know of a certain Hostility officer who always goes about in a pair of sea-boots, though he goes no further than from his cabin to the wardroom!

At first, though, there is sometimes a little bashfulness, especially with such as have offered themselves in a lower capacity than that they held ashore.

A working-party was marching through one of our dockyards a short time ago consisting of eight men carrying a copper-punt—a thing like a huge butcher's tray—and a petty-officer in charge. This latter happened to be a fashionable doctor in the town. All were in working-rig, which is a costume rather resembling that of a dilapidated convict, and even these unbecoming suits had seen decidedly better days. Suddenly there appeared round a corner a party of well-dressed people—visitors come to see over the dockyard. On seeing them, the petty-officer in charge of the party immediately dived beneath the copper-punt, and was heard to murmur as he disappeared, "Oh, mine offence is Rank!" It was a struggle for the poor man to keep up with the others on his hands and knees, but he managed it somehow, and at last emerged flushed and breathless, but well pleased at his escape. "You see," he explained, "it wouldn't have done very well for them to see me in this rig; those were some of my best patients!"

Chapter 42

Wool and Water

I steal a chapter-heading from that incomparable book which is as much loved by every naval officer as by any other children; and then proceed to commit a further crime by calling in Apt Alliteration's 'Ateful Aid to help me in wording to the war-workers in wool-work the well-won thanks of those who wear their welcome work upon the water.

Respice finem—look to your extremities; take care of your legs, and your lungs will take care of themselves. It was on this sound medical principle that I based an appeal for Sea-Boot Stockings for the Fleet a year ago; for although there is not a man in the navy who suffers from "cold feet" in the metaphorical sense, yet in the literal significance this distressing sensation is ever lying in wait to entrap the feet of our sailors, who, if they are protected against the nautical equivalent of "trench-leg," need not fear the most vigorous assaults of a northern winter against the rest of their bodies.

It is not for nothing that our keen-witted Allies, the Italians, speak of knitted things in general as "Mail"; for the resemblance to chain-armour lies in its protective results as much as in its outward appearance.

One can imagine the man who laboriously pieced together the first coat of mail showing his handiwork to his wife, and saying, with triumphant pride: "Look, my dear, what a splendid invention I have hit upon all by myself!" While she, bending her head to hide a smile, would see at a glance that he had unconsciously been imitating the product of her busy needles; though, of course, she would not for all the world let the dear stupid know anything about that!

Of this soft armour every needful piece with one exception was provided by gentle fingers in the early days of last winter: helmets, *hausse-cols,* breastplates, wristlets, arm-guards, and gauntlets, guarded the naval warrior against the attacks of the fierce enemy. But, like Achilles, he was still vulnerable in the heel—and in the leg besides; greaves were lacking in his equipment of mail.

It was a new experience for the sailor to find himself the recipient of gifts and attentions from the outside public. This, and the lavishness with which the presents were showered upon him, had the effect, it must be admitted, of making him a little careless and wasteful at first. When, for example, the discovery was made that for brass-cleaning purposes nothing could approach a soft woollen muffler, who could refrain from turning one to such base uses, seeing that mufflers cost nothing, and half a dozen more were to be had for the asking? Or, if applied to its original purpose, and worn till it became dirty, the simplest way to solve the washing-day problem was to burn the thing in the incinerator, and draw a new one.

On the top of all these private and unofficial gifts came an Admiralty free issue of warm winter clothing, in some cases supplementing the private gifts, in others merely adding to the existing profusion. Long stockings, however, were still not provided.

Just at this point a many kind ladies stepped into the breach, aided by the friendly offices of the *Westminster,* and welcome parcels of long, thick stockings began to arrive on board.

I wish I could have seen these ladies at work. They hardly knew what was wanted—the request was put in such a thoroughly stupid, man-like way, just asking for "sea-boot stockings," with careless disregard of the mysteries of plain and purl, length, breadth, and the turning of the heel, and whether the wool should be double Berlin or plain Scotch winsey. But they worked on in the dark, evolving sea-boot stockings from their inner consciousness, and, of course, intuitively arriving at precisely the very thing needed. And how they must have smiled, at times, thinking how other loving fingers had once knitted wee bootees for the same feet that now required these huge and heavy monuments of wool-work!

Not for the first time, surely, the ladies have given an example to the official guardians; this year—quite recently, in fact—the Admiralty has made a free issue to the Fleet of these same stockings—one pair to a man. In spite of this, there is still a demand for all that are privately sent, for there are limits to the unwashed life of one pair, after all!

Many requests have been made for details as to the true nature of the perfect sea-boot stocking. Perhaps it is a little late in the day, but

I would answer them all by saying that the only essential qualities are length, roominess, and warmth. Stockings have been sent, some made with heels and some without, blue ones, brown ones, white ones, of weight ranging from one to four pounds. And all were equally acceptable.

I hope I may be forgiven for doing so, but I *must* tell the story of a lady who wrote to me saying she had never made such stockings before, but she had modelled the pair she was sending upon the legs of her brother-in-law, who was a bishop, and hoped they would do. The stockings were of such generous proportions that I could not help saying, in my letter of thanks, that if her brother-in-law's legs were really of this mould it was no wonder he had been raised to the episcopate!

Possibly those who have worked so hard at these welcome gifts may have now and then tried to picture something of the men who wear their handiwork. Sailors are by no means ungrateful men—quite the contrary—but they are shy, and extremely diffident about expressing their thanks on paper. Yet their thanks have not been unuttered. Many a time, I fancy, when away in the picket-boat in a heavy sea on a cold winter's night, with the white waves half-burying the tiny craft; when kneeling to scrub ice-covered decks on a raw morning before daybreak; when away aloft a hundred feet above the deck, where the chill blast tries to benumb a man's feet, and send him headlong down; or in many another case of the seaman's life, these two war-winters, a grateful thought has come from the sailor's heart for the one who worked that he might be kept warm.

Chapter 43

"Wireless"—and a Cat

Have I mentioned that we have a very nice puss on board? It is the pet and property of the Wireless operators' staff, and, on the analogy of most of the books pertaining to this specialised signalling, it is generally described as "Wireless Cat, with Addendum One." It waves its Addendum when it is annoyed.

This rightly privileged animal has the free run of the wireless office; and, to quote a formula so often used gratefully by naval people when shore-goers make us honorary members of their club, this is "a privilege of which it gladly avails itself"—except with regard to a certain portion of the room, where two terminals lie just in a convenient position for the investigations of a creature endowed by Nature with an aptitude for the pursuit of science. The first—and last—inquiry into the *Practical Uses of Applied Electricity* led to such a leap into the air as has not been equalled since first in old Egypt the Cat leapt up to her pedestal in the Pantheon to take her place among the gods.

To mere humans, however, the wireless room is one of the most sacredly secret places in the ship. If you come on board to pay us a visit, when peace breaks out and we can once more have the pleasure of seeing what ordinary people look like—no, I don't mean "ordinary" people—we will show you the inside of the turrets and take you down into the engine-room, and anywhere else you please; but we shall diplomatically forget to mention the existence of the wireless room; and, if by chance you find yourself outside its hallowed portal, we shall point out to you a notice-board hanging thereon, which forbids even the officers of the ship to enter unless required to do so by their duty.

Without divulging any of its arcane mysteries, I may go so far as to say that it is very different in its general economy from the wireless room of a dozen years ago. At that period the whole of the apparatus was contained in a couple of small boxes which stood on the desk in an otherwise empty office; the messages were automatically printed in Morse code by a tape machine which always worked slowly and frequently failed to work at all, being powerless to respond to the more delicate vibrations. At the present time, however, the room is packed full with machinery and complicated instruments—the nature and uses of which have been carefully explained to me on several occasions by an enthusiastic P.O. Tel.; but, as the whole business is entirely beyond my comprehension, I always confine myself to the wise policy of replying with a non-committal "Yes, I see."

But even I can understand that the present achievements are simply marvellous; and that they are, furthermore, nothing compared to the vast range of its future possibilities, when the experimenter shall have learnt more about what he terms the "Ether," and tamed it to his will.

Personally speaking, the chief use for which I hitch wireless to my own particular wagon is in order to make it do duty as a Danger Signal; for my constant advice to anyone who is interested in spiritualistic or theosophic literature is that he should search and see if his book contains the words "Wireless Telegraphy," or "The Ether"; and, if it does, pitch it in the fire at once: the book smells of quackery! Because wireless certainly affords no proof, and is even only a very poor illustration, of the possibility of communication between the departed and ourselves; while, as for the Ether, no one can say positively that such a thing exists at all.

The wireless room is near my cabin, and the loud, insistent *zip-zip-zip* when messages are being sent is a disturbing sound that makes itself heard above all other ship-noises and takes a little getting used to. The cat, with that spirit of detachment which is the real halo of this super-animal, preserved from the first a complete imperturbability with respect to this noise. The operation of receiving messages, on the other hand, is a silent process, and I have been trying to deduce an appropriate moral lesson from this, but the only one I can think of is that if you haven't got anything to say you should dry up and keep quiet—which, after all, is well worth taking to heart.

The main principle underlying the whole business of Wireless Telegraphy is exactly the same as that which necessitates having a double-first to teach the junior form; namely, that in order to convey knowledge to any desired recipient there must be a highly concentrated and powerful force at the source of information, since most of it is going to be dissipated into space. There ought to be great consolation in this thought for all long-suffering schoolmasters—although I can't see exactly where it lies. The sending ship, it will be observed, is in the position of a man who wishes to talk to a friend in the middle of a crowd of people half a mile away; he has to talk very loudly to make himself heard at all, and everybody else in the crowd is going to hear what he says. The receiving ship, therefore, requires very little power indeed, and the only difficulty is that so many people are shouting; it is rather like being in Hyde Park on a Sunday afternoon, amongst a hundred leather-lunged preachers, each telling you the one and only true gospel of spiritual, political, or social salvation; or like taking in all the papers there are in order to get a clear idea of the conduct of the war.

The only thing to do is to close your ears to everything you don't wish to hear—a most pernicious doctrine for a chaplain to preach, but the only practical course for a ship that wishes to receive a wireless message. And so there have been invented many ingenious devices whereby a ship can cut off the sound of all but the one tune it desires to hear: devices foreshadowed long ago by the Wanderer in his many-oared ship—and in general use from Adam's day till now by men who, finding troublesome the loud, clear calls of Duty, Self-Denial, and Honour, discover means of shutting off those voices and listening only to the call which suits their own desires. I omitted to say that our Wireless Cat (with Addendum One) is of the gentler sex; she is—at present—*Télégraphie sans fille*.

Chapter 44
A Flap

We are not always in harbour—though you might think we were if you listened to the Germans, who in this as in every other matter act on the good old legal principle that if you have a bad case you should abuse the other side.

But neither are we always at sea, as some fond parents, unversed in naval ways, appear to imagine. The ship that can keep the seas for ever has yet to be designed; and, besides, what is the good of playing Prisoner's Base continuously if the prisoner will not leave his base and has no idea of playing the game?

So it happens that we are sometimes in harbour. Where, and when, and for how long, wild Tirpitz should not drag from me—and he *must* feel pretty wild, mustn't he?

Yet, if anyone should rush to the conclusion that while we are in harbour the safety of the seas and of our shores is left to look after itself, or that we are resting in idle and luxurious seclusion, he may take it from me that he is mistaken. At any time since the first day of the war we have been ready to fight the greatest sea-battle in history before our next meal-time; ready, to the smallest gun in the smallest ship; ready and willing. Never are any sudden preparations needed, nor laments for might-have-beens in the way of equipment or men; nor is one jot of expectation relaxed on account of being at an anchorage instead of out on the deep. It is difficult to write of such constant and thorough preparedness without the risk of descending to banal verbiage; but indeed the simile of eager hounds upon the leash, though trite, expresses the situation more completely than could be done by any less threadbare phrase.

Our comings and goings are, of course, secrets carefully hidden from public knowledge. Whether they are guessed at or discovered by our friends the enemy remains a question one which is answered in the emphatic affirmative by a member of our mess who believes strongly in the resourceful wiliness of the Teuton. "Why," said he, "it only needs a man to walk along the cliffs wearing a little red cap to give the whole show away at once!" Which thing has become a proverb to this day, so that whenever we are about to leave harbour we say that "*The Man in the Little Red Cap*" has been taking a walk.

Sometimes our departures are more than usually sudden and unexpected. The whole proceeding then becomes what is known amongst us as "A Flap"—which I will attempt to describe.

We have had an unwonted spell at anchor, and are getting a little fed up with it; the allurements of the beach are entirely absent, and even if they were not we couldn't get at them. It would be far better, we are all feeling, to be at sea. All the papers are stale, and the Russian Kromeskies and Caramel Custards of the messman fail to excite that interest which normally places food on a level with the weather as a topic for discussion. On deck the hands are employed painting ship, making the side look a little less disreputable than when we came in after our last buffeting by the paint-destroying waves.

Down below, in the ante-room, certain languid forms are reposing in various attitudes of boredom, too weak to stem the tide of the Navigator's flow of reminiscences. He, at this moment, is relating how the Rag, of which he is a member, was on one occasion closed for cleaning and renovating, and the homeless clubmen were offered the hospitality of the Athenaeum. "Well, I went in there," he narrates, "in the middle of one forenoon, and ordered a cocktail. Lord! I thought the roof would have fallen in! You never saw such a horror-stricken assemblage in your life! Several venerable waiters held a ruridecanal meeting to consult as to the form and manner of making a cocktail; and when they finally brought it I felt so ashamed of myself that I went out and drank it in the hall."

From this he goes on to recount his experiences out Chinaside, and how he won the Cherry Medal, and still nobody is strong enough to stop him.

Then there enters a signalman, in dripping oilskins, with a rain-blurred chit in his hand, which he presents in silence to the engineer-commander. This officer as silently took it, and adjusts his spectacles to read the communication.

"What's the news, Chief?" comes from several quarters in tones of newfound interest.

He informs us that it is an order to raise steam for a hundred knots at five minutes' notice—more or less.

And then the Flap really begins.

A minor thrill of excitement courses through the whole ship; a thrill, because the old questions still possess their power—"Is it a Stunt this time?" "Shall we have any luck at last?" But a thrill of the minor kind because of the proverb about Hope Deferred. We have been disappointed so many times.

On deck the Flap is in full swing. All the painting-stages are got in, and a procession of men shouldering the paint-spattered planks with dangling ropes fills the battery. Another crowd jostles them coming from the opposite direction with the tackle for getting in the nets. The order for steam on the capstan has already been given, as also for power on the motors and boat-hoists. And soon all these engines are moaning and humming together, an intricate mass of ropes and wires laid on the deck begins to move and straighten out, the torpedo-booms swing aft, and the nets coil up and repose on their shelves. Then the main derrick is topped up and turned outboard, its guys led to the motor-hoists, and the fifty-foot picket-boat swings high into the air, a shower of drops streaming from its keel along the wind. Other boats follow suit, and all in turn are safely lowered upon the crutches, the sea-boats alone being left to hang from the davits and lashed to their griping-spars.

All this means a busy time for the commander, whose chief trouble is not so much to get the right things done as to cater for people whose original sin prompts them to do the wrong things.

But what really breaks his heart is that the temporary surgeon, who hasn't even heard mention of the Flap at all, should come to him in the thick of it with the mild request, "Would you kindly arrange for a boat to take five dental cases to the Hospital Ship at eight-thirty tomorrow?"

And so the Flap continues, till we are peacefully at sea. And then—nothing happens! The situation is summed up with disgust by someone remarking, "I expect some man was reported to be going round oiling the lock-gates of the Kiel Canal!"

Chapter 45

The Beach

I went ashore for a walk a few days ago. This would scarce deserve mention were it not for the fact that shore-going has become a rare event with me these days; it is a good six weeks since I last essayed the terrors of the land previous to this occasion.

The sage in *Rasselas* speaks of the "barren uniformity" of the sea; and sapiently informs us that:

"The ocean and the land are very different. The only variety of water is rest and motion. But the earth has mountains and valleys, deserts and cities; it is inhabited by men of different customs and contrary opinions"

Sentiments in which are reflected the prejudices of the learned author, who declared that a man might as well live in a prison as aboard ship. But I wish that Dr. Johnson had continued his tour to the Hebrides a little further, and had landed where I landed; he wouldn't have had quite such a lot to say about the diversities of the land and its attendant pleasures! The catalogue of the surrounding scenery was rather on the lines of the schedule of midshipmen's uniform as it used to appear in the Quarterly Naval List, detailing, "*Hats: no hat, but a cap; Swords: no sword, but a dirk.*"

Similarly, enumerating the above-quoted features of the land, I traversed mountains: no mountains, but a bog; cities: no cities, but a hovel here and there, and a wretched and lonely farm; and amidst the general barrenness a few rare patches still more bare, where it seemed like expecting a miracle to hope to produce a scanty crop of that *tenuis avena* upon which the natives are reputed to cultivate the Muses. Three miles inland—and, thank goodness, the sea was in sight the whole of the way; it was the only thing worth looking at; then about turn, down to the boat, and so back to the comfortable and homely ship. Anybody can have my share of the land—at any rate, of *this* land!

And, when I got on board, a hostility officer spread out before me some snapshots he had just received by the day's mail—photographs of Oxford! A bit of scenery on Boar's Hill, with a misty glimpse of towers and spires in the distant valley; the lake in Worcester gardens; an upper reach of the Cher, reed-fringed, where drooping willows strive to caress the further bank with graceful outstretched finger-tips. Ah! what a land! Almost can one hear the very heart of England beating there. A land where a man might kneel and kiss the clods and not be ashamed; a land where still applies the verdict passed upon an earlier Paradise, Behold, it is very good!

I wished he had not shown me those photographs!

But after a while there supervened a feeling that even in the barren scene of my afternoon's perambulations Mother Earth still lived, the kindly nurse, ready to add strength to any pygmy Antaeus who might come to her broad bosom. There was a hurrying together of leucocytes and phagocytes, those cherubim and seraphim of the corporeal cosmos, singing and shouting praises for life given more abundantly, and in a million tiny arteries the rivers thereof began to make the city glad.

Yes; on the whole, it is a good thing to take to the Beach. I think I shall go again soon—perhaps in another six weeks or so.

Dr. Johnson was right in likening a ship to a prison to the extent that no one is allowed to leave it without permission, even for an hour. Senior officers, "Heads of Departments," must obtain leave from the captain in person before going ashore—though, usually, a general dispensation from this obligation is given at the beginning of a commission. Junior officers, however, have to observe the ritual on every occasion, and must approach the commander with the set formula, "May I go ashore, sir, please?" To which the proper response is "Please": a polite form which gives the desired permission as though it were a favour done to the granter, in the true spirit of ancient chivalry.

Young officers of branches other than the executive must also first ascertain from their own immediate superiors whether they can be spared; so the process of obtaining leave sometimes becomes quite elaborate; the most junior engineer-officer, for example, may be observed to enter the wardroom, cap in hand; first, he approaches the "Senior," and recites the appointed interrogation. "*Please*" is returned in a quiet voice. But this is not enough. The youngster steps across to where the engineer-commander is sitting, and again asks, "May I go ashore, sir, please?" once more getting *"Please"* to encourage him. Yet once again he stands a suppliant, before the commander now, till a final *"Please"* sends him away rejoicing to "shift into plain clothes."

The permission, of course, is readily given, as no officer would think of asking unless he knew that his work was all "clewed up" and his services could be spared. But as a general rule it is not considered good form to go ashore too frequently before about 4 p.m. though now in war-time this unwritten law is repealed, and everyone is allowed, even expected, when possible, to take to the beach

—*for the good of the Service,*
As much and as oft as may be.

There is always a "Boat Routine" posted in some prominent place, telling the times at which one may be prepared to taste the sweets of the shore. When the officers' boat is called away by the quartermaster's pipe, notice is given to all intending beachcombers by "sounding one G"; which is performed by one of the buglers, sometimes on the proper instrument of his office, but more usually by means of a hand fog-horn, which is a thing like a pair of bellows with a long blunderbuss-nozzle of brass. It gives forth a sound which is very raucous and loud, and would be most unpleasant to listen to but for the fact that it conveys the welcome appeal, *"Once more unto the beach, dear friends, once more!"*

The desire for going often ashore is one that is apt to wear off with length of service. I have known men, especially men of the lower deck, who have spent a three-year commission on a foreign station without once leaving the ship. The old stager rather affects a sort of good-humoured contempt for anyone who cannot content himself on board, and vents his feelings with the ironical comment, "Anyone would think you had been *born* on shore!" Or, again, quoting from some forgotten origin a phrase now become proverbial, *"Don't forget, the ship is your home!"*

Well, a very pleasant home it is, for the most part, and, if one cannot be living the normal life amongst one's family and friends, there is no place better to be in than a ship. Yet, after all, the beach is the final goal to which every sailor looks; and in a "Ship of War at Sea" we may be excused for looking forward to its attractions, since we are bidden to pray each morning, *"That we may return in safety to enjoy the blessings of the land."*

Chapter 46

Sunrise and Sunset

It is entirely typical of the navy that not the slightest notice should be taken of the sun's uprising, while his down-setting is attended by a good deal of ceremonial solemnity; as much as to say:

"When you've *done* your job and proved yourself of some good we'll give you all the respect you like, but till then just carry on with your work and don't expect us to treat you like a little tin god, because, if you do, you'll be mistaken."

So when the sun first peers over the horizon he finds the ship's company all hard at work—except at that period of the year when he assumes a virtuous fit of early rising—and not a man to doff a cap to him; but when he goes off duty, having placed himself at the service of the Admiralty for the whole of the day, bugles are sounded in his honour, and every man stands to attention as a mark of honour for the occasion.

Macaulay's schoolboy will deduce at once from this the reason why the Arabians have no navy and we have. I read once, in an old number of the *Quarterly Review*, a brilliant article on the Arabs, their extraordinary achievements and marvellous powers, and their inexplicable downfall as a race. But is not the latter feature of their history made obvious by the fact that as sun-worshippers—for this they originally were—they paid too much reverence to the sun at his rising? In many parts of Southern Europe, where traces of sun-worship still exist, though the present population would be horrified at being told so, you may see on many a cottage roof a pair of ox-horns—Baal's symbol—carefully orientated to catch the first rays of the god at his appearing; I have seen this myself, as a prevalent custom amongst what is perhaps the strictest Roman Catholic populace in the world. But I have never seen, and do not think that anyone else has, a pair of horns pointed towards the *setting* sun.

Over-elation at the promise of endeavour, too little regard to final accomplishment and to the maintained drudgery necessary thereto that is the true explanation of the pathetic limitations of the race that was once nearly master of half Europe; and the opposite of this, a fine disregard for the most pompous beginnings until they have proved successful endings, accounts for the pre-eminence of our navy—and of our country.

Many of our new Hostility-men do not understand this; they come to us with an inner knowledge of their own reputations and attainments, sufficient to give them, "*outside*," that standing to which they feel justly entitled; but once "inside," thrown into the navy's melting-pot, they find that no bugles are sounded to herald their rising; and some of them do not altogether like it.

But let them wait. It is the way of the navy. If an Archangel were to come aboard he would be messed with the ordinary seamen until he had proved himself good at his job.

Let me, however, describe a little more fully the complete ritual of sunset. To begin at the beginning, the correct time is made by wireless from Greenwich each day, and with this to aid him the navigator of the flagship works out the exact moment at which the sun is due to set. This is calculated at the Mean Solar Time, not the Apparent Time, so that the ceremonies are frequently observed while a part of the sun is still able to watch what is being done in his honour. The idea is that if he *hasn't* set he *ought* to have—and it is by this obstinate habit of looking at things as they ought to be rather than as they are that (well, anybody that likes can complete this sentence; I, personally, am not convinced that the moral of it is quite good).

Then, five minutes before the time, a preparative flag is hoisted in the Flagship, and certain "repeating ships "do the same for the benefit of such vessels as are not in sight of the Flag. As soon as this is hoisted, there is intense agitation up on the signal-bridge, every signalman having his eyes glued on this "preparative." At the same time one of their number reports the matter to the officer-of-the-watch, who in turn reports to the captain, with the formula, "Five minutes to Sunset, Sir," the captain replying, "Carry on, please"—thus giving the sun the official permission to set by order of the Admiralty. The five minutes pass. Suddenly the flagship "hauls down"; the repeating ships do likewise, and in every ship of the Fleet an excited signalman bawls loudly to the officer-of-the-watch "Sunset, Sir!" The bugler sounds the "Still" Everyone on deck drops his work or his recreation, and stands strictly to attention, facing The Colours. All officers raise their hand to the Salute. The assembled buglers sound a long call, weird and plaintive, a lament for the dying day, and the white ensign comes slowly down. Then sound the two sharp notes of the "Carry-on" and sunset is over.

And when during the summer in Northern latitudes the sun takes up the ridiculous attitude of refusing to set till midnight, if at all, the navy has a short way with its recalcitrant god like those West Africans who beat the image of their deity when he refuses to send rain; the order is issued, "Sunset will be at such-and-such a time"—and if the sun will not fall in with the navy's ideas, well, that is *his* look-out! Like many another servant of the navy, he is told to retire at a time when he feels he has a lot more work in him. But he continues to shine on the ship all the same, just as many a man "retired for age" is now digging out as hard as ever for the good of the service.

But when the sun plays tricks like this it is no wonder if he finds himself now and then distrusted. There was a ship "up North" last autumn, in which the men were holding a concert on the upper deck, in the dog-watches. The deck was housed-in with awning-curtains to screen off the chill winds, and inside this the electric lights blazed brightly. The captain and his officers occupied the front row of chairs and watched the performance, which was timed to finish well before the hour for "darkening ship"—for, of course, it would not do to have such a glare of light on the upper deck when that time came. It was observed that the captain seemed a trifle uneasy, and kept looking towards the awning-curtains where the sunlight still beat strongly; but not till long afterwards was the cause of his uneasiness surmised: the cause being that, like an inverted Joshua, he was anxious about the sun, for, although he *knew* that sunset was not due till eight o'clock, yet—well, you never can tell, and it is best to be on the safe side!

Sunset is just about to sound off as I write; let me go on deck and once more see that sight which never loses its impressiveness, and pray while the bugle peals forth its sad notes that the sun may *never* set upon our Banner of the Cross—the White Ensign.

Chapter 47

The Acting Sub

Amongst the mass of information to be absorbed by the young gentlemen who study navigation under the naval instructor comes the interesting fact that while the sun moves at a uniform rate it nevertheless appears to travel at a much increased speed at certain periods of its annual course.

How true this is, if applied to that other curve which the sun also marks—the curve of a lifetime! Those who were on the flat side of the ellipse—that is to say, in the period of Middle Age—when the war broke out, still find themselves moved onwards so little that they appear to themselves to be practically stationary; meanwhile, however, their little nieces have developed from unconsidered trifles into Cosmic Forces.

Yet I doubt whether in their case the flight of time is so marked as it is with those young gentlemen mentioned above. At the beginning of the war they were junior midshipmen, mere excrescences upon the body politic—or, to use their own briefer term, "*Warts.*" But now they shine in all their splendour as acting subs!

For you must understand that to be an acting sub is to be at the most glorious period of a naval career. He has two other and distant goals remaining; one is reached when he first gets a brass hat and is mentioned in the list of promotions to commander, and the other when he achieves flag rank; but neither of these can give him the thrill of exaltation and the happy sigh of satisfied ambition that are his when first he sees himself gazetted acting sub-lieutenant!

It marks the transition from childhood to manhood. When we commissioned, our present acting subs were mere squeakers, boys with piping treble voices, accepting the reproach of being youngsters with meek acquiescence.

But with time's insidious creep even junior midshipmen pass through stages of evolution; the white patches on the collar of the monkey-jacket—distinguishing marks of midshipmen's rank and relics of an age when the whole collar was white except for a space left blue at the back, so as not to show the soilings of a greasy pigtai—these patches grow less and less white; trouser-legs climb upwards, and there is a distinct suggestion of elbow-sleeves, the growing wearers wandering about like so many Smikes; then comes the period when they become senior midshipmen, holding a high hand over a new generation of "warts," and bearing the wisdom of the world written on their faces—and something of the wisdom of the sea besides.

A brief period of racking tension supervenes, during which their store of accumulated knowledge is tested by heartless officers from other ships, who coldly set them to perform practical tasks in seamanship and engineering, and the like; as, for instance, how to hoist in a picket-boat with the aid of a couple of capstan-bars and a fathom of spun-yarn; worse still, papers are set on navigation and half a dozen other subjects; and for a solid week the strafe goes on.

But—if the tortured victim finally hears that *he has passed!*—

Not merely is it a matter of transition to established manhood; it certainly is this, but in addition it is a glorious sea-change into something most extraordinarily rich and strange!

Can you imagine the feelings of a caterpillar when it wakes up and finds itself a butterfly? They may give you some faint indication of what it is to be suddenly transformed from a midshipman into an acting sub!

For the first time now he wears upon his sleeve that ring of gold lace which, though but a single one at present, will multiply like ripples on a pond until it becomes the insignia of an Admiral of the Fleet—perhaps!

Further, he becomes the equal in rank of a First Lieutenant in the army, and thus possesses a very real standing amongst men of considerably more than his own age.

For, mark you, the acting sub really has his proper dignity, and upholds it exceedingly well as a rule. Do not base your mental image of him upon his portrait as given in the weekly illustrated papers. I do not, of course, deny that there may be a certain solicitousness that the socks should be of exactly the same shade as the eyes—or whatever the mode of the moment may be; but you wouldn't have him otherwise, would you? Yet there can be no erring greatly on that side when a man has to do a man's work, as the acting sub has. Picture him rather as—well, let us avoid falling into the opposite error; here is no hero of short-story fiction, with steely, deep-set eyes, and determined, squarecut jaw, and all that sort of thing; but just a man, keen as mustard on the next thing that may happen to blow along, and only hoping that it may be a chance to do something a bit more exciting than coaling ship or keeping watch on the quarter-deck. Give him the opportunity to go as first lieutenant of a destroyer, or even a torpedo-boat; he will think himself lucky—and you, if you live in a coast-town on his patrol, may sleep at peace, knowing that while the acting sub is looking out for you there won't be much going wrong on *his* particular portion of the ocean!

CHAPTER 48

Storm

There is only one storm worth considering in all prose literature, and that is, of course, in *David Copperfield*. This, however, is a storm as seen from the shore, and describes to the landsman something which he already knew; but would that the writing-master had lent his pen to a description of a storm on the high seas! Then the dwellers in inland cities might have been able to realise something of all its terrible grandeur; but I do not see how this is possible now.

Unless someone in a destroyer or a patrol-vessel takes up the task, someone of the hundreds of young officers who have had a daily battle with the elements ever since the first day of the war, up and down off the coast and out in the North Sea, for these men see the works of the Lord and His wonders in the deep; and, though they may possess but little knowledge of literary conventions, they have the one essential thing—knowledge; not the knowledge absorbed by quiet meditation, but knowledge beaten and buffeted into them, washed into them, blown into them by sweeping seas and shrieking winds.

The thing could not be done by anyone in a big ship, because from such a point of view a storm is like the one in *King Lear*—not convincing. For, unless the weather is very, very bad, it is quite difficult to realise there is any storm in progress worth calling a storm.

The other day I watched from this ship a patrol drifter coming towards us with the wind and sea on her beam; she rolled and played in the tumble of the waves like a gambolling porpoise, now heeling over till her keel was nearly visible, and a moment later turning all her upper deck into view, the while a heavy curtain of white spray dashed funnel-high across her just as though some playful sea-giant were splashing her in fun. Then, to test the amount of motion in my own ship, I went to my writing-table and stood a long lead-pencil on its end: it remained upright, and did not fall for several minutes.

The biggest ships, however, can be lively enough on occasions, and move about sufficiently to satisfy the veriest sea-dog that dislikes a still ship. Build we our leviathans as big as we may choose, Nature still retains the mastery, and if the mood pleases her is capable of tossing about the hugest battleships as if they were mere cock-boats. There is a theory that the crests of two successive waves can never be more than a definite maximum distance apart, and that therefore you have only to build a vessel long enough to span two wave-crests, and she is bound to remain supported without pitching; the theory might work out all right if only your vessel would be certain of steering a course at right angles to the long waves—but, unfortunately, that is not always the case. Big ships generally take a long time starting to knock about in a storm, but when once fairly on the move they are correspondingly long in quieting down again.

I have seen a squadron of super-Dreadnoughts giving a very fair imitation of submarines, their decks so swept by the breaking waves that no man was allowed to appear there unless absolutely obliged. Then is the time that newly joined ship's boys find a certain consolation for the horrors of sea-sickness in their pride at being regular deep-sea sailors who can boast of their hardihood to the next batch of raw recruits; then, too, in the wardroom it is advisable to make a careful choice of seats at meal-times, for there never yet was a man-of-war skylight that did not leak—and some leak worse than others, as I have found out by personal experience.

The worst storm is that which falls upon a flat sea. The *"calm before the storm"* is no mere figure of speech. The sea appears turned to sluggish oil, and the air tastes as if it had "gone bad." The sky may be clear, except for a long low line of clouds in one quarter, and there is a sinister silence, a period in which the world seems holding its breath against the great effort which it knows full well is coming soon. Then a slight and steady breeze springs up, and simultaneously those low-banked clouds advance *against the wind*, and imperceptibly thin out and spread a veil of lurid greenish-grey over all the heavens. The surface of the sea becomes disturbed by curious little lines of oncoming rollers, which lip and curl and break upon the flat ocean as upon a level beach.

Then, while you are watching the sea, you forget the rising wind, till a whistling through cordage and wires and a cold blast upon your face remind you that the powers of heaven are unloosed at last; and, turning to the sea again, you find that in a few moments it has changed to a welter of heaving, tumbling, leaping billows, confused and disordered as yet, and seeming to be quarrelling for place before they get properly into their stride. An hour later, and they have settled down to their attack, and the massed battalions sweep steadily on, one after the other, hurling themselves against the ship-fortress in endless succession.

It is all very majestic, and perhaps nowhere better viewed than from a fighting-ship. And the naval officer, who in spite of his professed scorn of the sentimental is quicker than most to perceive the grandeur and the beauty of Nature, probably realises the wonder of it all, though he is silent about it.

Chapter 49

Ranks and Ratings

I have been asked for the elucidation of a mystery which seems to have a perennial interest for naval officers—namely, the relative ranks, duties, and positions of officers of the Church. I have many times been called upon to explain these unknown quantities, and have found that the easiest way is to give x in terms of y—y being the relative position of naval ranks; and it may possibly prove of some interest to those to whom ranks and ratings are an unknown quantity if I reverse the process and give y in terms of x.

The commander-in-chief, then, is our Archbishop of Canterbury. He is *primus inter pares*, and may have one or two suffragan admirals on his staff. Under his orders are a number of other admirals in command of squadrons, like bishops in charge of dioceses, the flagship representing the Cathedral, and the flag-captain answering to the dean. At this point the parallel breaks down a little, because although the "private ships" represent the parishes, with their captains as rectors, it is a little difficult to say whether the commander should be classed as a vicar or merely as the senior curate. (By the way, it is curious to the outsider that the commander is not the officer who commands the ship unless he happens to be appointed as captain of a small vessel.) Then the further difficulty comes in that captains, commanders, and lieutenants are all distinct ranks, whereas the imposingest rector and the mildest curate are both priests of the same order.

Other naval ranks have their curiosities also; we have a fleet-surgeon and fleet-paymaster, who have nothing whatever to do with a fleet, and a staff-surgeon and staff-paymaster, who are not on the staff. The same prefixes were formerly applied to engineer officers, before the invention of the terms engineer-commander and engineer-lieutenant; and now we have yet another name for officers performing engineering duties, since the "New Scheme" has given us "Lieutenants E."

Two new ranks have quite recently been invented—namely, that of lieutenant-commander, who is a two-and-a-half striper, and that of mate. The main advantage to the holder of the former seems to be that if he is court-martialled he cannot be reduced below the lowest of this rank, whereas formerly he was liable to be set back to become a lieutenant of no seniority at all! "Mate" is a revived term; at least, there used to be "Master's Mates" in the old days, when the navigating branch was distinct from the executive. Mates are now chosen from the warrant officers, or even straight from the lower deck. The institution of this rank is a very great privilege to the men, since it leads on to further advancement, and the old dream of *"Powder-Monkey to Admiral,"* unheard of since Nelson's days, has once more become something of a practical possibility.

From ranks let us now turn to ratings. The next step above boy is ordinary seaman the very last term that ought to be applied to him, for as a rule he is a most extraordinary seaman! Being newly emancipated from the restrictions which are maintained over the boys, he is apt to misuse his novel privileges at times, before he has learnt enough of his trade to palliate his shortcomings; so that the "rorty young O.D." is at once a holy terror and an object of scorn to all right-thinking men; and if you want to flatten out anyone of your acquaintance who brings you a feeble and obviously inadequate plea in mitigation of— say, for instance, failing to keep an appointment—just remember to make the crushing rejoinder, *"Don't come here with any of your ordinary seaman's excuses"*

Next above him comes the able seaman, who represents the splendid rank-and-file of the navy.

If you really *want* to talk to a bluejacket, and don't know his name or rating, you should address him as "*Sailor*"

Some of the ratings are redolent of the good old "costume" days. "Master-at-arms," and "Armourer"—do they not smack of hauberks and bucklers and jousts? Alas for those degenerate times! The former is but the head policeman of the ship, and the latter no more than a glorified blacksmith!

As to my own branch, it is easy to state our rank in the navy. Chaplains have *no* naval rank.

Chapter 50

Boy Giblets

Giblets was the "Pusser's Name" with which he joined the navy; and a vast amount of persuasion was exercised upon him, both at Shotley and when he was drafted to his first ship, to make him pronounce the initial "G" hard—"for the sake of euphony," as the old-fashioned French grammars used to say about the interpolated "-t-." Vain, however, were all such efforts. The youthful owner of the anatomical patronymic persisted in pronouncing himself as an important part of a fowl's interior; in truth, he was a vulgar little boy!

After the first fortnight of ship life he decided that the navy was not all it was cried up to be, and that as a career it was not sympathetic to his temperament; so he planned to forfeit his earlier hopes of becoming an admiral and to deprive the navy of his services.

An attempt at getting invalided out by simulating fits with the aid of a piece of pusser's soap proved a lamentable failure, owing to the uncanny knowledge of a brutally suspicious fleet-surgeon, and only resulted in six cuts with the cane laid on by p ship's corporal who appeared to take a pride in his job.

Despairing of any chance of leaving the service by such a recognised channel, he next made up his mind to desert; and seized his opportunity when the boys were landed for a football party.

Four days later he was ignominiously brought back to the ship by a policeman. Subsequent investigations revealed that the intervening time had been spent in a lively and varied manner, which must have taxed fairly heavily even an imagination nourished on penny "Deadwood Dicks."

It appears that on the first day he presented himself at a lonely cottage of an old woman of the labouring classes in the character of a shipwrecked mariner who had swum ashore from a torpedoed merchantman; but his achievements at suppertime convinced the old lady that feeding distressed seamen was not her *métier*, and he was shown the door. Exactly how he managed to procure a suit of civvies never leaked out, but he owned up to having condescended to give the army a trial, though he was refused on the score of size. From the army proper it was a natural step to the Salvation Army, where he posed as a reformed burglar's apprentice, and so procured free meals for a day. His capture took place some few hours after his joining a travelling circus, where he was completely given away by his free use of nautical swear-words, in which part of his professional studies he had from the first proved himself remarkably proficient. The manager of the circus, who didn't want to have trouble with the police, took immediate steps to place his feet once more on the lower rungs of the ladder of naval glory—in other words, he handed him over to the local constable.

A wise captain turned a deaf ear to the charge of desertion, and prescribed an outward application, as before. For a few days after this Boy Giblets's conduct was exemplary. The only break in his monotonous life was when his messmates jeered at him for getting no letters or parcels—a jibe which was true at the moment; but within three days he rounded on his persecutors by receiving a stupendous mail—seventy-eight letters, mostly containing photographs of fair ladies, and nineteen parcels of various kinds of food—though there was also tobacco, two mufflers, a bundle of tracts, and a French horn; the mystery of this embarrassment of riches remained sealed to everyone except the censor, who could have told of an advertisement inserted in a provincial paper, wherein a certain lonely sailor, considered strikingly handsome, presented a moving appeal to the sympathetically minded.

In the ordinary course of events the tobacco should have been confiscated and doled out on coal-ship days, when alone the boys are allowed to smoke; but Giblets had a master-mind, and made friends with the mammon of unrighteousness by presenting it all to the ship's corporal, in hopes of getting it laid on more lightly next time.

The French horn he swapped with a member of the band for a boot-cleaning outfit, with which he set up a little business on the lower deck until he had amassed eleven and ninepence. From this point he changed his views, and came round to the opinion that the navy was not such a bad place after all; the boot-cleaning business was changed for the more lucrative one of snobbing; out of the proceeds of this he kitted himself up till he was the smartest-dressed boy in the ship—invested also in a spelling-book and a *Complete Letter-Writer,* and shone conspicuous amongst the boys of the intermediate class at Ship's School. In fact, he progressed so rapidly that he is now recommended for promotion to Ordinary Seaman at 17½; and I should not be surprised if one of these days you were to hear of Lieutenant Giblettes—with the "G" sounded hard, and the accent on the *second* syllable, please!

Chapter 51

Singing Sailormen

Sailormen are always singing—Westoes especially; one passed my cabin door just now, carolling in a way that would make a martinet of the old school say that the navy was going to the dogs. But you can't stop them—even if you wanted to, which no sensible person does; a sailorman must sing, whether he does it entirely on his own, undisturbed by the clatter and talk around him, or in conjunction with half a dozen others sitting at their mess-table, to the accompaniment of a mouth-organ or a *mandoline*, or else in the grand style at a shippy concert 'tween decks, with the captain and officers in the front seats of the audience; the music that is in his soul has to come out somehow!

Sea-songs are of two classes: those which are written by landsmen for sailors' use, and those which spring Aphrodite-like from the sea itself. Of the former kind there is nothing to be said except that sailors don't sing them—won't look at them, in fact. The smart epigrammatist who announced that, Let him make a nation's songs, and anybody that liked might write its history, might have written sea-songs till he was blue in the face—but he would have had to sing them himself! Dibdin's collection, for example, is very interesting; but you never hear them sung on board ship.

The *real* sea-songs are those which grew naturally out of oft-repeated phrases used every day at work, mostly in the old sailing-ship times; the common expressions of orders, words of encouragement or complaint, uttered at first in an ordinary speaking-voice, taking on a musical form until every part of the day's work had its own appropriate "chanty"; the leading hand became the choragus, and the other men took up the burden in response. Most of these old chanties are unknown, however, to the seamen of the modern navy, though I dare say they are still to be heard in "windjammers."

Then there are others of a slightly more ambitious order, such as "Farewell and *Adieu*" and "Cawsand Bay." You never hear these on the lower deck, but they are still great favourites in the gunroom. Not many evenings ago I listened to a lusty young giant singing without the least suspicion of tune an endless ballad about the love-affairs of a downtrodden pressed man and his ultimate release by his lady-love, the culminating passage of which appeared to be:

And out from her boo-zum she drew his discharge!

We all repeated this line at the top of our voices and with great fervour.

There is not much scope for the spontaneous growth of genuine sea-chanties to meet modern occasions; not only has machinery replaced manual labour in most of the operations that used to call for vocal encouragement, but in such jobs as are still man-handled it is recognised that noise and efficiency do not usually go hand-in-hand; singing is a recreation nowadays, not an aid to work.

Such ditties as are sung mark a very pronounced decline from the simple ballads and chanties of former times. In an annual review of musical production I read lately:

"As to the countless ballads and drawing-room ditties which have been published, all one can say in their favour is that they are generally within the vocal means of those who care to sing such things."

About as nasty a criticism as could be made, I imagine, but sadly appropriate to the majority of the songs to which the sailor has in these days descended. He delights in the so-called comic song of the halls, and still more in sloshy, sentimental vapidities; you should hear him, for instance, in "The Pore Blind Boy," with its refrain of "We luv 'im, we luv 'im, we luv 'im bee-coz 'e is blind!"

Not for the sailor is that elusive search for The Method which seems to be at once the joy and the despair of so many musical amateurs. He wastes no time in trying to acquire the sensation of a curtain of water falling at the back of his nose, nor in endeavouring to feel as if the top of his head were resting upon his chin. Such a quest—akin to that of the good folk who pass delightfully anguished years in trying to "git religion"—is unknown to him, with all its bitter-sweets; as is also the triumph of having Got It; he is a very heathen, a Gallic, with respect to The Method. Only in one particular does he put in any specialised work, and that is in Nasal Resonance; and how extremely nasal his resonance is must be heard to be believed!

Chapter 52

"Small Cords"

Our uncompromising Number One would have it that they were all mealy-mouthed, white-livered swabs. Schooley, more discriminating, stood out for the Moral Courage theory: to face public obloquy argued the highest kind of bravery—and so on. The first lieutenant waved this aside with contempt. "Find me," he said, "a single one of 'em who is simply longing to fight, but doesn't on account of his principles, and I'll begin to believe in them; at present, their opinions square a dashed sight too well with their inclinations!"

"But it's absurd to deny that many of them are utterly sincere," retorted the naval instructor.

"So is every self-opinionated blighter that walks this earth! What you call their moral courage is nothing more than just abysmal conceit! They thoroughly enjoy making martyrs of themselves, so there's nothing in that just as there's nothing particularly brave about the fighting man who by nature revels in a good scrap. No; these puffed-up cranks won't be content to abide by the decisions of their betters—no excitement or self-glorification in that! They prefer to take their own line, and everybody else is wrong!"

Schooley thought this unfair, and said so. Minorities, he argued, were not always in the wrong; these people based their case upon Christianity, and it was notorious that the Christian Church, now as at the beginning, was always a discredited minority. Christ and His disciples made themselves thoroughly unpopular by running counter to all the received opinions of respectability.

"Oh," exclaimed Number One, "if you're going to take the argument of Christianity, it's no use my going on! Especially as the *padre* here will chip in to back you up."

"Nothing of the sort," said I; "I don't back him up at all!"

Incredulous and inquiring looks from both.

"I don't say that they are not sincere or not brave," I explained; "they may be both these things; but what I do most emphatically state is that your Conscientious Objectors—so far as their objections are concerned—are certainly not Christians."

"But surely these are their ideas—please don't take them for my own altogether," argued Schooley: "Christianity aims as breaking down all barriers of race and nationality. *There is neither Jew nor Gentile*—why not say *neither British nor German?* All are meant to be one brotherhood. I read the other day of a magistrate at an Exemption Tribunal who sneered finely at an appellant who said that England was not his country, and he was only passing through it on his way home to Heaven; but the man was only paraphrasing such phrases as *Strangers and Pilgrims*, and *Here we have no continuing city, but we seek one to come*. Christ deliberately stated that His was not an earthly kingdom; evil was not to be resisted; blows, theft, and oppression were to be accepted, even gladly accepted. You cannot imagine Christ countenancing fighting and bloodshed. He refused aid for Himself, and gave the final proof of His belief in the principles of passive non-resistance by allowing His persecutors to kill Him. And no one can deny that if we were all to follow His example there could never be any war. If we were *all* Conscientious Objectors to bloodshed not a man would consent to carry a rifle—and the world would be at peace. This was what Christ aimed at; not violent coercion—His was the gentler way; He would draw men *with cords of a man, with bands of love.*"

"But don't forget the other cords," I said, "the small ones."

"I don't quite follow," said Schooley; "you mean—"

"I mean *He made a scourge of small cords and drove them all out of the Temple*. Brutal violence, wasn't it? Remember, small cords sting hard. Your Christian exquisite, had he been present, would probably have accused *Him* of profaning the Temple. *O my dear friend*, he would have said, *how bewtifull is Peace! What is Peace? Is it toe beat, is it toe whip, is it toe scourge with small cords?* Schooley, I've no patience with your one-sided travesty of Christianity! It seems to me just as bad, in the opposite direction, as the doctrine of those German divines who preach the blessed gospel of bloodshed. Christ was frowned upon in His day for being too thorough-going; I have no doubt that if He were to reappear He would be treated with great suspicion by many who would consider Him not thorough-going enough. To say that we ought to refrain from all resistance to evil is only a parody of what Christ taught. Non-resistance to wrong-doing very often means acquiescence in it. It is all very well to turn your own cheek to the smiter; but if you see a bully ill-treating a little child you are not called upon to grip the child's head and turn *his* other cheek.

"You say that if everyone were to refuse to bear arms there would be an end of warfare. Why not complete your truism, and say that if everyone were kind, unselfish, contented—in short, Christlike, there would be no need for a call to arms? A man ought logically to conscientiously object, not to warfare itself, but to those private and national habits of greed, jealousy, and malice that finally result in warfare as either their consequence or their cure; just as it is more reasonable to disapprove of burglary than of a policeman, of a plague than of its resultant furuncles. The real trouble is that a very large number of people deliberately reject the formula of living which Christ enunciated, and in some cases a whole nation does so. Then comes war, which is never anything else but a struggle between right and wrong. You always find, on one side, the money-changers and dove-sellers; and on the other the man with the scourge of small cords. So I say that to refuse to wield this scourge in flaying greed and thievery, in cleansing the Temple of God from pollution, *may* be conscientious, but certainly isn't Christian—unless Christ was no Christian."

"Then you are on my side," said the first lieutenant, greatly surprised.

"On the side of the angels," I answered; and tried not to make the words sound so priggish as they look when written.

Chapter 53

"Tonal'"

Thrown into the vast melting-pot of the navy, and into that particular portion of the crucible wherein our ship's company is collected, came a raw, loose-limbed Hebridean, with flaming hair and high cheek-bones, a wild and rugged son of the Western Isles.

Donald McLeod was the name on his parchment-certificate, and his birthplace Stornoway, in Lewis. Somehow he had drifted from Ultima Thule to London, and there, at the beginning of the war, had joined the Royal Naval Division, and in course of time was drafted to us.

Amongst his messmates on the lower deck he became generally known as "Tonal'," because that was how he pronounced his Christian name; and as in that elementary society any personal peculiarities are seized upon as subject-matter for jests, his manner of speech was a godsend to the mess-deck wits. "I haf not the Engliss—not ferry well at all," he would plaintively say; and, indeed, when he talked—which was not frequently—he reminded you of one of the characters in William Black's novels.

For the other Scotsmen in the ship he had nothing but a withering contempt, because it so happened that they were all Lowlanders, from Glasgow and Dundee mostly.

It was quite early discovered that Tonal' claimed to have the gift of second sight. With some of the men this created an atmosphere of superstitious awe; others, however, ridiculed the matter, and made it another opportunity for provokingly pointed jests. They besought him to foretell when the 'Uns would bring their Canal Fleet out— when the end of the war would come—and, with greater interest still, when they were going to get some leave.

These requests angered Tonal' very greatly. Vainly he tried to explain to his tormentors that "the *Sicht*" was in the nature of things sacred, and not to be lightly considered as a mere method of fortune-telling jugglery—that it could not, in fact, be exercised save when the proper mood was on, a mood not under human control. When such explanations were useless, as they always were, he would turn upon the mockers and curse them roundly in a flood of what was presumably Gaelic; this caused much delight, and was regarded as part of the entertainment.

A tragedy very nearly resulted from one of these occasions. Having baited the angry Highlander to the limit of his endurance, a certain Simpkins committed the final act of unseemly levity by asking which cutter would win in a race taking place next day—"because I want to 'ave a dollar on it with Nobby Clarke, an' I'd like to make certain of it first!"

Tonal' rounded on the wretched Simpkins fiercely: "I haf the *Sicht* on me now," he roared, "and I tell you *this*—in three days you will be a dead man!"

For the rest of that day Simpkins walked delicately; the next morning he was sickly white and trembling, growing visibly worse towards the evening.

A sense of dread and mystery spread over the ship. Men talked in hushed voices, and always on the one topic, and stole away from their work every now and then to note how Simpkins was getting on. For the victim had not reported himself sick, and, in fact, denied with several forcible expressions, that there was anything the matter with him. For all that, he was obviously getting very near to a state of collapse. The fleet-surgeon talked learnedly about hypnosis—for all the officers, of course, knew about the affair and was for ordering the man to the sick-bay, to be kept under observation. But the first lieutenant asked to be allowed to try a different treatment, and got his own way. The first lieutenant, you understand, was not a sympathetic soul. He had also been on the West Coast, and said that he wasn't going to have any of this qualified *Voodoo* business going on in the ship, not if he could help it!

He sent for Simpkins, and, as the corporal of the gangway expressed it, "proper rattled him." "You just dare to die, that's all," was the end of his discourse; "you just try it on, and I'll make your life a perfect misery to you!" He also sent for Tonal', and said several things to him.

What the outcome would have been will never be known, because

Simpkins, doing some job on the foc'sle, and being uncertain-footed through failing nerve, fell overboard, and was picked up after some little time unconscious and with his lungs half-full of water, developing pneumonia before he recovered his senses. And when he eventually came to himself he was so pleased to find that the three days were gone and he was still alive that he made a very rapid recovery.

Tonal's reputation was much enhanced by this; some arguing that Simpkins would have died if it hadn't been for an unfortunate accident; others crediting the accident itself to Tonal' as a very sporting attempt which nearly succeeded.

But a short while after, Tonal' himself went sick—canteen salmon being the immediate cause. He suffered very severe pain, and voiced his griefs in tones which, to put it mildly, caused much astonishment.

"Ow, the pyne, the pyne!" he wailed; "fer Gawd's syke give me somefink to stop it wiv, doctor, carn't yer?"

"The man's pure Cockney," the fleet-surgeon reported to the wardroom, "no more Highlander than I am!"

"But what on earth possessed the man to act like that?" we asked.

"Your own question supplies the answer," said the man of science; "it was just simply *acting*, right through. A desire for notoriety, perhaps, coupled with the aids of his appearance and name though even the name—may not be genuine. A little abnormal streak—some men are built like that; it comes out in different ways."

But the first lieutenant said, "I always knew the man was an epithetical impostor; all the McLeods are black, not red!"

CHAPTER 54

The Advantage-Party

The practice of giving leave to men in small batches applies, fortunately, to sailors as well as to soldiers; no appreciable loss of efficiency is felt by the absence of a small number over a short period, and to the actual pleasure of going on leave is added the anticipatory excitement of wondering when it may be your luck to go.

Those who are chosen to be the first to proceed upon this pleasurable errand are termed, officially, the Advance-Party; but unofficially they are more generally known as the Advantage-Party—because when they go they do go, therein having the advantage over those who have not yet gone and don't know when they may go or even if they will go at all.

"Are *you* going on leave with the Advantage-Party?"

"Don't know, yet; it hasn't been settled at present—at least, so far as I know; have you heard anything?"

So might the expectant aristocrats of the Bastille have questioned one another with regard to the next day's proceedings in which they calculated on playing so prominent a part—only, in our case, the release is less permanent and more agreeable.

Not the least unpleasing feature of the whole business to those who are not amongst the chosen ones is to see coming alongside the small vessel detailed to transport the Advantage-Party to the beach. She remains alongside perhaps for some hours; we look well over her, possibly go aboard her, and note curiously upon the tablets of our mind that these very decks on which we are now treading will presently be a magic carpet to waft a certain number of people exactly where they wish to go, and we shall not be there then. We never quite realised before what it must feel like to those boys who are left at school during the holidays when they stroll down to the station and watch the outgoing trains—poor little blighters!

These pioneers, about to break into an almost forgotten land, are charged with any number of commissions for the far country. There is, it seems, one special kind of trout-fly that can only be procured at one special shop in London; a zealous watch-keeper has compiled a book of notes for the guidance of the officer-of-the-watch, a monumental *liasse* pasted on the back of old charts, which he desires to have taken to the one and only bookbinder who can be trusted not to make a pot-mess of the whole caboodle; the members of the Gourmet Club draw up an order for peaches and oysters, to be purchased at the latest possible moment; and our most musical member begs as a friendly act that his 'cello may be brought back from Herefordshire: "It won't take you long to nip down there, old man, and my people will be awfully glad to see you!"—all these commissions, and many more in addition, are undertaken with the utmost light-heartedness; and, strange to say, are most of them carried out faithfully.

Next to going on leave oneself the best thing is to try to take a vicarious pleasure in another man's prospective pleasures, to pick out his theatres for him, to select little dinners—even to wrestle with Bradshaw on his behalf. Many are the questions as to the locality in which the few brief days are to be spent; though, generally speaking, to all such queries may be applied the answer given by a young lieutenant of our ship, who explained: "Well, it doesn't make much difference where I make up my mind to go when on leave—somehow or other I always *manage to foul London!*"

On the analogy of men returning from a visit to the trenches, the suggestion was made that those who went on leave with the Advantage-Party should give a lecture, on coming back to the ship, and relate their experiences. The idea was received with marked coolness; particularly by one whose alternative sobriquets are *The Roué* and *Flaming Bill*; yet I feel sure that his narrative would have proved of enthralling interest.

However, in spite of the absence of any formal discourses on the subject, one was able nevertheless to glean a good deal—not of news about the war, for that appears to be almost as much a minus quantity in England as it is in the Grand Fleet—but of our messmates' doings, and still more of their impressions.

These latter prove most extraordinarily interesting to us, penned up in our ships and largely cut off from the world. Anyone who goes from us goes into a strange and unknown country, and it is just possible that the relation he brings back with him of the facts and ideas prevailing in the places he visits may seem, when written down, not more novel to us than to the inhabitants of that land who may be so habituated to them as not to be aware of them.

Perhaps the most striking impression was that of a strange kind of rivalry of pride which is springing up in so many homes. Everywhere one goes—so it was reported—one sees people dressed in mourning clothes (what must it be, though, in Germany!); elderly people, for the most part, comparing notes; in the parks, at restaurants, in shops, they meet one another: "My boy was killed at Gallipoli," says one; "Mine was killed in France last week," says his friend; "and my second lad was badly wounded in Mesopotamia."

Only a couple of years ago, such announcements would have been made, if made at all, with a choking voice and after much hesitation; but now they are issued with an abruptness which would almost seem callous, were it not that there rings in the words the resounding note of pride in a sacrifice gladly borne, a gift freely given. We might have imagined, up here, that our losses would have made a melancholy England, with dark sorrow brooding everywhere; and no doubt the sorrow exists, but to us, at least, it is a revelation to find it gilded with such a glorious spirit.

It was said, also, that it is very much rarer now than it was a year ago to see a man of military age in plain clothes. Obviously, of course, this must be so, after all the enlistment which has been going on continually; but none the less, it was much more striking to see the change made than to watch it in the making; possibly the enemy would not talk quite so glibly about our "phantom armies" if he could have the veil lifted after many months, and see our towns as they were seen by the Advantage-Party!

Yet another impression, lamentable or the reverse, according as one looks at the matter, was that there appears to be no appreciable tightening of the purse-strings amongst the generality of people. Not only were the shops crowded, but all theatres and places of amusement of every kind were doing a roaring trade. Very wrong, perhaps, in face of the urgent appeals to economise; but, on the other hand, surely it shows that the vast spending power of our country has barely been touched yet.

A psychologist may object that luxuries and amusements are the very last things on which people exercise economy; but though they may not do so spontaneously, they can be made to do so when necessary, and it is a comforting thought that the money is there, ready to take. If good Dr. Helfferich imagines that we have come to the limit of our resources, let him procure a safe-conduct, and come and see for himself, under the auspices of our next Advantage-Party.

CHAPTER 55

An Indeterminate Equation

Navvy would have it that the whole thing could be done on the back of a visiting-card; but, then, Navvy has been to China, where visiting-cards are measured by the square foot.

Schooley had not at this time joined the ship, so we had no professional mathematician to whom to refer; nevertheless, we all agreed that Navvy's statement was wrong, simply because on general grounds we saw no reason why he should be right.

Upon this, he shifted his ground at once, and offered a mild wager to each and all of us that we could not do it in an hour; to which we replied in that monosyllabic expression of offended pride and confident assertiveness generally written as "*Huh!*"—and at once produced our pencils and hunted around for signal-pads, old band-programmes, or the fly-leaves of those innumerable letters in which kindly-disposed gentlemen plead with us to accept anything up to fifty thousand pounds on our note of hand alone; any bit of paper would do to figure out this simple calculation.

What diabolical motive induced the disturber of our peace to spring this problem upon us I cannot say; unless the moving cause may be sought in the fact that Satan finds some mischief still for navigating-lieutenants to do; but when once the apple of discord was thrown in our midst—no, it was not an apple really, it was a nut. The odd nut was the crux of the whole matter.

Perhaps I had better explain at this point exactly what the problem was.

We were informed that a band of robbers had stolen a large bagful of nuts; which seems a silly sort of thing for robbers to do, because they couldn't have been satisfied with a nut-diet; who ever heard of vegetarian robbers?

Anyhow, they did. There were five of them in this silly business—and they also had a pet monkey; destroyer officers frequently keep a pet of the same species on board their pirate craft, so there appears to be some verisimilitude about this part of the story.

The robbery having taken place late in the evening, the five agreed to defer till next morning the sharing of the spoil, and went to bed.

In the night, however, one of the robbers, having the astute foresight of a company-promoter, arose stealthily and divided the nuts into five equal portions—one nut being left over, which he tossed to the monkey. Then he put his twice-stolen nuts under his pillow and went to sleep again. And the same brain-wave occurred to each of the remaining four robbers in turn; on every occasion one nut being left over for the monkey. In the morning, the residue of the nuts was shared equally amongst the five, and an odd nut still remained for the monkey. What, we were asked to discover, is the least number of nuts that meets the case?

It looks easy, doesn't it?

At the end of an hour the wardroom was strewn with papers all covered with algebraical fractions, longer than any fraction has a right to be in these days, when everything is being cut down and strict economy practised in all directions; and the worst of it was that these fractions were obviously only stepping-stones to larger fractions still.

Some of the struggling competitors gave in at this point, and weakly alleged that pressing duties claimed their presence elsewhere. Those who remained tore up their calculations and announced that of course this wasn't the proper way to work it; they should have tackled it from the other end, working backwards, which would make it quite a simple matter.

After another long interval the bravest of us said what we all wanted to say, but were ashamed of saying: "Of course, it's *easy* enough," he exclaimed; "*anybody* could do it if he cared to give the time to the thing; but it isn't worth while to waste hours over a stupid problem like that!" Whereupon he left the ward-room.

We would gladly have followed his example, but another suggestion held us. "Let's work it out practically," urged a persistent member. "Not enough nuts in the ship," was objected to this. "Never mind, we can get some haricot beans from the ship's steward; there are six of us here. You can be the monkey, young feller-me-lad, and we'll be the robbers!"

But the officer familiarly addressed as "young feller-me-lad" took umbrage at being cast for the monkey's part; expressed his objections not alone in words but in deeds; and leapt across the wardroom table upon the suggester's stomach with an agility that went far to justify his selection for the simian role.

The proceedings then took a livelier turn, and proved an agreeable diversion to the mathematical discussion.

The problem itself, needless to state, remained not only indeterminate, but undetermined!

******

I should like to thank my unknown correspondent at the Admiralty who sent me a solution of the "nuts" problem, giving 15,484,371 as the answer; this Admiralty estimate, however, is a little extravagant. The correct answer, as kindly supplied by a chaplain and naval instructor, is 15,621.

Chapter 56

Aftermath

Written a few days after the Jutland Battle (June, 1916).

The next morning broke misty and dull as the evening before; the noise of gunfire which had resounded at intervals during the night had died away; a light breeze was beginning to spring up, and already stirred the waves to leap mercifully upon all the flotsam, human and other, and sink it down to its long quiet rest. Fitful clouds spread and broke across the sky, with gleams of brightness in between, and lights and shadows chased one another over the surface of the leaden waters like the sad thoughts and the cheery satisfaction that swept across the minds of all of us.

So many gallant men and gay comrades gone! Men to whom we had been talking only a few days before, when we went aboard their ships or they visited us. Old shipmates, old station-mates; men who had pulled in boat-races against our men; partners at golf, people of the same term at Osborn or the *Britannia*, of the same lot at Keyham, students at the same hospital.

And all men of the same loves and hatreds as ourselves, the same tastes and ways, the same weaknesses, and the same joy in living: what had we done that they should be taken and we left?

Yet could we feel now more fit to take our stand beside our brothers of the army—who lose as many as this in a day's land fighting that is scarce judged important enough to put in the *communiqués*; that was our unspoken pride—not altogether, I think, an ignoble boast.

And we had won the day. Though at first we hardly knew what we had done, until reports began to filter through, and rumours one after another became confirmed as facts. Our own losses we knew, as the world knew them very shortly after; but not, at that time, our gains. Each ship, indeed, knew what it had contributed to the victory, but the fleet as a whole could not know so soon; and, indeed, had to bear the bitter comments of certain journals which in their omniscient wisdom adjudged the navy to have failed. But this flickering shadow soon passed, when the true tale was told; or, more correctly, half-told, for not till the war is over shall we know how very much greater were the German losses in that sea-fight than even our most optimistic estimate of them. I should very much like to know how many undamaged ships of the line the "Admiral of the Atlantic" could show at this present moment.

It was left for the *Kaiser*, of all people, to provide the inevitable Comic Relief! We had smiled very contented smiles before, but we laughed for the first time—the whole British Navy rocked with laughter—when the *Kaiser* made his famous speech, and said that:

The nimbus of British naval supremacy has departed.

Why *does* the dear man say these priceless things? Isn't it simply splendid of him to do it? He is surely about the last man in the world you would pick out to add to the gaiety of nations; and yet he has succeeded in doing it! Who now will dare to say that he is not superman? We are still enjoying the joke. One of our lieutenants was discovered wandering disconsolate about the wardroom, wearing a worried look and apparently searching for something. When asked what was the matter, he replied complainingly, "I *cannot* find my nimbus anywhere!"

Another aftermath, again a most sad one, when, in addition to the great harvest of the sea, a scantier reaping was laid up on shore, in a wild spot within sound of the waves, where, however, they that rest beneath the coarse grass and the brown turf shall rest tenderly, and their honoured graves shall be cared for, for they lie in consecrated ground—consecrated not so much by that Episcopal act which set apart that place for ever, as by their own hallowed and hallowing bodies, cast willingly off in God's service and the King's.

Such sacred thoughts are not for us to dwell on overlong, though doubtless their impression is one that will recur constantly to us. For the present, it is perhaps the reaction that helps us to utter our comments in a lighter style. "We had," says one of our sailors, "a bit of a spring-cleaning last week, and started to tidy things up a little."

ALSO FROM LEONAUR
AVAILABLE IN SOFTCOVER OR HARDCOVER WITH DUST JACKET

THE 9TH—THE KING'S (LIVERPOOL REGIMENT) IN THE GREAT WAR 1914 - 1918 *by Enos H. G. Roberts*—Mersey to mud—war and Liverpool men.

THE GAMBARDIER *by Mark Severn*—The experiences of a battery of Heavy artillery on the Western Front during the First World War.

FROM MESSINES TO THIRD YPRES *by Thomas Floyd*—A personal account of the First World War on the Western front by a 2/5th Lancashire Fusilier.

THE IRISH GUARDS IN THE GREAT WAR - VOLUME 1 *by Rudyard Kipling*—Edited and Compiled from Their Diaries and Papers—The First Battalion.

THE IRISH GUARDS IN THE GREAT WAR - VOLUME 1 *by Rudyard Kipling*—Edited and Compiled from Their Diaries and Papers—The Second Battalion.

ARMOURED CARS IN EDEN *by K. Roosevelt*—An American President's son serving in Rolls Royce armoured cars with the British in Mesopotamia & with the American Artillery in France during the First World War.

CHASSEUR OF 1914 *by Marcel Dupont*—Experiences of the twilight of the French Light Cavalry by a young officer during the early battles of the great war in Europe.

TROOP HORSE & TRENCH *by R.A. Lloyd*—The experiences of a British Lifeguardsman of the household cavalry fighting on the western front during the First World War 1914-18.

THE EAST AFRICAN MOUNTED RIFLES *by C.J. Wilson*—Experiences of the campaign in the East African bush during the First World War.

THE LONG PATROL *by George Berrie*—A Novel of Light Horsemen from Gallipoli to the Palestine campaign of the First World War.

THE FIGHTING CAMELIERS *by Frank Reid*—The exploits of the Imperial Camel Corps in the desert and Palestine campaigns of the First World War.

STEEL CHARIOTS IN THE DESERT *by S. C. Rolls*—The first world war experiences of a Rolls Royce armoured car driver with the Duke of Westminster in Libya and in Arabia with T.E. Lawrence.

WITH THE IMPERIAL CAMEL CORPS IN THE GREAT WAR *by Geoffrey Inchbald*—The story of a serving officer with the British 2nd battalion against the Senussi and during the Palestine campaign.

AVAILABLE ONLINE AT **www.leonaur.com**
AND FROM ALL GOOD BOOK STORES

www.ingramcontent.com/pod-product-compliance
Lightning Source LLC
Chambersburg PA
CBHW031559170426
43196CB00031B/233